MW01096810

Arizona Game Birds

Mearns' Quail, Both Male

Arizona
Game Birds

David E. Brown

with frontispiece and drawings by Paul Bosman

The University of Arizona Press
and The Arizona Game and Fish Department

Financial support for this publication
was provided by the Arizona Game and Fish
Department Publications Revolving Fund.

THE UNIVERSITY OF ARIZONA PRESS

This book was set in 10/13 Galliard.
Manufactured in the United States of America.

93 92 91 90 89   5 4 3 2 1

⊗ This book is printed on acid-free, archival-quality paper.

Library of Congress Cataloging-in-Publication Data

Brown, David E. (David Earl), 1938–
    Arizona game birds.

    Bibliography: p.
    Includes index.
    1. Upland game birds—Arizona.   I. Title.
QL684.A6B74   1989   598'.6'09791   88-27797
ISBN 0-8165-1019-9 (alk. paper)

British Library Cataloguing in Publication data are available.

Contents

Illustrations

Tables

Preface

I was in unfamiliar country and somewhat uneasy. The dense vegetation obscured any landmarks, and the late November light was waning. Not knowing my location, I suddenly realized that I might not get back to camp before dark. Soon the calls of poor-wills would be heard and I would have only minutes to find my way.

I glimpsed birds threading their way through the thornscrub ahead of me. Their soft worried calls were quail-like and familiar. I quickened my pace to see them better. Thus pressed, the birds ran ahead of me and then took flight. Their rustling *whir* on take-off, instant speed, and short determined flight proved them to be quail. I had encountered my first Elegant Quail (*Lophortyx douglasi*), a Mexican species sometimes called Yaqui quail, Benson quail, or Douglas quail.

My worries were put aside as I marked the landing site of the laggard of the covey. How long would it take for the birds to regroup? Would they hold on landing, or alight to scurry somewhere else? What would their assembly calls sound like? Would they roost on the ground or spend the night in a shrub or tree? Such were the things that interested me now.

These questions and more were answered as I followed the quail. The covey appeared to be a family group, the young having hatched late the previous spring. I had expected younger birds, hatched after the onset of the summer monsoon when the other Mexican species—Mearns' Quail

and Masked Bobwhite—nest. The birds did run on landing and soon became intermingled with a large covey of Gambel's Quail on their way to
roost. The Elegant Quail kept more to the dense cover, however, and their
multinote assembly calls were harsher and more distinct than those of their
more numerous cousins. Their behavior seemed to be intermediate between that of Gambel's and Scaled quails. Within twenty minutes the seven
birds had regrouped to spend the night in a dense *Phaulothamnus* bush
next to a large wash—a wash that I recognized as the one leading to my
truck and the comforts of camp.

What outdoor experience is not made more enjoyable by the presence of
game birds? The sight of cranes on their way to roost, the heart-stopping
flush of an underfoot grouse, the gathering calls of quail at daybreak, all
quicken the senses and sharpen our instincts. Perhaps it is the primeval
recognition that these *are* game birds that so fixes our attention. Such birds
are not valued solely by their pursuers; their special character has always
captured the attention of observers and artists as well.

Game birds have always been hunted more for sport than for their flesh.
Most species are instinctively wary, capable of explosive flight, and gregarious by nature. Much of the pleasure of hunting them involves the use of
dogs. A properly trained bird dog epitomizes the sport in its purest form,
and there is no better example of joyful cooperation between man and
beast, a bond recreated whenever game birds are shot over dogs. Once a
bird is bagged, its culinary aspects should not be overlooked. Properly
prepared, wildfowl are superior tablefare to any domestic bird, and their
firm flesh and slightly nutty flavor make for epicurean dishes. Finally, there
is the science of game birds. To know the life history of a bird, to realize its
limiting factors, and to understand its habitat requirements and ecological
needs is to ensure its welfare and its continued availability as a source of
pleasure.

CHAPTER 1

Introduction

Arizona is justifiably famous for its wide variety of birds. Only the adjacent state of New Mexico can claim more species of native game birds, and no other U.S. state has more doves and quails. Furthermore, generous amounts of public land make these resources available to all. Sportsmen come thousands of miles to shoot doves and bag quail; bird watchers come equal distances to see Mearns' Quail and observe Sandhill Cranes.

Why does Arizona possess such a varied bounty of wildlife? The answer is geography. Arizona's southern latitudes and great topographic relief (from 100 to more than 12,000 feet elevation) allow for tremendous variation in climate. One can, within a few hours, go from shooting White-winged Doves in the Neotropical Sonoran Desert to searching for Blue Grouse among subalpine meadows bordered by spruce, fir, and other boreal trees.

Although the focus of this book is Arizona game birds, the descriptions, life histories, population data, and field advice are applicable throughout the Southwest and North America. Accordingly, generalized distribution maps are provided for each species. Not included are the waterfowl, covered in a previous volume (D. Brown 1985a), and other primarily wetland game birds as coots, gallinules, rails, and shorebirds, not generally accepted as game in Arizona and not yet studied in depth.

TAXONOMY AND NOMENCLATURE

Taxonomy is an arrangement, or classification, of plants and animals based on anatomical similarities. Anatomical features are genetically determined, and thus taxonomy is based on evolutionary history. A particular bird's classification, then, depends on its systematic relationship to similar forms and the relative length of time that these forms have been separated from common ancestors.

Species are populations of potentially interbreeding individuals, reproductively isolated from all other species. The scientific name of each species is given by two Latin names: a generic name, or *genus*, for the group of plants or animals to which it belongs, followed by a descriptive *species* name for that specific kind of plant or animal. Populations of a species geographically or otherwise imperfectly isolated from others of the same species, and possessing physical characters differentiating it from other members of the species, are called *subspecies*. A third latinized name, after the genus and species, designates a subspecies.

The use of scientific names provides a universal language and a traceable chain of nomenclature for describing and discussing the different taxa. This value becomes apparent when one realizes that the common names of many Arizona species have changed since 1900: Mearns' Quail were then known as Massena Quail, White-winged Doves were more commonly called Sonora Pigeons, Mourning Doves were Carolina Doves, Lesser Sandhill Cranes were Little Brown Cranes, and so on. Nonetheless, it should also be noted that scientific names change as much as, or more than, common names. Biologists periodically propose changes in taxonomy on the basis of precedence, systematic evidence, or logic. (I would suggest, for example, that the New World Quails be elevated to family rank, equivalent to the Turkeys, Grouse, Pheasants, and Partridges.) For the sake of conformity, however, the taxonomic hierarchy and scientific nomenclature used in this volume follow the sixth edition of the *Check-list of North American Birds*, published by the American Ornithologists' Union in 1983. The sources of subspecific names are cited in the text and in Table 1.1.

Thirteen species of game birds, representing ten genera, six subfamilies, and three orders, are recognized as occurring in Arizona. As many as nineteen subspecies or races may be, or have been, present in Arizona (Table 1.1).

Each species of bird has at least one common name in general usage. Names vary with location as well as over time. Mearns' Quail, for example, are still known as Fool Quail in much of central Arizona. In an attempt to standardize popular usage, the American Ornithological Union has also compiled a checklist of designated common names for North American birds. Names of game birds in this volume follow AOU nomenclature, except when another name (often the subspecies) is predominantly used in Arizona: for example, Mearns' Quail instead of the AOU name of Montezuma Quail. Local and colloquial names are provided in the discussion of each species.

Common names are used for plants throughout the book unless no English name is in usage or the common name is confusing. The source for plant names in the United States is Nickerson et al. (1976). For the names of Mexican plants that do not occur north of the international boundary, see D. Brown (1982a) and Shreve and Wiggins (1964).

IDENTIFICATION, SEX, AND AGE

Differentiating the various species of upland game birds is not as difficult as identifying waterfowl. The fewer numbers of species within each genus make for less confusion between closely related forms. With a little experience, observers may easily identify most game birds by such distinctive field characters as calls, plumage, and behavior. Proper identification is essential for hunting, for regulations require that one must be able to differentiate between White-winged and Mourning doves in flight, and the season opens later on Mearns' Quail than on Gambel's and Scaled quails. Masked Bobwhite are totally protected. This book, or any of the numerous field guides available, should answer any identification questions raised by even the novice observer. It should be kept in mind that all quail fly in a similar fashion. If there is any doubt, subsequent behavior, assembly calls, or simply a better view should permit a positive species identification. To ascertain a bird's sex and age usually requires careful examination, however.

Every student of game birds needs to know the anatomy and plumage of his subjects (Fig. 1.1). Such knowledge assists in identification and allows the bird to be classified as to sex and age. For wildlife managers age and sex classification is essential for obtaining data on population structure, productivity, and mortality. Using the classification techniques described in the species accounts, an observer may be able to ascertain a bird's sex and age, and a hunter, by classifying the age of birds in his bag, can gain insight

TABLE I.I
Taxonomy of Arizona Game Birds

Class Aves—Birds
    Order Galliformes—Gallinaceous Birds
        Family Phasianidae: Partridges, Pheasants, Grouse, Turkeys, and Quails
            Subfamily Phasianinae—Partridges and Pheasants
                Genus *Phasianus* (Linnaeus)—Pheasant
                    Species *P. colchicus* (Linnaeus)—Ring-necked Pheasant
                        Subspecies *P. c. bianchii* (Delacour)—Afghan White-winged Pheasant
                        Subspecies *P. c. torquatus* (Delacour)—Chinese Ring-necked Pheasant
                Genus *Alectoris* (Kaup)—Partridge
                    Species *A. chukar* (Gray)—Chukar
            Subfamily Tetraoninae—Grouse
                Genus *Dendragapus* (Elliot)—Blue Grouse
                    Species *D. obscurus* (Say)—Blue Grouse
                        Subspecies *D. o. obscurus* (Say)—Dusky Grouse
            Subfamily Odontophorinae—New World Quails
                Genus *Callipepla* = *Lophortyx* (Wagler)—Quail
                    Species *C. gambeli* (Gambel)—Gambel's Quail
                        Subspecies *C. g. gambeli* (Gambel)—Western Gambel's Quail
                        Subspecies *C. g. fulvipectus* (Nelson)—Fulvous-breasted Gambel's Quail
                    Species *C. californica* (Shaw)—California Quail
                Genus *Callipepla* (Wagler)—Scaled Quail
                    Species *C. squamata* (Vigors)—Scaled Quail
                        Subspecies *C. s. pallida* (Brewster)—Arizona Scaled Quail
                        Subspecies *C. s. hargravei* (Rea)—Hargrave Scaled Quail
                Genus *Colinus* (Goldfuss)—Bobwhite
                    Species *C. virginianus* (Linnaeus)—Northern Bobwhite
                        Subspecies *C. v. ridgwayi* (Brewster)—Masked Bobwhite

---

into a population's productivity during a given year. If nothing else, classifying birds into age classes permits the separation of the older, tougher birds from the younger, more tender ones prior to cooking.

Sex and age classification of game birds can be easy or difficult, depending on the family of birds involved. Classifying the sex and age of quails is remarkably easy; age separation of grouse requires experience, and distinguishing the sex of juvenile doves is difficult. The sexes of coots and cranes are impossible to differentiate in the field. Because sex and age classifica-

TABLE 1.1 *(Continued)*

Genus *Cyrtonyx* (Gould)—Harlequin Quail
    Species *C. montezumae* (Vigors)—Montezuma Quail
        Subspecies *C. m. mearnsi* (Nelson)—Mearns'
        Quail
    Subfamily Meleagridinae—Turkeys
      Genus *Meleagris* (Linnaeus)—Turkey
        Species *M. gallopavo* (Linnaeus)—Wild Turkey
          Subspecies *M. g. merriami* (Nelson)—Merriam's
          Turkey
          Subspecies *M. g. mexicana* (Gould)—Mexican
          Turkey
Order Gruiformes—Cranes, Rails, Gallinules, and Coots
    Family Gruidae—Cranes
      Genus *Grus* (Pallas)—Crane
        Species *G. canadensis* (Linnaeus)—Sandhill Crane
          Subspecies *G. c. tabida* (Peters)—Greater
          Sandhill Crane
          Subspecies *G. c. canadensis* (Linnaeus)—Lesser
          Sandhill Crane
Order Columbiformes
    Family Columbidae—Pigeons and Doves
      Genus *Columba* (Linnaeus)—Pigeon
        Species *C. fasciata* (Say)—Band-tailed Pigeon
          Subspecies *C. f. fasciata* (Say)—Interior
          Band-tailed Pigeon
      Genus *Zenaida* (Bonaparte)—Dove
        Species *Z. asiatica* (Linnaeus)—White-winged Dove
          Subspecies *Z. a. mearnsi* (Ridgway)—Western
          White-winged Dove
          Subspecies *Z. a. monticola* (Saunders)—Highland
          White-winged Dove
        Species *Z. macroura* (Linnaeus)—Mourning Dove
          Subspecies *Z. m. marginella* (Ridgway)—Western
          Mourning Dove

SOURCE: Modified from American Ornithologists' Union (1983) and Johnsgard (1973a)

tion is important to researchers and managers and of interest to many hunters, external sex and age criteria are included in the accounts of the various species. Otherwise, the sex and age must be determined by internal examination.

To ascertain the sex of pigeons and doves internally, place the bird on its back, tail forward. Bend the vent area downward with your left hand while manipulating the cloaca with the fingers of your right. If the bird is a male, the penis should emerge. Care must be taken not to confuse roundworms

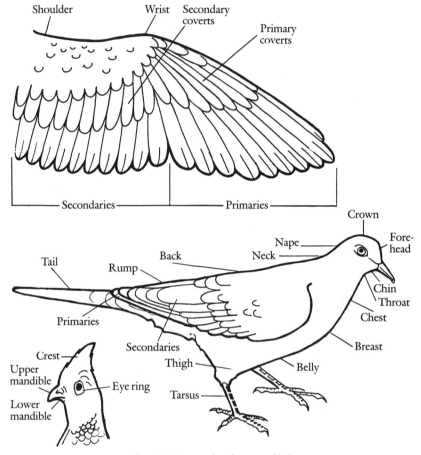

Fig. 1.1. Topography of a game bird.

or other internal parasites with this organ. Gallinaceous birds do not have a visible penis and sex must be ascertained by internal examination. If the bird is dead, the sex of any species can quickly be ascertained by removing the intestines and noting whether testes or an ovary are present along the lower back (Fig. 1.2).

Juvenile birds can almost always be distinguished by plumage characters. The ninth and tenth juvenile primaries in most species are not replaced until the bird's second year, allowing for separation into juvenile and adult age classes (Fig. 1.3). If still in doubt, examine the lower intestine for the presence of a bursa of fabricus, a large blind pocket found only in immature

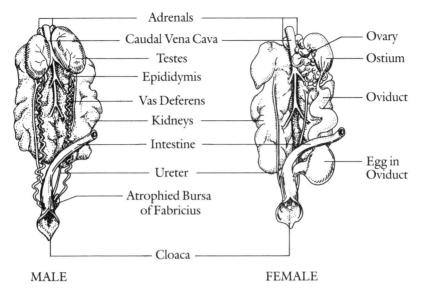

MALE		FEMALE
Adrenals		
Caudal Vena Cava		Ovary
Testes		Ostium
Epididymis		
Vas Deferens		Oviduct
Kidneys		
Intestine		
Ureter		Egg in Oviduct
Atrophied Bursa of Fabricius		
Cloaca		

Fig. 1.2. Ventral view of a bird as seen when looking at the lower back of an eviscerated specimen. Adapted from A. J. Godin (in Schemnitz 1980:158).

Fig. 1.3. Wing of an adult grouse (top) compared to that of a juvenile. The outer two primaries (9 and 10) of the adult are not pointed or frayed and are of uniform appearance. These feathers in the juvenile are pointed and worn.

birds (Fig. 1.4). This feature can be located with a blunt probe in live birds or upon dissection in dead birds. Most game birds cannot be accurately classified to age after their second year to other than an adult category.

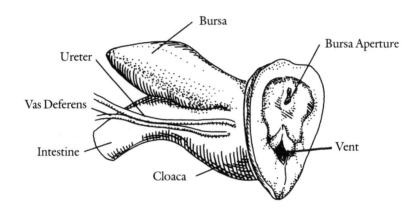

LATERAL VIEW   (After Johnsgard, 1973)

Fig. 1.4. Bursa of fabricius and lower intestine of an immature pheasant. Adapted from A. J. Godin (in Schemnitz, 1980:160).

GAME-BIRD MANAGEMENT IN ARIZONA

The Territorial Period

When Anglo-Americans began arriving in Arizona after the Mexican War, they found a landscape little affected by settlement. With the important but limited exception of the southern river valleys, where livestock had been grazed, most wildlife habitats were in pristine condition. Turkeys and quails appear to have been inordinately abundant (Davis 1982), but the expense of ammunition, a need or desire to obtain large game animals, and the seasonal nature of doves and other migratory species often caused small game to be ignored. This attitude was to change greatly in the settlement era (1865–1925), the end of which saw the use of almost every available acre and every natural resource.

Even as late as the 1880s there was little concern for game birds. The few cities and poor transportation facilities relegated market hunting to only local importance. The prevalent attitude and abundance of game in the back country are attested to by a letter published in the *Arizona Weekly Star* in September 1886:

I am just back from the Arizona White Mountains, and had a splendid time hunting and fishing. Dr. Davis caught 302 mountain trout, while I only caught 235, and the men caught countless numbers. We shot at one bear and one Indian—both escaped unhurt, but we got the Indian's horse. We killed several deer. I shot fifteen wild turkeys and numerous grouse.

The only wildlife protection laws thought to be necessary were prohibitions against year-round hunting and the shipment of game by commercial hunters with the arrival of the railroads in the mid to late 1880s.

The first Territorial Game Code for the Preservation of Game and Fish was passed in 1887 and restricted the taking of most small-game species to between September 1 and the last day of February. Quail and turkeys could be trapped only on one's own premises; there were no bag limits, and game could be sold in season. Doves were not protected at all, but there was a closed season on grouse and Prairie Chickens (even though none of the latter was ever present in Arizona). Any shortage of game was blamed on the displaced Indian, who attempted to make a living at hunting wildlife to sell at the forts and mining camps (Harrison 1893; Secrist 1896).

The impact of commercial hunting on wildlife was nonetheless minimal when compared to the cumulative effects of settlement and ranching. Always settling in select habitats and appropriating whatever limited surface waters were available, homesteaders steadily displaced large, water-dependent species such as the Wild Turkey and Sandhill Crane. The settlers' systematic shooting, trapping, and egg robbing also adversely affected populations of these game birds in the 1880s (Mearns 1890; Howard 1900). Moreover, subsistence hunting could hardly be outlawed, nor could any law against it be enforced.

The arrival of the railroads opened markets on the Pacific Coast, and the commercial hunting of quails and doves became conspicuous if not pervasive. These activities prompted the Tucson Gun Club to prevail on the territorial legislature to amend the game code in 1893 to extend the sport hunting of quail and other small game through March and to outlaw the shipping as well as the sale of wildlife during the closed season.

By the 1890s, environmental conditions had deteriorated considerably. Overgrazing and drought had taken a tremendous toll of southern Arizona wildlife, game birds included (Brown 1900). New homestead laws opened up montane and forested regions previously considered unsuitable for settlement (D. Brown 1985b), and Arizona's abundant wildlife heritage, except

in the more remote desert regions, appeared to be doomed. Yearlong grazing, or rather overgrazing, was the major culprit (Brown 1900; Ligon 1927).

Relief was coming. National Forest reserves were created that would
eventually assist the Wild Turkey, Mearns' Quail, Band-tailed Pigeon, and
other montane species in making a comeback. In 1897 the territorial legislature amended the game code to prohibit all commercial trapping of quail
and the collecting of eggs, and to establish a closed season on doves between March 1 and June 1. The general small-game season was shortened to
October 16 through the end of February. These laws were to be enforced
by the Territorial Fish and Game Commissioners and their appointed assis-
tants. The commissioners' biennial report for 1897–98 reported the destruction of sixty-seven quail traps along the Gila, Salt, Verde, and Agua Fria
rivers and "closing down" the sale of quail in Phoenix.

Even though the state's rangelands were showing evidence of recovery
from the overstocking and droughts of the 1890s, the "nesters" kept coming. The sale of all game was finally outlawed in 1905, but as long as people
lived year-round off the land, both range and game laws were largely cosme-
tic. In spite of these problems, there was still plenty of good small-game
hunting. Wheat farming and an abundance of riverbottom vegetation gave
Arizona a reputation for quail and dove hunting par excellence (O'Connor
1939). As today, quail hunting had its ups and downs, and some banner
years were reported. The laws prohibiting market hunting appear to have
been effective, however, according to the *Arizona Daily Star* (October
16, 1903):

Yesterday was the opening day of the quail season, and many local nimrods tried
their luck with the gun. The little brown birds at one time bid fair to be an unknown
quantity in Arizona, but of late years a wise law for his protection has been in
operation and his call can now be heard on all the hills and in all the valleys. At one
time trappers captured the quail by the thousands and shipped them by the car load
to the markets of California. The sportsmen became alarmed at the rapid extermination and the legislature did the rest. Quail are now plentiful all over the country.

Management under Statehood

The advent of cities and commerce meant that sport hunting had come
to stay. On Arizona's admission to the Union, the state game code of 1913
specified:

Game Birds.—Bobwhite, grouse, pheasant: no open season. Quail, open Oct. 15 to
Feb. 2. Dove and white-wing, June 1 to Feb. 2. Duck, geese, brant and coot, Oct.
15 to Jan. 31. Rail, Sept. 1 to Nov. 30. Woodcock, Nov. 1 to Dec. 31. *Gun.*—Every

person who shall use a shotgun of a larger caliber than No. 10 gauge, for killing any wild turkey, dove, quail, bobwhite, partridge, grouse, pheasant, wild duck, wild goose, snipe or rail, shall be guilty of a misdemeanor.

A hunting license was required for the taking of game, only no one had printed any licenses—a situation not corrected until the bird season was well underway.

The mid-1920s were a low point for southwestern wildlife (Ligon 1927). The number of rural settlers was at an all-time high (Bahre 1977), overgrazing was ubiquitous, and most game laws were little heeded and poorly enforced. The state game warden was without a professional staff, and all regulations were promulgated through the political processes of the state legislature. Thoughtful Arizonans knew that, unless positive steps were taken, their wildlife heritage was in jeopardy.

Action had been taken elsewhere. A political constituency for the protection of game and fish had developed among gun and sportsmen's clubs, and in 1911 the American Game Protective Association was formed in New York. As early as 1913 a New Mexico Game Protective Association was founded in Albuquerque, and under the leadership of such conservationists as Aldo Leopold, J. Stokely Ligon, and several influential ranchers, progress was being made. The key to game abundance was thought to be strictly enforced closed seasons, a system of unhunted refuges for the game to expand from, and vigorous predator control. Small game was subject to the same prescriptions as big game except that restocking with pen-reared and exotic game birds was much in vogue. Although these concepts were later found to be simplistic if not outright erroneous, such thinking was to dominate southwestern wildlife management for thirty years.

In 1927 an Arizona Game Protective Association (AGPA) was formed. Consisting of affiliate sportsmen's clubs from throughout the state, the organization began almost immediately to exert political influence. One of its first actions was to publish a magazine, *The Arizona Wildlife Sportsman*. This organ soon became a vehicle for what was to be the AGPA's first major achievement—a referendum repealing the state game code so that a new one could be adopted. After much debate and opposition (mostly in Tucson), this movement succeeded, and in 1929 the state legislature adopted the code that the AGPA had helped draft.

The game code of 1929 established permanent seasons and regulations that could be modified without being voted on by the legislature, defined game and hunting methods in a more relevant context, and most importantly, established a three-man Game and Fish Commission with broad authority to protect and propagate game mammals, birds, and fishes. An expanded and salaried field force under the state game warden was to report directly to the commission. The status of the state's wildlife was to be assessed annually and steps taken to combat any negative influences.

Although good numbers of deer and turkey were still to be found in the state's remote reaches, small-game hunting opportunities were poor by modern standards. After the dry years of the mid-1930s, even populations of such prolific species as quail were much reduced (Gorsuch 1934). There was no open season on pronghorn antelope, elk, bighorn sheep, Mearns' Quail, Blue Grouse, or Sandhill Cranes. In 1939 the season on mule deer south of the Gila River was closed, and the quail season lasted only fifteen days.

The depression years, however, provided an atmosphere for the beginnings of improvements in resource management. The small homesteaders were giving up. As goat ranches, small cattle outfits, and rural farms were abandoned and absorbed by their larger neighbors, the U.S. Forest and Grazing services were able to gain some semblance of control. The Taylor Grazing Act brought rationale, and eventually range improvement, to the public domain, and the establishment of federal refuges after 1939 promised some measure of habitat management other than the prohibition of the taking of game. Subsistence hunting declined as people moved to town.

Wildlife management was still a seat-of-the-pants proposition, though. State refuges proliferated, and by 1938 there were seventy-six (Fig. 1.5), few with any real provisions for improving the habitat. Predator control was considered a panacea for every species of game, including quails, doves, and turkeys. Closed seasons were advocated to "bring the game back." The propagation of such exotics as pheasants was touted as the solution to wildlife shortages. It remained for the U.S. Biological Survey (now U.S. Fish and Wildlife Service) and the University of Arizona's College of Agriculture to assist the Arizona Game and Fish Department in the progression toward sound game management. This progress was accelerated by the AGPA's earlier efforts to create a professional department that welcomed effective cooperation and participated in such studies as Gorsuch's *The Gambel Quail in Arizona* (1934) and Vorhies and Taylor's 1933 investigation of Arizona's jack rabbits. Although dated by today's standards, these findings were important in dispelling erroneous beliefs and showing how environmental factors controlled wildlife populations.

In 1937 Congress passed the Pittman-Robertson Act, which established a federal tax on firearms and ammunition, the proceeds of which were distributed to state wildlife agencies. All monies were to be spent on wildlife investigations, and particular emphasis was to be given to making life-history studies, developing survey techniques, and collecting harvest data. Because of its early hunting season and an observed decline in numbers, Arizona's most controversial game bird was then the White-winged Dove, and a cooperative life-history investigation of that species was immediately begun (Neff 1940a, b). By 1941, quail and turkey studies were underway and game management in Arizona can truly be said to have originated with implementation of the Pittman-Robertson Act.

Through the 1950s, predator control, refuges, and restocking were still popular game-management prescriptions, but these approaches were now subjected to the scientific method. Studies carried out by the Arizona Game and Fish Department and the Arizona Cooperative Wildlife Research Unit established the state as a leader in game-bird investigations. The cumulative effect of this surge in research was a major change in game-management perceptions. Refuges were abandoned. Predator control was shown to be ineffective for small-game species, and native birds were shown to provide more recreation than exotics. Most importantly, the understanding that small-game numbers were determined by habitat condition and climatic patterns became widely accepted.

Modern Management

By 1960 the life histories of the more popular southwestern game birds had also been studied, and the foremost question was how hunting affected small-game population numbers. Quail populations, for example, were erratic from year to year. Reproduction and populations rose after wet years and declined after dry years. Did hunting affect base population levels, and if so, should quail be hunted in "bad" years? Studies by Hungerford (1960a, 1960b, 1962, 1964) and Smith and Gallizioli (1965) on Gambel's Quail in Arizona, by Campbell et al. (1973) on Scaled Quail in New Mexico, and by R. Brown (1978) on Mearns' Quail were conclusive: quail numbers were determined by climatic factors, and nonhunted populations rose and fell to the same extent as hunted ones. Other findings showed hunting to have little effect on grouse and other gallinaceous game birds and resulted in the setting of generous, standardized seasons.

The status of migratory game birds was more complex. Their populations are affected by conditions on both nesting and winter ranges as well as various points in between. Banding studies, long used to gather migration data, were now used to measure harvest levels and mortality rates.

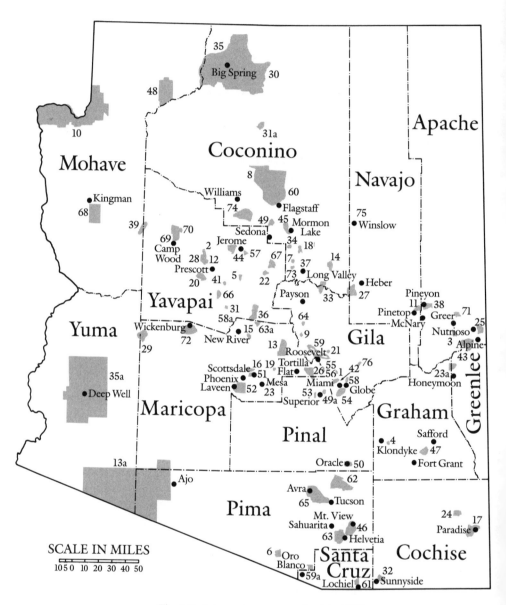

Fig. 1.5. Arizona state game refuges in 1938.

1 — Alamo
2 — American Ranch
3 — Apache Lake
4 — Arivaipa
5 — Ash Creek
6 — Baboquivari
7 — Banfield Springs
8 — Big Lake
9 — Blue Hill
10 — Boulder Canyon
11 — Brushy
12 — Burnt Ranch
13 — Bush Highway
13a — Cabeza Prieta
14 — Cabin Draw
15 — Cahava
16 — Camelback
17 — Chiricahua
18 — Coconino Turkey
19 — Coon Bluff
20 — Copper Basin
21 — Cottonwood
22 — Cottonwood Canyon
23 — Desert Wells
23a — Eagle Creek
24 — El Dorado
25 — Escudilla
26 — Fish Creek
27 — Gentry
28 — Granite Basin
29 — Harquahala
30 — House Rock Valley
31 — Horse Thief Basin
31a — Hull Tank
32 — Huachuca
33 — Indian Garden
34 — Jones Mountain
35 — Kaibab
35a — Kofa
36 — Lime Creek
37 — Long Valley
38 — Los Burros
39 — Mohan Mountain
41 — Mayer
42 — Miami
43 — Middle Mountain
44 — Mingus Mountain
45 — Mormon Mountain
46 — Mt. Fagan
47 — Mt. Graham
48 — Mt. Trumball
49 — Munds Park
49a — Oak Flat
50 — Oracle
51 — Papago Park
52 — Phoenix South Mountain
53 — Picket Post
54 — Pinal
55 — Pinto Creek No. 1
56 — Pinto Creek No. 2
57 — Quail Springs
58 — Rambo Wash
58a — Rock Springs
59 — Roosevelt Lake
59a — Ruby
60 — San Francisco Peaks
61 — San Rafael
62 — Santa Catalina
63 — Santa Rita
63a — Seven Springs
64 — Sheep Trail
65 — Tucson Mountain
66 — Tuscumbia
67 — Walker Creek
68 — Wallapai
69 — Walnut Creek
70 — Walnut Creek Area
71 — Water Canyon
72 — Wickenburg
73 — Wilbur Canyon
74 — Williams
75 — Winslow
76 — Wood Camp

Band recoveries of Western Mourning Doves indicated that only a fraction of the state's population was taken by hunters, but such was not the case for White-winged Doves. High recovery rates, coupled with declines in the statewide call-count index, harvest, and hunt success, indicated that this species was in trouble. Seasons and bag limits were adjusted and bandings intensified.

Investigations began to focus on species previously thought to be too few in number to be hunted or otherwise "managed." In spite of some controversy, the 1960s and 1970s saw studies and eventual seasons on Blue Grouse, Mearns' Quail, Band-tailed Pigeons, and Sandhill Cranes—game birds that had not been legally hunted in years. Some of these studies were federally funded under the Accelerated Research Program For Migratory Upland Game Birds, in effect between 1967 and 1982. It was found that carefully regulated hunting had no effect on population numbers and served to increase public interest in the welfare of these species. Valuable data was collected concerning those factors that did control population numbers and distribution. By the 1980s even coots and rails were being studied, not because biologists were worried about their status, but because they were of biological as well as management interest. The cessation of

Accelerated Research funds after 1982 has halted this work, however, and such birds as the Common Snipe remain virtually uninvestigated.

Further research is needed. Wild Turkey populations appear to be declining, or at least fluctuating more markedly than formerly, and the causes have yet to be identified. Some turkey populations have disappeared entirely. The role of disease in decimating population levels remains largely unstudied in the Southwest except for determining the incidences of bird malaria in quails and trichomoniasis in Mourning Doves. Other problems needing attention are the incidence of lead in dove populations, the effects of timber practices on Wild Turkeys, and the source and destination of Arizona's snipe populations. Necessary management measures include finding the means to preserve and increase wintering crane populations near Willcox and on the Lower Colorado River, managing White-winged Dove populations for maximum productivity, and retaining blocks of quail habitat in public ownership close to population centers.

The most difficult, yet crucial, research involves applied studies to determine the effects of changing land-management practices on selected species. Such investigations require duplicate studies on a treatment area and a control area and must be conducted over a period of five to ten years. Data obtained from such studies are needed to allow an informed public to participate in land-management decisions affecting wildlife.

How Regulations Are Set

Southwestern quail, grouse, partridge, and pheasant populations are no longer systematically censused. Seasons are set for public convenience and at a time when the young are raised and the largest numbers of birds are available. Because the seasons on resident game birds are relatively uncontroversial, there has been an increasing tendency to pass standard seasons, renewable each year at the spring meeting of the Arizona Game and Fish Commission. The seasons are set for varying lengths, and each species of bird is subject to a particular bag and possession limit (the latter usually double the former).

Setting season dates and bag limits for doves, Band-tailed Pigeons, Sandhill Cranes and other migratory birds follows a more circuitous route. Primary management responsibility for these species resides with the U.S. Fish and Wildlife Service, but because this agency has no field biologists in Arizona, it is left to state biologists to coordinate dove surveys, supervise banding and other studies, and collect harvest data. Each state has a biologist on the Migratory Upland Game Bird Technical Committee within a regional Flyway Management Unit. Findings and recommendations from each state are presented to the U.S. Fish and Wildlife Service, and seasons and bag limits are approved by the director and his staff.

After frameworks for each of the management units are published in the federal register, season dates, bag limits, and other hunting arrangements within these frameworks are selected by the states and recommended to their game and fish commissions. There is still opportunity for organizations and individuals to present arguments for additional restrictions on or variations in the hunt regulations. Public interest and involvement may be high, and some regulations adopted may be based largely on public comment.

MANAGEMENT TECHNIQUES

Small-game management methods need not be sophisticated. Most studies of game birds require only a survey, capture, classification, and marking technique. It is also helpful to examine significant numbers of birds (or wings) in order to record sex and age ratios, index population levels, and evaluate their physiological condition. Hunter-killed samples are of great assistance in this regard, and experimental hunt seasons are often recommended when a study is undertaken.

Trapping and Banding

The banding of birds is one of the most useful management tools. Recovered bands can be used to measure harvest levels of hunted species through first-year recovery rates (e.g., Braun et al. 1975). Recoveries and/or trap returns over a period of years are used to construct life tables and estimate annual survival and mortality rates (e.g., Davis and Winstead 1980). Recovery rates can also be used to identify differential vulnerability of sex and age cohorts. With allowances for crippling loss, annual mortality, and incomplete reporting rates, recoveries can even be used to estimate population levels (Seber 1973).

Banded birds also enable biologists to evaluate population discreteness, learn wintering and summering areas, and obtain data on migration chronology. Knowledge of Band-tailed Pigeons, White-winged Doves, and Mourning Doves in Mexico, for example, is primarily derived from U.S.

bands recovered there and returned by cooperative Mexican hunters. Large samples of banded birds may also be used to calculate annual and cumulative survival rates (see, e.g., Schemnitz 1980).

Of course, banding studies cannot be carried out without a suitable trapping technique to capture large numbers of birds. Doves and most quails are easily captured in baited Stoddard or funnel traps. Turkeys, Sandhill Cranes, and Band-tailed Pigeons are usually best secured by firing a cannon net over a bait site or using a drop net or other specially designed trap (Evans 1972; Day et al. 1980). Mearns' Quail can be located with the aid of a pointing dog, night-lighted, and captured with a throw net (R. Brown 1975).

Surveys

Monitoring any species requires a census technique to determine whether the population is stable, increasing, or decreasing. Although a direct count is sometimes used to inventory such highly visible subjects as cranes, most birds do not lend themselves to this technique. A better census method is systematically to sample representative portions of the population and monitor or index trends in population levels. This can be accomplished through either visual or auditory surveys in selected areas.

Call-counts are widely used as a census technique. These surveys consist of randomized (or at least systematic) counts of the announcement calls of territorial male birds. Such counts have been found to adequately index populations of Gambel's Quail (Smith and Gallizioli 1965), Scaled Quail (D. Brown et al. 1978), pheasants (D. Brown 1973a), Band-tailed Pigeons (Fitzhugh 1974), and Mourning and White-winged doves (D. Brown and Smith 1976). Some of these counts have the added advantage of being able to predict the coming year's reproductive and/or hunting success (e.g., Smith and Gallizioli 1965; D. Brown and Smith 1976). The male grouse's *hoots* are too low in volume to census, however, and this species is surveyed by conducting late-summer brood counts. Mearns' Quail are painstakingly surveyed by counting their "diggings" (R. Brown 1976), but an acceptable census technique for Wild Turkeys remains to be determined.

An inexpensive method of surveying hunted species is the use of postseason hunt questionnaires. One of the best indices of annual abundance is hunter success. If a statistically valid number of hunters is sampled and the same sampling method is used each year, population changes can be ascertained from the reported number of birds bagged per hunter day.

Harvest Data

An obvious advantage of a hunting season is that it facilitates the gathering of large samples of birds for biological data. For a researcher to collect similar samples over such large areas would be costly if not impossible. Most game birds are readily classified as adults or juveniles (first year), and these data can be used to measure reproductive success and the number of young birds recruited into the population. Check stations and wing-collection boxes are a convenient means of obtaining age and sex ratio data as well as information on hunt success. Along with population indices, these data can be used to provide measurements of recruitment, survival, and mortality.

Recruitment can be expressed as the ratio of juveniles to adults, or of juveniles to adult females, or the percentage of juvenile birds in the population. An important consideration is the higher vulnerability of males and juveniles. Such differential vulnerability can be measured through banding studies and by comparing recovery ratios of the different age and sex classes.

Variations in recruitment rates among years can be compared with environmental measurements (precipitation, mast production, etc.) to see if these variables are related to the number of young birds coming into the population. Such correlations have shown, for example, that Gambel's Quail nesting success depends on the amount of rainfall received during the preceding October–March period (Smith and Gallizioli 1965).

Population levels of other species, such as Mearns' Quail, are determined more by annual variations in survival rate than by variations in recruitment. Once a method of indexing annual population trends and measuring recruitment has been established, the rate of survival can be measured from one year to the next. Annual survival rates, or the reciprocal mortality rate, can then be compared with any of several environmental variables, including hunter numbers. Should any of these factors prove to be significantly correlated with survival, reasons for population increases or decreases can be hypothesized and tested. For example, the estimated annual survival rate of Mearns' Quail is correlated with precipitation amounts received during the summer before the current year's harvest of adults. Because summer precipitation determines perennial grass production in southeast Arizona (Cable 1975), these data suggest that Mearns' Quail survival rates and population levels are related to the amount of residual grass cover produced the preceding year.

Obviously, summer rainfall itself has no more direct effect on Mearns' Quail survival than winter precipitation does on Gambel's Quail nesting. The correlations only provide clues as to what factors might be affecting the quails. Knowing these clues enables the researcher to ask the right questions. These investigations allow resource managers to prescribe management practices beneficial to the species's needs—in this case, reduced livestock grazing. Such knowledge also forestalls unwarranted actions such as season closures.

The value of gathering population data lies not so much in the manipulation of wildlife populations, although that may be a desirable option from time to time, but in the knowledge it provides about a species's population dynamics. If the environmental variables that determine wildlife densities can be identified, population highs and lows can be foreseen. In addition to providing the public with desired information, wildlife managers can explain the reasons behind low population densities and educate the public against futile management prescriptions.

PART I

Partridges and Pheasants

Partridges are Old World galliforms that are sexually monotypic (males and females have a similar appearance) and form extended pair bonds to spend at least part of the year as a family group. Two species have been widely and successfully introduced into North America: the Gray, or Hungarian, Partridge (*Perdix perdix*) and the Chukar (*Alectoris chukar = A. graeca*). The former has adapted to farming areas within the intermountain and prairie regions, and the latter is found throughout the arid mountains of the Great Basin. Introductions of Chukars, "huns," and such other partridges as the Black Francolin (*Francolinus francolinus*) and Gray Francolin (*F. pondicerianus*) have nonetheless generally failed in the Southwest. Only the Chukar can be said to be established in Arizona, and then only in the extreme northwest portion of the state.

Pheasants are largely Oriental galliforms, more closely related to grouse than are the partridges. They are sexually dimorphic, that is, the males differ from the females not only in plumage—which among male pheasants is exaggerated and often gaudy—but often in size and even in habitat preference. The polygamous males take no part in nest preparation, incubation, brooding, or chick rearing. Because of their long adaptation to agricultural lands, several races of Ring-necked Pheasant have been introduced to farming areas in Europe and North America, often with notable success. Numerous such attempts in Arizona have been mostly unsuccessful, probably due to the arid climate and low spring humidity.

PAUL BOSMAN

CHAPTER 2
Chukar

Blue Grouse are just as good to eat. Gambel's Quail are infinitely more abundant. Scaled Quail can be just as challenging, and Mearns' Quail are a more sporting proposition. So why the Arizona hunter's fascination with Chukars? Maybe it is because the Chukar is the number-one game bird in Nevada and an important species in the bags of California, Washington, and Idaho hunters. Whatever the reason, the number of inquiries for information on this species in Arizona is markedly out of proportion to the bird's limited distribution, remote occurrence, and generally low numbers in the state.

There is no mistaking a Chukar. The staccato of short cackles that gives the bird its name is unique. The black-barred flanks, purplish blue backs and breasts, coral beaks and feet, and black line passing through the eye and encircling the white throat are easily recognizable. The birds look and behave like oversized quail. Adult males weigh from 19 to 26 ounces; females are between 16 and 19 ounces (Christensen 1970).

The sexes have similar plumage. The larger, older males tend to have stockier beaks and brighter-colored bills and feet than the hens, but birds of the year, and some individuals, are difficult to classify to sex externally. Chukars in hand can be classified to sex and age by examining their ash-brown wings. Juveniles up to sixteen weeks have mottled secondary feathers, and because all but the outer two primaries are replaced in the postjuvenile molt, the "newness" of the other primary feathers and the outer two juvenile primaries' narrower shape, faded color, and worn condition can be used to distinguish them from those of adults. In adults, if primary number three is longer than 5.35 inches, the bird is a male; if this feather is 5.35 inches or shorter, the bird is a female (Weaver and Haskell 1968).

Chukars in Arizona are derived largely from an Indian strain, *Alectoris chukar chukar* (Christensen 1970). Transplants of wildtrapped Turkish stock, *A. c. kleini*, released at Burnt Corral near Apache Lake, failed to become established.

DISTRIBUTION

The only populations of Chukars currently established in Arizona are restricted to the Arizona Strip north of the Grand Canyon and possibly the environs of Cataract Canyon south of the Grand Canyon. These birds are therefore limited to a relatively small area of canyons and broken country between Great Basin grassland and desertscrub (Fig. 2.1). Most Chukars are seen between 4,500 and 6,500 feet elevation on points and in canyons leading into Snake Gulch, Hack's Canyon, and other tributaries of Kanab Creek. Their distribution usually depends on the availability of water, although in May 1975 I was amazed to see and hear a lone "sentinel" bird atop a boulder on waterless Fishtail Mesa now in Grand Canyon National Park. In the 1970s Chukars were reported in the upper reaches of Cataract Canyon northeast of Williams (G. Dickens, pers. comm.) and in canyons leading into Paria Canyon. The latter birds are believed to be the result of introductions just to the north in Utah.

I know of no sightings along the Colorado River in the Grand Canyon, despite ample opportunity for the bird to become established in such well-watered and appealing terrain. Without repeated releases, the Chukar is also absent from other Mohave Desert locales, including the western portions of the Arizona Strip. Fears that the Chukar would displace the native Gambel's Quail are therefore unfounded, and the two species are largely allopatric. Nonetheless, in 1968 John Russo and I shot two Gambel's Quail out of a small covey when hunting Chukars in Snake Gulch. This species has never been encountered there again, and it may be that Chukars have displaced some marginal populations of Gambel's Quail in some drainages in the Great Basin.

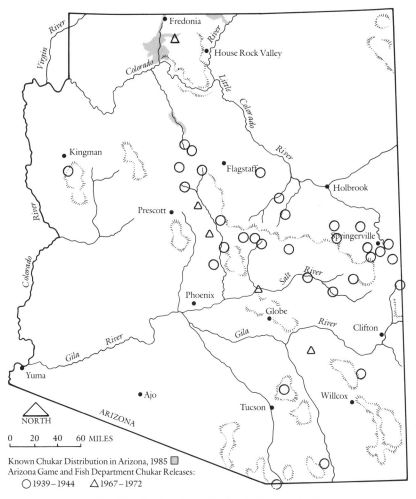

Fredonia

House Rock Valley

Kingman

Flagstaff

Holbrook

Prescott

Springerville

Phoenix

Globe

Clifton

Yuma

Ajo

Willcox

Tucson

ARIZONA

NORTH

0   20   40   60 MILES

Known Chukar Distribution in Arizona, 1985 ▨
Arizona Game and Fish Department Chukar Releases:
○ 1939–1944   △ 1967–1972

Fig. 2.1. Distribution of the Chukar in Arizona in 1985.

Fig. 2.2. Arizona Chukar habitat: a side canyon draining into Snake Gulch on the North Kaibab Plateau. The low shrubs are big sagebrush, other sagebrushes, a few junipers, and pinyons.

HABITAT

Steep hillsides, dry canyons, rock outcrops, cliffs, and talus slopes characterize Chukar country everywhere (Fig. 2.2). Chukar habitat is universally arid with moderately cold winters and warm summers. Precipitation averages between eight and twelve inches a year, and although some rainfall can be expected to occur sporadically throughout the year, the most regular precipitation comes during the winter months.

The Chukar is a bird of arid grasslands or shrub-steppe grading into desertscrub. Its habitat in both the Old World and the New is populated by coarse bunchgrasses and such drought-resistant shrubs as sagebrush, horsebrush, rabbitbrush, and joint-firs, interspersed among bare ground and annuals. In the American West a few Utah junipers and Rocky Mountain pinyon pines may be scattered about, but it is the spring annuals such as fiddleneck and red-stem filaree that are the Chukar's staple food. Indeed, if such exotic annuals as filaree, Russian thistle, and cheatgrass are lacking, so are the Chukars. These partridges were not really introduced to new habitats—the essential vegetative components of their homeland preceded them. Because cheatgrass and other annuals increase with grazing and range fires, overgrazing is not detrimental to Chukars and in fact greatly assists in their establishment and success. Free water is important, however, and the birds cannot exist without it.

LIFE HISTORY

Although there have been no studies of Chukars in Arizona, Christensen's (1970) definitive work on the species in Nevada is applicable to the populations here. Covey break-up and pair formation depend on temperatures and plant phenology and usually take place between late February and mid-March. The male becomes increasingly aggressive, giving a threatening *chak-chak-chak*, or "steam-engine," call and engaging in "waltzing" displays in front of the female with one wing extended downward (Stokes 1961). The monogamous pairs then disperse to form territories around a base water source. If the winter's rains have been adequate and a sufficient supply of green annuals is available, most of the birds will have paired by late March.

Egg laying and incubation begin in late March and usually continue into mid-April. Although the male defends the nest area and may remain in attendance through the nesting period, it is believed that the female does all the incubating. Afterward many of the males form bachelor coveys accompanied by females unsuccessful at nesting—a not uncommon occurrence in drought years.

The nest is a mere scrape sparsely lined with leaves, twigs, and possibly a few feathers, but it may be well concealed under a sagebrush or among rocks and difficult to locate. The eggs may number as many as twenty or even more, but more commonly there are between eight and fifteen. They vary somewhat in size, shape, and color but are distinctly ovoid and average approximately 1⅝ x 1¼ inches. Their color is a creamy white or buff, speckled or splashed with purplish, red, or brownish spots. Incubation requires twenty-two to twenty-three days.

Most hatching occurs in late May and early June, the driest time of year in much of Arizona. Should the breeding condition of the bird be at a high level, renesting will occur if the first nest is destroyed, and some nesting may persist into August. There is little evidence that hens raise more than one brood, even though the males may return to assist with chick rearing and parental duties. The birds commonly "hold tight" at this time and may have to be almost stepped on to flush. Either parent may feign being crippled in an attempt to lure an intruder away from eggs or downy young.

Clutches may be large, particularly in favorable years, and brood size varies from under four to more than twelve. The downy gray young feed almost entirely on insects for their first weeks of life before turning to the new growth of cheatgrass and other greens. From May through early fall, water becomes increasingly important to the Chukars' movements and distribution. Single and broodless adults usually water early in the morning; hens, pairs, and broods may not come in to drink until three hours after sunrise. During the summer the integrity of family groups breaks down, and large aggregations of adults and young become common. Groups with fifty to one hundred young have been reported at this time, some of them still only small chicks.

Greens, taken so avidly during the late winter and early spring, are gradually replaced in the diet by insects, particularly grasshoppers, during incubation and brood rearing. As the summer continues, seeds become a staple. The most important are those of the Russian thistle, filaree, fiddleneck, and especially cheatgrass (Fig. 2.3)—some two thousand seeds of this exotic grass were found in one crop. Most foraging takes place in midmorning as the birds walk and fly up to a mile or more from their watering source to select feeding areas (Phelps 1955). A *took-took* call is common during feeding.

Chukars invariably roost on the ground, often beneath a big sagebrush (*A. tridentata*) or other large shrub, under a rock outcrop, or even among sparse cover. Dusting is an almost daily activity, and dusting bowls—oblong depressions in fine dirt—are common in the shelter of the roosting site and around water. Some feathers and droppings are usually present, and during spring and early summer, "clockers," the unusually large droppings of incubating hens, may often be found in dusting bowls and at water.

In July and August the Chukars have a regular daily routine of watering and feeding. This is usually the best time of year to conduct surveys, as the birds are concentrated and ratios of adults to young can be readily observed. Counts are best carried out from sunrise to about nine o'clock in the morning, when most birds are through watering.

When Chukars are disturbed, one or more birds may let out a loud piercing squeal followed by a series of descending *whitoo—whitoo* calls. Although startled Chukars may fly up to a mile or more, most of the covey will usually alight within a distance of fifty to four hundred yards. More

Fig. 2.3. Cheatgrass. This exotic annual is the Chukar's staple food source, both when green and as seed.

often than not, they will then begin running uphill, easily eluding their pursuers. They sound their rallying or gathering cadence of *chuck, chuck, chuck, chucker, chucker*, which increases in tempo to become a rattling chuckle reverberating off the canyon walls. It is also used by both sexes early in the morning and late in the evening to call the covey together. Commonly given from a commanding rock or other elevated perch, this call may also serve to space male birds during the breeding season.

The young attain adult size at sixteen weeks of age, and most coveys consist of full-grown birds by October. With the advent of fall, the seeds of spring annuals become increasingly difficult to glean and the Chukars again seek out the new blades of cheatgrass and other greens, provided that the winter rains have arrived and temperatures permit. Although deep and prolonged snow has been known to kill Chukars in more northern states, there is no evidence that such a phenomenon has yet occurred in Arizona. The few birds taken by hunters is certainly no drain on the population, and the cause of most mortality among Arizona Chukars has yet to be determined. There is also no indication that Arizona's Chukars regularly migrate downhill during winter months as has been observed farther north.

MANAGEMENT HISTORY

The Chukar is a superb game bird. Its sporting character, well-deserved reputation as table fare, and ability to adapt to some of the West's bleakest landscapes have made it almost a panacea to game managers. Since World War II, western states have spent hundreds of thousands of dollars trying to get Chukars established on depleted rangelands, sometimes with phenomenal success.

In Arizona, private releases were conducted at least as early as 1941 on the Maricopa Indian Reservation. Some reproduction was noted, and the initial results were deemed promising enough that in 1942 the Game and Fish Department purchased nineteen Chukars for release on the newly acquired Raymond Ranch west of Winslow. Another eighty were purchased by the San Carlos Apache Tribe and released at Warm Springs and Bear Springs crossings on Black River.

Introductions accelerated in the late 1940s. Almost ten thousand Chukars from the Cluff Ranch Game Farm near Pima were released by the Game and Fish Commission at twenty-nine different locations between 1946 and 1949 (Fig. 2.1). Two hundred or more birds were recommended for each release site, selected to be in well-watered canyons and in areas of open junipers and oaks or in areas of good grass and weed cover. Most of the sites were between 4,000 and 7,000 feet elevation (Lawson 1949a).

Follow-up investigations in 1950 and 1951 showed Chukars to be still present in the Graham Mountains, in the Catalina Mountains, near Saint Johns, at Raymond Ranch, along the Little Colorado River from near Springerville to below Lyman Reservoir, on the OW Ranch (where several broods had reportedly been raised), in upper Sycamore Canyon, in Lime Creek, in the Phoenix and White Tank Mountains, in upper Cataract Canyon, and along Kanab Creek near Fredonia. None of these localities had what was thought to be a huntable population, and the department's small-game biologist, L. L. Lawson (1951a), recommended against additional releases of game-farm stock. Lawson was pessimistic that Chukars would ever provide a resource of any magnitude in Arizona and recommended that if any more were to be introduced they should be wild-trapped birds from the Middle East.

The enthusiasm for Chukars was hard to cool, and following Lawson's recommendation, birds were obtained from Turkey. Between February 1951 and the spring of 1954, 873 wild-trapped Chukars were released in and around Burnt Corral in the Three Bar Wildlife Area across from Apache Lake (Webb 1953a, 1953b, 1954a; Fig. 2.1). Chukars were seen as far as seventeen miles from the release site, but no reproduction was noted by department personnel. Webb (1955) recommended against further releases, not so much because of past failures, but because he feared that such exotics would compete with Gambel's Quail for winter foods.

Sycamore Canyon, east of Dugas in the Prescott National Forest, was selected as the next release site. This area was thought to resemble the Pilot and Excelsior mountains in Nevada where Chukars had become successfully established. Forty-six wild-trapped Chukars from Nevada were traded for javelina and released east of Dugas in September 1956. Chukars were meanwhile still being reported at a number of earlier release sites, and there seemed to be some hope for the program.

After evaluating Chukar habitats in Nevada, Utah, and other Great Basin states, Webb (1958) recommended the Snake Gulch area on the North Kaibab as the most suitable Arizona locale. During the autumn of 1958, 238 wild-trapped Chukars from Nevada were released here (Webb 1959a). The following deer season, hunters were asked to report any Chukars they observed. Although some young birds were reported, the relatively few observed and the lack of sustained sightings in any one area did not bode well for the success of the transplant.

In 1960 a supplemental release of ninety-five wild-trapped Chukars from California was made in Snake Gulch. Broods had been documented at this locality each year since the initial release, and in July 1961, fifty-six Chukars, more than half of them young, were observed. Two broods were also reported from Mingus Mountain near Jerome (Webb 1961a), stocked in 1957 and 1959, but no reports were received from the Apache Lake or Dugas areas.

In 1963, 123 wild-trapped Chukars from Nevada were liberated in Aravaipa Canyon approximately five miles west of Klondyke (Webb and Robeck 1963). This was the department's last attempt to establish this exotic game bird in Arizona. A few Chukars were subsequently reported, but the introductions in the Mingus Mountain–Jerome and Dugas areas were judged to be failures. Since Chukars had been released in all potential habitats, further introductions were not advisable. The only hope for Chukars appeared to be in Snake Gulch and adjacent canyon areas on the Arizona Strip and North Kaibab.

Reports of the birds persisted, and a Chukar season was opened concomitant with the quail season in 1965 and 1966. A similar season was offered through 1971 in the Snake Gulch area, but interest in this remote population by hunters other than department personnel was almost nonexistent. No season was recommended for 1972 and 1973.

TABLE 2.1
November–March Precipitation and
Chukar Hunt Information in Arizona, 1974–78

Year	Number of Hunters	Hunter Days	Chukars Bagged	Chukars per Hunter	Nov.–Mar. Precipitation[a] (inches)	March Drought Index[b]
1974	57	152	26	0.5	3.99	−22
1975	55	131	125	2.3	4.11	13
1976	51	155	8	0.2	4.04	5
1977	71	167	13	0.2	1.86	−18
1978	19	38	0	0.0	10.90	23

[a]Mean of Tuweep and Pipe Springs Climatological Stations
[b]Northwest Arizona (Palmer 1965)

A general Chukar season concurrent with the quail season was again established in 1974, with the proviso that hunters obtain a special bird-hunting permit to provide a sample frame for postseason hunt questionnaires. The bag limit was set at five Chukars a day and ten in possession. That year fifty-seven hunters reported hunting 152 days to bag twenty-six Chukars. The special game-bird permit requirement remained in effect for five years, during which time the number of hunters in any given year never exceeded one hundred, and 125 Chukars was the maximum bag reported (Table 2.1). In 1979 the special-permit requirement was dropped, but the season and bag-limit arrangements established in 1974 have continued.

POPULATION DYNAMICS

Christensen (1970) maintained that the size of Chukar populations in Nevada is determined by the amount and timing of spring precipitation and the number of adults surviving from previous years. He and others have noted that almost no young are produced during drought years but that abnormally heavy precipitation in May and June can also cause chick mortality. The cessation of freezing temperatures and the phenology of the key annual plants that determine Chukar breeding conditions are thought to be the factors that most affect reproductive success.

The limited amount of hunt data available on Chukars in Arizona is compared with winter–spring precipitation and regional drought data in Table 2.1. It appears that here as in other western states there is a relationship, but no direct correlation, between winter precipitation amounts and Chukar population levels.

ARIZONA CHUKAR HUNTING

It was John Russo, Arizona's Game Management chief, who introduced me to Chukar hunting. We were working the Kaibab deer-hunt check station when he woke me well before dawn. "Why so early?" I protested. "Our shift doesn't start until noon."

"We're going Chukar hunting" was the only response.

I have to admit that I was more interested in John's recollections of the days of the huge Kaibab deer herds than in hiking after some almost mythical bird. As we passed through "The Gut" and into the west-side winter range, John regaled me with vivid descriptions of how many deer there used to be. Looking north through the open landscape of sagebrush and junipers, we could see the red cliffs of Zion country and the grandeur of the Pine Valley Mountains in Utah. There was little doubt that, if they existed, Chukars enjoyed the most spectacular scenery in Arizona.

As we approached Willow Point, John cautioned me to watch for Chukars in the patches of cheatgrass scattered among the big sagebrush. Sure enough, a small covey of eight to ten birds flushed out of a patch of cheat toward the rim of the canyon wall separating Willow Point Ridge and a tributary of Table Rock Canyon. The birds scattered along the canyon rim, and after interminable delays in finding and loading shotshells, we hiked down toward the spot where most of the partridges had settled in.

The Chukars had not gone far and John let me take the best position. When we were within twenty yards the birds began to flush, but instead of flying out over the canyon as I had envisioned, they arched down over the lip of the ridge. John was effectively thwarted but I powdered one and hit another just as the birds were dropping out of sight. I let out a loud yell and rushed to the rim where the birds had disappeared. The Chukars had presented challenging targets and I was proud of my shooting. John stood there grinning, enjoying the sight of another convert to "Chukar fever."

The birds had fallen a hundred yards or so down into the canyon. At least one had; I could see a pinkish gray pillow lodged against a pinyon tree. It took at least ten minutes, as I eased my way across broken talus and bypassed some small but sheer cliffs, to get to my prize. Then I noticed a trail of feathers leading to the second bird, which lay exposed on a bare rock another fifty yards below.

A full thirty minutes had passed before I clambered back to the truck. My initiation to Chukar hunting had been typical, though perhaps more

productive than usual. A note from Russo stated that he had gone on to
Table Rock Springs. I could hear the broken covey of Chukars calling in a
high-pitched cackle as they reassembled. Reloaded, I headed off to follow
Russo's tracks in the patches of crusted snow.

It was with no little effort that I worked my way down to the spring,
having gone up two false side canyons before I recognized Table Rock.
Russo was nowhere to be seen. Not quite knowing what to do, I went up
to inspect the overhang that shielded the springs. Chukar tracks were prominent in the soft duff under the ledge; so was the waffle pattern of John's
boots. Some of the quail-like tracks appeared to be on top of John's, and I
was wondering if someone else had been here earlier, when I heard a shout.

On the slope just across from the springs John was yelling "Chukars!" I
could neither see nor hear any. Then a great swishing filled the cavern as
the flock came in to drink. On seeing me, the alighting birds doubled back
on themselves in their haste to retreat; others, perturbed at having their
drink interrupted, remained just outside the recess of the ledge. One I
could have shot on the ground but did not, a decision I would later regret.
Inhibited by the confines of the overhang, I scrambled out from beneath
the ledge.

The remaining Chukars scattered immediately and headed uphill, some
flying and others proceeding on foot. Both methods of locomotion were
expedient, for I never got a shot off. John pulled down on a long-range
stray but without success. Not knowing better, I took off up the pinyon-
studded slope after them. Russo, more experienced, staked out the spring
to await another covey.

The birds were never again within range. Several times I glimpsed them,
always farther ahead and higher up on the steep incline than before. Their
intermittent cackling, answered by other coveys calling on the rimrock
above, kept drawing me on. After an hour of rigorous climbing, I was
forced to give up. The Chukars were nowhere to be seen and I no longer
had the energy to drop back down into Snake Gulch and climb the
thousand feet or so to the birds calling on the north rim. I had learned
what Chukar hunting was about. Only luck and some exceptional shooting
had given me a two-bird bonus to go with the lesson.

I made several subsequent expeditions after Chukars, usually accompanied by Paul Webb and other Game Department personnel assigned to
work the Kaibab check station. Never did I kill more than three of the wily
birds, and we came back from most of our trips empty-handed. One hunt
I especially remember was an evening run into Wild Band Springs. Halfway

there, a covey began flushing wildly from heavy sage cover in Snake Gulch, the first bird rocketing off while I was still seventy-five yards off. Typically, the Chukars did not all get up at once, and I managed to scratch one down that held until I had approached to within forty yards.

I hurried to the base of the cliff where they had alighted, just in time for a most unusual shoot. One by one, the big birds got up at my feet to fly straight up a sheer wall of rock before angling out over the slope a hundred feet above. I bagged two of the ascending partridges, but both fell back onto me as I hastily and unsuccessfully tried to reload before the remaining birds departed. Only one other time, while hunting Prairie Chickens, have I shot a game bird that was flying straight up.

My most memorable venture after Chukars was on an outing with Paul Webb and Dick Todd. Leaving at dawn, we dropped off Willow Point with the intention of working out the entire length of Snake Gulch down to Kanab Creek. We arrived at the stream at about two o'clock that afternoon. No Chukars had been seen or heard, and the long march back promised nothing but drudgery. My dog, at first so energetic in the cool November air, gave out around four o'clock. We stopped to check the map: eleven miles to go, and we had already gone fifteen. Zombielike, we began trudging back, grateful that we were traversing the soft alluvium along the bottom of Snake Gulch.

I was carrying my dog when somebody said "Chukars!" About a dozen of the elusive birds were partaking of a late afternoon snack just ahead of us in a patch of cheat. On hearing our approach they immediately fanned out toward a jumble of talus to our left. The sight of Chukars once again pumped enough adrenalin into my system for me to jog after them. No one else paid them any attention whatsoever.

As before, I soon found myself losing ground in a footrace I could never win. The birds were now fifty yards off and almost invisible in the tumbleweeds and failing light. I jumped up on a rock and sluiced one running. That big male was the only Chukar I have ever shot on the ground. My only regret, however, was the distance back to the main trail— just two hundred yards, but with my excitement subsided, it took the better part of a half hour to catch up with my companions. Carrying that pound-and-a-half Chukar was like carrying another dog. It was after ten o'clock when we got back to Table Rock Springs and our prearranged ride.

That was more than a dozen years ago. I have not bagged any Chukars since, although I have participated in a hunt or two. It's probably time to go after them again. On second thought, maybe I'll just hunt quail instead.

PAUL BOSMAN

CHAPTER 3
Pheasant

While stopping to enjoy the chorus of a colony of White-winged Doves, I was startled by the unforgettable, two-note *korrk-kok* of a cock pheasant ahead of me on the canal bank. As if realizing that his crow had given him away, the bird took flight, and I was treated to a raucous cackle and show of metallic bronze plumage. Strong wing beats carried him across newly planted alfalfa, where he cupped his wings to glide down into a ripening barley field. His dark, iridescent head revealed just a tinge of a white neck-ring, which, coupled with white wing epaulets, showed him to be of mixed Chinese Ring-necked and Afghan White-winged blood. Long, recurved tail feathers trailing from a silvery rump made a memorable departing impression as he dropped into the barley.

I knew the bird's habits well. He would not stay in the barley but would continue running down the row to the cover of a dense arrow-weed thicket. Nor would he be content to stay even there but would sneak off to some hidden retreat beyond view. If any hens were about, they kept their presence to themselves as befits their more secretive nature.

No other Arizona bird can be taken for a pheasant—no other bird near the pheasant's size inhabits agricultural fields bordered by weedy hedgerows and riverbottom jungles. Adult males of the small Afghan White-winged race (*Phasianus colchicus bianchii*), which constitutes most of Arizona's pheasant strains, range from a mean of 2½ pounds to 2 pounds 10 ounces, depending on the year and the bird's condition; grain-fattened cocks may exceed 3 pounds. The more delicate adult hens average about 1 pound 14 ounces in November, when first-year cocks weigh between 2¼ and 2½ pounds and first-year hens weigh between 1 pound 9 ounces and 1 pound 14 ounces.

The cock, or rooster, is truly spectacular. Its iridescent green head is set off by ear tufts and a crimson-wattled cheek patch; its purplish chest, soot-colored belly, and distinctively dotted golden flanks make it a bird of un-rivaled plumage—even minus the ridiculous but handsome barred tail. The beige and sand-colored hen also has long, pointed tail feathers, and though not as impressive as the male's, this feature serves for easy species identifi-cation. No other gallinaceous bird in Arizona has a pointed tail. And al-though the hen is often less vocal on take-off, both sexes get up with a clatter of wings that startles the uninitiated into immobility. With all these attributes, it is no wonder that farmers, game-bird fanciers, and hunters take a proprietary interest in any pheasants within their jurisdiction.

Pheasants can be classified to sex, but not age, by examination of their wings. In contrast to grouse and other galliforms, the ninth and tenth primaries of pheasants are commonly replaced during the postjuvenile molt. The length of the male's spur is also an unsatisfactory age measure-ment, as some older roosters have worn stubs that are hard to distinguish from a juvenile spur. The most reliable age-classification technique for birds in the hand is to measure the bursa of fabricus, the blind pouch extending from the end of the lower intestine. This organ in adult birds rarely meas-ures more than 0.3 inches; juvenile birds have a measurably longer bursa through their first winter (Schemnitz 1980:190).

DISTRIBUTION AND HABITAT

The major pheasant populations persisting in Arizona are largely the result of releases in adjacent states. The pheasant has done well in parts of Nevada, Utah, Idaho, and other Great Basin states whose climates, vegeta-tion, and agriculture are similar to those of the bird's native habitats. Pheas-ants have been able to maintain themselves in Arizona only in limited and fluctuating numbers in humid river valleys having small, irrigated farms with row crops of alfalfa and grain bordered by unkept fence rows. A prox-imity to sumps, drains, and other wetland sites is also essential. Otherwise, Arizona is just too dry to sustain any race of pheasant.

The only sizable population of pheasants in Arizona at present occurs south of Yuma, where mature citrus trees and an understory of irrigated grasses provide relatively moist nesting conditions. Self-sustaining populations elsewhere are limited to remnant citrus and agricultural areas near Mesa, intermittent farmlands along the upper Gila River Valley between Geronimo and the Arizona–New Mexico line, along the Virgin River Valley between Littlefield and the Arizona-Nevada boundary, and a few farms between Camp Verde and Clarkdale (Fig. 3.1).

LIFE HISTORY

There have been no life-history studies of Arizona pheasants, but management investigations and observations here and in adjacent states show biological and chronological parallels with White-winged Pheasants in their native habitat near the Russian-Afghanistan border as reported by Kozlowa (*in* Delacour 1951).

Beginning in March, the male becomes solitary and sets up a territorial beat that is traveled and defended each day. Early morning crowing, accompanied by wing flutters and a loud whirring, announces his presence and serves to attract any hens within hearing distance. An increasing frequency of calls and displays coincides with gonadal development. If the male has chosen and maintained a productive territory, he will acquire a harem of one to three hens, sometimes more. Mating begins in early April, with the peak of nest initiation concomitant with the peak of calling activity in late April or early May. By mid-May most of the hens are nesting and of no further interest to the rooster, who does not participate in nest construction, incubation, or chick rearing. By the end of May he abandons his now-solitary patrols.

The nest is commonly in grass or in an irrigated substitute such as barley or alfalfa. The herbaceous understories of Bermuda grass and exotic forbs found within the humid confines of mature citrus groves are among the more productive nesting sites in Arizona (Fig. 3.2). A bush, loosly lying brush, or other protective structure may shield the nest and setting hen from sun and predators. The nest itself is sparsely lined, usually with grass or soft downy feathers, and measures about a foot in diameter. The eight to fourteen (rarely up to seventeen) pale, glossy, grayish olive eggs measure about 1½ by 1¾ inches.

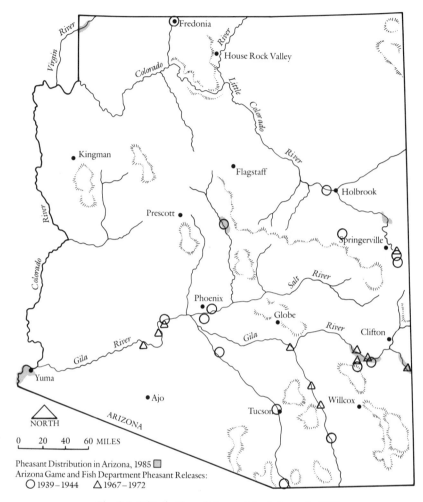

Fig. 3.1. Distribution of pheasant in Arizona in 1985.

Pheasant Distribution in Arizona, 1985 ◻
Arizona Game and Fish Department Pheasant Releases:
◯ 1939–1944 △ 1967–1972

Fig. 3.2. Herbaceous understory in old-growth citrus, an artificially humid microhabitat conducive to pheasant nesting success.

Incubation takes about twenty-three days after the deposit of the last egg, placing the peak of hatching in the last weeks of May—the most arid time in Arizona. The hen does not feign injury when approached by an intruder but instead runs off from the nest for ten to fifteen paces before taking wing. If flushed repeatedly, the hen abandons the nest, and many nests are destroyed by the cutting of alfalfa and barley fields. With the approach of hatching, the hen becomes increasingly loath to flush and must be almost stepped on before revealing itself.

Eggs continue to hatch through June. The youngsters are covered with yellow and brown down, striped in brown and black, and are remarkably self-sufficient. They feed by following the hen about and following her example, much like domestic chicks. Should the hen flush, the chicks will scatter and hide in the nearest cover. After only about two weeks they are capable of flight and remain with the hen for only about another two months before setting off on their own.

Pheasants roost on the ground or, if circumstances allow, in the low branches of trees. Roosters when flushed emit a guttural cackle that descends in tone and frequency. A flushed hen may give a subdued chuckle, but her usual call is a harsh *kia-kia* that announces her presence and assists in keeping her brood together. Typical hiding cover is a neglected patch of rank weeds or, if available, reeds or cattails.

Except during incubation and chick rearing, when insects provide much of the hen's diet and most of the chick's, pheasants feed primarily on culti-vated greens and waste grain—alfalfa and barley sprouts, and kernels of maize, barley, and corn. A great variety of weed seeds are also taken along with incidental insects, and from late summer through the winter, several birds may forage together in newly planted fields or stubble. Such aggrega-tions are not typical, however, as most birds remain solitary or form small, loose flocks of the same sex.

MANAGEMENT HISTORY

Because of their great sporting qualities, fine flavor, and adaptability to agriculture, pheasants have always been high on the list of desirable intro-ductions. When the first transplants of Mongolian Pheasants to Oregon were promoted in the 1890s as the answer to game shortages, strong pro-posals were voiced to obtain similar birds to "colonize favorable Arizona localities" (Harrison 1893).

One of the first acts of the first state game warden in 1913 was to appro-priate five hundred dollars to determine the adaptability of the "Chinese Pheasant and other imported game birds to the food and climate condi-tions of Arizona" (Willard 1914). Because there was no game farm or other state facility to hold birds, the pheasants purchased were apportioned out to various individuals. A lack of accountability made the success of this venture inconclusive, and requests were made to obtain additional birds and to purchase or lease a state game farm. Interest in pheasants continued, and by 1919, gun clubs, bird fanciers, and youth groups were releasing pheasants in the Salt River Valley and probably elsewhere (Lawson 1940a). By 1929 a state game farm on West Glendale Avenue north of Phoenix was supplying Arizona Game Protective Association affiliates with pheasants and turkeys to transplant and release.

Pheasant populations, however, appeared unable to sustain themselves. Interest in establishing this species in Arizona might have lagged except for the eruptions of pheasant populations in California and the northern Great Plains. Why was this fine game bird not becoming established in similar cultivated habitats in Arizona? With the availability of Pittman-Robertson funds in the late 1930s, an effort was made to find out. One of the first projects to be approved was an investigation of potential introduction sites and a systematic evaluation of any releases. More than one thousand pheasants from Arizona game breeders and the Ligon Game Farm in New Mexico were released at twelve locations between 1939 and 1942 (Lawson 1940b; Arrington 1942a; Fig. 3.1).

Despite prerelease screening procedures, predator control, and some early encouragements in the more promising sites, pheasants refused to proliferate in Arizona (Gambrell 1941). By the end of the release program in 1942, their outlook was rated as good only in the Buckeye, Stafford-Thatcher, and Camp Verde areas, with the birds considered established only in the northern vicinities of Richville, Springerville, Snowflake, and Fredonia. Releases in the more populous and extensive farming areas— Mesa, Casa Grande, Phoenix, and Tucson—were recommended to be discontinued barring more conducive farming practices or new information. Lawson (1940a) suspected that low humidity might be contributing to reproductive failure in the Salt River Valley and other desert locales, despite reports of numerous pheasants from private releases at Gillespie Farms near Gila Bend.

Pheasant observations persisted through the 1950s and 1960s near Springerville, in the Lehi area, in the Virgin River Valley, and in the Verde Valley between Camp Verde and Clarkdale, where two to three hundred birds were thought to be present in 1961 (Webb and Robeck 1962; Dickens 1979). These areas were subject to periodic releases from private parties, and the true status of pheasant populations was difficult to evaluate. In any event, there appeared to be little hope for a huntable population of any magnitude. With only an outside chance of the establishment of a self-sustaining population, interest in pheasant hunting was relegated to shooting preserves.

In the early to mid-1960s a "new" arid-lands pheasant became popular in the West. The Afghan White-winged Pheasant from cultivated valleys in Russia and northern Afghanistan was thought to be better adapted to the arid basins of the intermountain states. These birds were leaner than those of the Ring-necked race (*P. c. torquatus*) introduced previously, and the cocks possessed a pronounced white shoulder patch on the wing coverts and lacked the white neck collar. The hens were said to have a slightly more pinkish tinge to their plumage. Although climatic comparisons between most Arizona farming locales and the Afghan's native habitat showed several dissimilarities, including lower humidity in Arizona during the critical January–June period, an introduction program was scheduled (Project Personnel 1968a).

Between 1966 and 1968, 2,278 Afghan White-winged Pheasants were released along the Gila River in the Arlington, Robbins Butte, and Painted Rock wildlife areas, and in the vicinity of Safford. All releases were in midwinter and of game-farm stock. Released birds were banded, and crow call-counts, brood counts, fall density counts, and sex-ratio surveys were scheduled. Hunts were recommended to determine the extent of natural reproduction by comparing ratios of banded to unbanded birds.

Spring call-counts showed a good breeding population and proved to be a valuable census technique. Another thousand pheasants were purchased and released along the Gila River near Duncan and in the Pima-Thatcher area near Safford, and 228 were purchased from Magma Game Farm near Queen Creek for future propagation.

Arizona's first pheasant hunt took place in November 1968. The open area took in both the Arlington and Robbins Butte wildlife areas, and permit-holders had to check in and out of the hunt area. The bag limit was two pheasants of either sex during each of the two days of the hunt.

A total of 184 hunters participated, taking forty limits and harvesting 164 pheasants (Table 3.1). The ratio of roosters to hens was approximately 1:1, and 40 percent of the pheasants were juveniles hatched in 1968. Twenty-five percent of the birds taken were banded, and it was estimated that 30 percent of the population was removed by the hunt and that the mean annual survival rate of the adults had been 58 percent (Project Personnel 1969). The crop contents were almost entirely milo maize. Nineteen blood samples all tested negative for fowl spirochetosis.

TABLE 3.1
Pheasant Hunt Information at Arlington, Arizona, 1968–71

	1968	1969	1970	1971
Permits issued	225	225	150	150
Hunters in field	184	158	116	93
Hunter days[a]	271	203	166	118
Pheasants harvested	164	45	28	10
Pheasants per hunter	.89	.28	.24	.11
Pheasants per hunter day	.61	.22	.17	.09
Limits (2 per day)	50	5	2	0
Limits per hunter day	.15	.02	.01	.00

SOURCE: D. Brown 1972b
[a]Any part of a day was counted as a full day

Despite the removal of an estimated 218 birds, including crippling loss, and no additional releases during the winter of 1968–69, crow call-counts in the area increased 11 percent, and the prognosis for establishing a pheasant population near Arlington appeared to hold some promise. What was not considered at the time was that spring moisture conditions had been considerably above average in 1968 and were slightly above the norm in 1969 (Palmer 1965; Table 3.2).

The remaining stock of White-winged Pheasants at the Ligon State Game Farm were purchased the following winter and released at Duncan and at two locations on the San Pedro River near Redington and Mammoth. Another 138 birds were purchased from Magma Game Farm and released at three locations in the Springerville area. No further release areas were recommended until it could be shown that a population could maintain itself through natural increment and support limited hunting (Project Personnel 1970).

In 1969 a hunt similar to the one in 1968 was held in the Arlington area, and in addition, two rooster-only hunts were authorized in Graham County. Each of the Graham County seasons was for one weekend and opened to 250 permittees. Only forty-five pheasants of both sexes were harvested at Arlington and forty-seven roosters were taken in Safford Valley (Tables 3.1, 3.3). Less than 50 percent of the birds at both Arlington and in Graham County were birds of the year, and weights were lighter than in 1968 for all age and sex cohorts. Although band recoveries indicated a mean annual survival rate of 66 percent for roosters in Safford Valley, the survival rate for both sexes at Arlington was only 5.4 percent. These figures cast doubt as to whether pheasants would be able to maintain themselves during dry years.

Underscoring this concern, the 1970 call-counts were lower in all areas except Duncan, where pheasants had been released in the winter of 1969–70. May drought indices were below average and the pheasants now had to contend with more typical Arizona conditions (Table 3.2).

The hunts in 1970 at Arlington and in Safford Valley were reduced to 150 and 300 permits, respectively, and harvests and hunt success declined at both areas when compared to 1969 (Tables 3.1, 3.3). The spring of 1971 was one of extreme drought, and call-counts were lower than previous years on all comparable routes. The success of the entire program was in doubt (D. Brown and Project Personnel 1971)—the releases at Springerville and in the San Pedro Valley already being judged failures.

TABLE 3.2

Afghan White-wing Pheasant Crow Call-Count Information in Arizona, 1966–73

Location	1966	1967	1968	1969	1970	1971	1972	1973
				Number of Crow Calls Heard[a]				
Hassayampa-Arlington	28	73	114	101	40	22	15	—
Robbins Butte-Arlington[b]		19	63	97	27	9	3	—
Painted Rock		26	59	30	25	6	1	—
South of Yuma	—	—	—	—	—	—	—	124
			May Drought Severity Index (South-Central Arizona)					
		−23	33	8	−5	−27	−33	64
				Number of Crow Calls Heard				
Safford Valley (Thatcher-Eden)			29	29	101	Discontinued		
San Jose-Hollywood		—	—	11	2	4	1	—
Safford-Bryce-Eden		—	—	58	11	13	6	13
New Mexico Line-Clifton		—	—	11	53	16	12	—
Winkelman-Mammoth		—	—	—	11	11	7	—
			May Drought Severity Index (Southeast Arizona)					
		−25	41	−10	−17	−31	−25	59

[a] Highest count recorded on minimum of two surveys during last week of April or first week of May each year
[b] The last half of the Robbins Butte route is near the Arlington release site

TABLE 3.3

Pheasant Hunt Information in
Graham County, Arizona, 1969–71

	1969[a]	1970	1971
Permits issued	500	300	300
Hunters in field	296	145	135
Hunter days[b]	422	228	103
Pheasants harvested	47	18	16
Pheasants per hunter	.16	.12	.12
Pheasants per hunter day	.11	.08	.08
Limits (2 roosters per season)	6	4	3
Limits per hunter per season	.02	.03	.02

[a] Total from two seasons
[b] Any part of a day was counted as a full day

Hunts in 1971 were similar to the previous years' seasons, but only ten pheasants were harvested at Arlington and sixteen in Safford Valley (Tables

3.1, 3.3). The spring of 1972 was even drier than in 1971, and call-counts declined further on all areas surveyed despite the release of the department's remaining brood stock the previous winter at Arlington. In 1973 more feral pheasants were heard on call-count routes in the citrus orchards south of Yuma than had ever been heard in the release areas (D. Brown 1973a; Table 3.2). Arizona's experimental introduction of White-winged Pheasants was at an end.

Call-counts continued to show a thriving pheasant population in and adjacent to old-growth citrus groves on Yuma Mesa. These birds, which appear to be of mixed Ring-necked–Afghan White-winged stock are thought to have originated from long-established populations in Baja California Norte and California (see, e.g., Leopold 1959). Because the prime pheasant habitat was privately owned and the growers did not want their fruit pierced by shotgun pellets, a firearms season was out of the question. However, the Arizona Game and Fish Commission did authorize a month-long, statewide falconry season in 1975.

In 1980 this season was extended to forty-four days and opened to both falconry and archery hunting. To obtain a questionnaire sample and determine how many pheasants were being taken, a special game-bird permit was required for the 1981 season which was extended to coincide with the general small-game season from the second Friday in October through February 15 of the following year. A bag limit of two birds and possession limit of four was also established, an arrangement that has continued to the present time.

Questionnaire data collected from permit-holders showed an annual harvest of one to three dozen pheasants by fewer than one hundred hunters for the years 1981 through 1985 (Table 3.4). Most of the pheasants were taken by archers near Yuma, with a few birds also reported from the upper Gila River near Safford, the Mesa area, and the Virgin River Valley.

TABLE 3.4
Pheasant Hunt Information in Arizona, 1981–85

Year	Number of Hunters	Days Hunted	Pheasant Bagged
1981	94	391	12
1982	89	440	36
1983	16	71	19
1984	66	429	30
1985	74	472	19

THE LAST PHEASANT

Things were looking bleak. I was working the checking station and unable to participate in what was to be Arizona's last shotgun pheasant hunt—the last one not in a shooting preserve, anyway. Having participated in the original releases of the Afghan whitewings and having monitored the experiment from start to finish, I coveted taking and possessing at least one of the birds. But I could see that the chances for validating my permit and bagging a pheasant were slim. The cloudy sky parted; the western position of the December sun told me that in another two hours this final day of the season would be over. The returning hunters had diminished to a trickle, and most of them were empty-handed.

My relief finally arrived. Wasting no time, I drove to Fort Thomas and a recently flooded maize field behind the Mormon church. The field was well hidden, and, being next to the river, offered as good a chance as any place for a fast pheasant. I had seen a good number of the showy birds here prior to the season and knew from the poor showing at the check station that most of them had escaped the hunters' guns. The pheasant is a crafty bird, well conditioned to the ways of man and his dogs.

But I was not alone; another hunter was working the rows of unharvested grain with a German Shorthair. Leaving him the field, my Brittany and I went to work the tamarisk-lined Gila. A patch of cockleburs between the maize and the river made an ideal hiding place; if any cover held the promise of a pheasant, this was it. Sure enough, no sooner had the dog gotten into the cockleburs than two hens clattered out. My adrenalin surged: there had to be a legal rooster in there somewhere.

The cackle was off to my right and not close. I turned to see a rooster flushing wildly out of the maize a good sixty yards off. No chance for a shot. He had probably run the first fifty yards while the hens were getting up. The spooked bird flapped purposefully across the field, unaware of the other hunter until it was almost too late. Seeing his danger, the bird wheeled, and I knew the hunter would shoot, even if it was maximum range. He had nothing to lose.

A slight shudder and ruffle of feathers preceded the bark of a 20 gauge; the cock had been dusted, but nothing fatal. Setting his wings, the pheasant sailed across the field to land in an isolated weed patch next to a drainage ditch. As fast as mud-sodden boots allowed, both hunters headed for the spot where the bird had dropped in. The sense of urgency was communicated to the dogs, who became visibly excited.

I kept my eyes glued to the open ground beyond the weeds, watching for a pheasant headed for more spacious cover. Nothing. Either he was still in the weeds, or I had missed his escape. Sixty yards, fifty, forty, thirty; still no sign of a crouched bird scuttling off across the sprouting barley on the other side. If he flushed now, one or both of us would get a crack at him—unless he had mysteriously disappeared as pheasants so often do.

By unspoken agreement, we partitioned the weed patch. The cover could not exceed ten acres, but it was dense. The shorthair was bounding above the seed heads, the bell on his collar jangling frantically. My Brittany was too short-statured for such a vigorous attack. I could see the weeds part as she tunneled through the stalks and only briefly glimpsed her twitching tail signaling the scent of game. Few birds entice a dog like a pheasant; each bird must smell like a whole covey of quail.

Forty yards apart, we staked out our positions and let the dogs work, waiting for the moment of action. The back of my neck was sweating. Not once, but several times, the dogs covered the weed patch, never losing interest, but without getting the pheasant up. Neither dog gave the empty barley field any sustained attention, confirming my opinion that the bird had not left by that route. But where could it be? Remembering my youthful forays after pheasants in California, I recalled how they would sometimes backtrack. Maybe the wily bird had doubled back into the maize field. I would try that tack. There was no time to go anywhere else anyway.

I called Rosie back and sent her crisscrossing the maize looking for fresh scent. Suddenly, she showed new interest—hyper-interest. No sooner did she drop her nose to the ground than the cock exploded in front of her. Even as prepared as I was, the rustling and clapping startled me. It did not keep me from swinging, though, and I was on the bird in an instant. What kept me from shooting was the other hunter. He had followed my lead and entered the field with his dog. I could see them in my peripheral vision just beyond the ascending rooster. We would both have to wait. I started to swing anew.

He was quicker than I. Too quick. His shot was ineffective. The bird was now forty yards off, but I was on him, and my modified choke Model 12 was ideally suited for the shot. I squeezed off a 12-guage load of #6s, and the still-rising rooster halted midair and began windmilling down. His neck remained extended, though, and I knew the game was not over yet. There is not another bird as tenacious of life as the pheasant. Besides, the other hunter might think the bird was his; we had shot only a second apart.

Dogs and men rushed to the crash site. My fears were justified. Neither dog had a pheasant in its mouth. Still, the bird was hard hit and on foot. The dogs should be able to trail him up. But whose dog? The competition took on a new dimension as we helplessly stood by to watch the dogs trailing fresh scent. My Brittany was slow and methodical; the shorthair was aggressive and fast. I had to give the odds to the shorthair. Both dogs disappeared into the stalks of maize.

We were now joined by Tom Waddell, wildlife manager from Pima. Tom had spotted the action and had come over to see the results of what was sure to be the last shots of the season. In the descending shroud of evening the three of us joined the search for a crippled bird in what was now a race with time.

Rosie came through. I could not believe how far the pheasant had traveled with two broken wings and a broken leg—a good sixty yards. I was just about to call Rosie back when she stuck her muzzle into a clump of maize and pulled out the prize. The bird was dead. I felt proud; it was a great way to end the season.

The other hunter came over to congratulate me. His wry smile could not hide the disappointment in his eyes. Even his dog seemed chagrined, while Rosie lay in front of us, panting and what had to pass for grinning.

"Nice shot," he said and put out his hand.

"Thanks," I replied, relieved at his magnanimity. "You got a few feathers yourself."

"I know," he said.

I put the rooster in my game bag, noting the long spurs and lack of a band on his legs. This fellow had been raised here and knew the ropes. He had given us a great hunt and some good dog work. Tom sidled over to me.

"That guy really wants the pheasant," he whispered.

"I know, but it's not his; it's mine. Rosie's and mine."

"Come on. Give it to him," he coaxed. "You've killed plenty of game. That pheasant doesn't mean anything to you. He'll never get another one. You hunt all over the country. You will."

I felt guilty now. Maybe I should offer it to him. The trouble was I knew he would take it. There would not even be a gesture of protest to renege on. The fact was that the pheasant was mine and we both knew it. The pheasant stayed in my bag as we slogged our way back to the trucks. The only sounds were the mournful whistles of wintering White-crowned Sparrows in the gathering gloom.

I had that pheasant for Christmas dinner, but I do not recall anything about the meal. All I remember are the details of the hunt and that it was the last wild pheasant shot in Arizona. If I had given it away, I might not have remembered that. But maybe I would just have remembered it differently. Tom was right. I should have been bigger. Now it's too late. The opportunity to be generous is over in a few seconds. Regret lasts for years.

PART II
Grouse

Grouse are a boreal, or northern, subfamily of galliforms, restricted to North America and Eurasia and reaching their southernmost distribution in North America in the Southwest. Of nine species endemic to North America only the Blue Grouse is found in Arizona. By way of contrast, the adjacent, colder state of New Mexico has, or had, populations of Blue Grouse, Sage Grouse, Lesser Prairie Chicken, Sharp-tailed Grouse, and White-tailed Ptarmigan.

Like pheasants, most grouse species are sexually dimorphic. Many species also exhibit bimaturism: the males are not reproductively active until after their second winter, whereas the females attain sexual maturity their first spring. Breeding is usually promiscuous, and the females select dominant males at individual display sites or communal *leks*. With the notable exception of the ptarmigans, no lasting pair bonds are formed and the precocial chicks are raised solely by the hen. Only one nesting per season can be expected.

Paul Bosman

CHAPTER 4
Blue Grouse

The chickenlike Blue Grouse is easily recognizable when seen foraging on the ground or taking flight. A flushed bird that is only glimpsed may be more difficult to identify unless it lands in a nearby conifer (an almost sure sign of a grouse) or starts up other birds in the covey. Most confusion involves mistaking other birds for grouse. I have seen wildlife biologists take Band-tailed Pigeons flushed from the ground for grouse and have heard competent naturalists describe what I knew to be Northern Goshawks, Band-tailed Pigeons, or Wild Turkeys as grouse.

On close examination or in the hand, Blue Grouse are unmistakable and need only be identified to age and sex. Hens with broods (the most common summer and fall observation) have an overall brownish gray appearance with white and black markings on shades of brown. If all of the birds in the covey appear close to the same size, the juveniles can sometimes be differentiated by their pale buff or white breasts and absence of any gray on the belly. First-year birds in the hand can be distinguished from adults by their wings and tail feathers. The outer two juvenile flight feathers (9 and 10) are not replaced until the second year and are more pointed, more frayed, and lighter and more mottled than a primary of an adult (VanRossem 1925; Bunnell et al. 1977). The outer tail feathers of juveniles are narrower (less than ⅞ inch wide half an inch below the tip) and more rounded than the squarer retrices of adult birds, which are 1¼ inch wide or

Aftershaft —

Fig. 4.1. Body feather of a galliform showing the aftershaft.

wider (Boag 1965). Like all galliforms, grouse possess a heavy, conical beak adapted for terrestrial foraging on greens and seeds and have a secondary feather, or aftershaft, attached to the main shaft of their body feathers (Fig. 4.1).

Males, including adults not in nuptial plumage and the older juveniles, have blue-gray flanks and dark slate breasts; unlike the browner females, they have no barring on the top of the head, nape, and interscapulars (Johnsgard 1973). Males also usually have some yellow over the eye, leg feathers that extend to the base of the middle toe, and the base of their neck feathers, even in first-year birds, is white. Both sexes have bluish, unmarked tails ending in a distinct light gray band, but only males have gray marginal wing coverts; these feathers in hens have an extensively mottled brown pattern. All Arizona birds are the subspecies *Dendragapus o. obscurus*—the Dusky Grouse.

Second-year males, or cocks, commonly exceed 2 pounds and males more than two years old may attain weights exceeding 3 pounds. The smaller females average 1¾ and 2 pounds. Early September weights of juveniles range from 16 to 28 ounces and average between 20 and 24 ounces (LeCount 1970a).

DISTRIBUTION

Blue Grouse in Arizona are almost entirely confined to subalpine forests and meadow regions above 8,500 feet elevation. Grouse are therefore restricted to the highest portions of the White Mountains and nearby mountaintops, the North Kaibab Plateau, and the Chuska and Lukachukai mountains on the Navajo Indian Reservation (Phillips 1937; P. Ryan, pers. comm. 1985). The more limited boreal forests on the San Francisco Peaks, atop the Pinaleño Mountains, and in the Chiricahua Mountains were historically uninhabited by grouse (Fig. 4.2).

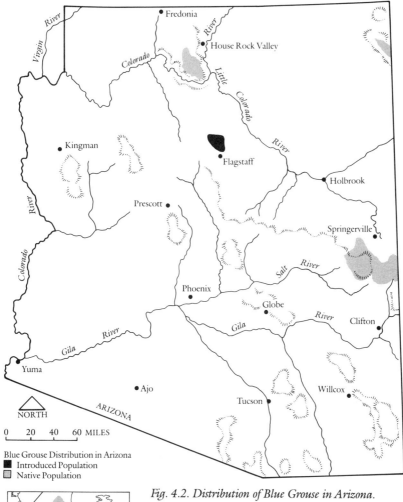

Fredonia

House Rock Valley

Virgin River

Colorado River

Little Colorado River

Kingman

Flagstaff

Holbrook

Prescott

Springerville

Salt River

Colorado River

Phoenix

Globe

Clifton

Gila River

Gila River

Yuma

Ajo

Tucson

Willcox

ARIZONA

NORTH

0   20   40   60 MILES

Blue Grouse Distribution in Arizona
■ Introduced Population
▢ Native Population

Fig. 4.2. *Distribution of Blue Grouse in Arizona.*

Even in the White Mountain region, which supports the largest grouse population in Arizona, the bird's range is discontinuous and principally confined to such high peaks as Mount Baldy, Greens Peak, Pole Knoll, McKays Peak, and Escudilla Mountain, all in the Apache-Sitgreaves National Forest or on the Fort Apache Indian Reservation. Only in the wetter mountains around Alpine are grouse occasionally seen below 8,000 feet elevation.

Although good numbers of grouse have been observed on the North Kaibab Plateau, the bird's density and distribution there appears to be more restricted than in the White Mountains. The assumption that grouse habitat on the Kaibab and in the Chuska Mountains is of poorer quality than in the White Mountains is untested. Grater (1937), Bailey (1939), and Rasmussen (1941; pers. comm. 1973) considered grouse to be formerly generally distributed and common on the Kaibab Plateau. The reasons for lower numbers of grouse on the Kaibab after the 1930s and for the sparse population in the Chuska Mountains are unclear, but overgrazing of high-elevation meadows by livestock, fire suppression, and overbrowsing of forbs and aspen by deer and livestock may have had a more pronounced effect on grouse numbers and distribution on the North Kaibab than in the wetter White Mountains.

HABITAT

Arizona's Blue Grouse are closely associated with the subalpine forest belt of Engelmann spruce and subalpine fir, the lower reaches of which are interspersed with quaking aspen. Of lesser importance are patches of white pine on wind-swept ridges and drier sites, and blue spruce in mesic, colder canyons and meadow margins. At the subalpine forest's lowest elevations there is much intermingling with Douglas fir, white fir, and even ponderosa pine.

Except for dwarf juniper, understory shrubs are in short supply, and where the forest is closed, considerable duff and debris may accumulate. Few if any herbaceous plants occur in such places, and the only ground cover may be sedges, mosses, liverworts, lichens, and fungi. However, in seral stages, natural openings, and at the edge of the forest such shrubs as red elderberry, creeping mahonia, shrubby cinquefoil, currants, raspberries, and snowberries may be present. Herbaceous species tend to be abundant in aspen groves or where the forest is opened after fire or logging, and

Fig. 4.3. Foraging habitat of Blue Grouse within subalpine conifer forest.

it is in these locations that grouse are most likely to be seen (Fig. 4.3). A number of flowering herbs may be found in these situations, including vetches, fireweed, wild pea, strawberry, mountain dandelions, mountain parsley, balsamroot, groundsels, primroses, and sneezeweed, among many others. Grasses include spike trisetum, Arizona fescue, nodding and fringed brome, oat grass, mountain timothy, mountain muhly, and bluegrasses.

*Fig. 4.4. Summer habitat for Blue Grouse: subalpine
meadows in the White Mountains used as brood cover.*

Adjacent subalpine grasslands provide summer habitat for hens and
broods and are commonly dominated by perennial bunchgrasses with varying numbers of forbs and shrubs. Included are many of the above species,
plus larkspur, asters, yarrows, and clovers (Fig. 4.4). These high-elevation
prairie plants are replaced in the wetter cienega sites by sedges and rushes,
often in combination with a variety of the more moisture-dependent forbs
and grasses such as mountain timothy and tufted hairgrass.

LIFE HISTORY

Unlike more northern populations of Blue Grouse, Arizona grouse
show no evidence of migrating upslope in winter and appear to winter on
the same high knolls and mountains that they spent the summer on: there
is nowhere higher for them to go! Much of the winter is spent in preferred
roost trees, where solitary individuals forage on needles and buds of Douglas fir and other conifers. Males, especially, appear to winter close to their
breeding ground and may remain in the same general area throughout
the year.

As soon as the snow melts, males two years old and older leave their winter roosts and establish a strutting, or breeding, territory. The cocks are strongly attached to these areas and may return to the same site year after year. Most territories are small openings or clearings on a slope or ridge and are commonly the site of an earlier disturbance within the forest. Territories may range in size from less than an acre to about two acres. A stump, fallen log, rock, or other prominent display site is characteristically present. Aspens and at least one stand of large conifers are typically nearby for escape and roosting cover (Severson 1986). Breeding territories are claimed in early April and defended well into June (LeCount 1970b).

Territorial males put on a spectacular display. The full-plumage cock struts about with this tail spread and tilted forward, head and neck stretched out, yellow eye combs enlarged, and wings arched downward. His neck feathers are ruffled out and the purplish gular sacs are inflated and exposed. Air expelled from these throat sacs produces a so-called hooting noise. These low-pitched, hollow *hoots*, usually given from the ground or a fallen log, are only faintly discernible to the human ear and, at best, cannot be heard much farther than a distance of fifty yards or so. "Flutter flights," in which the bird tumbles through the air are also part of the performance, and aggressive attacks can be elicited through the use of tape-recorded hen calls as well as by the arrival of a hen or a competing male. At this time the males behave with much bravado and show little fear of any intruder, man included.

The hens appear to not be tied to a particular breeding area and, although they exhibit some territorial behavior toward other grouse, are not as bold as the males. Hens are intercepted and displayed to as they travel up and downslope, which probably explains the selection of ridges as favorite display sites. Receptive hens may emit "whinny" or "quaver" calls prior to copulation (Stirling and Bendell 1970). First-year males are commonly silent but highly mobile, and they appear attracted to the breeding territories of adult grouse. Such birds can on occasion assume ownership of an unoccupied territory or one vacated by a departed male. Peak mating activity takes place during the last week of May and the first week of June (LeCount 1970b).

Upon completion of the courtship ritual and copulation, the hens continue about their business and most eventually nest. Males remain in their breeding territories to display and attract any other hens that come along. The cock takes no part in nest-site selection, nest building, incubation, or chick raising.

Before nesting, hens must have a mixture of forbs and grasses seven to eight inches high covering the ground (Mussehl 1963; LeCount 1970b). The nest is a shallow scrape or depression on the ground, lined with grass and needles and often partially concealed by exposed tree roots, fallen branches, bunches of grass, or shrubbery. Even first-year females may attempt to nest, although their success rate is poorer than that of older hens. The mean clutch size varies from year to year but usually averages between five and ten. The eggs average 2 by 1.4 inches and are a pale pinkish buff, evenly covered by minute, clay-brown dots. Most chicks in Arizona hatch between June 15 and July 15 after an incubation period of twenty-six days.

The chicks are extremely precocial. They begin feeding their first day and make short grasshopperlike flights when between six and seven days of age. Few birds need to be brooded after three weeks. The average brood size varies by location and year, but after the first two weeks of mortality can be expected to be between four and six. Brood cover is extremely important, and LeCount (1970b) found that females with broods avoided cover under twelve inches in height. Insects are eaten ravenously and compose almost 75 percent of the diet of chicks up to three weeks old. As the season progresses, both adults and youngsters begin taking more and more vegetable matter.

LeCount (1970b) found Blue Grouse in September to feed on eighteen plant species and six families of insects. The most frequently chosen items were wild pea and vetch. Raspberries were preferred, along with spiny gooseberries. Other selected foods were dandelions, silverleaf cinquefoil, aspen leaves, and Douglas-fir needles. Mountain parsley seeds were taken relatively frequently but constituted only a fraction of the volume of the crop contents and were probably used principally as grit.

Males remain in the timbered areas and take more aspen leaves and forest forbs than the hens. They also feed earlier in the year and more often on Douglas-fir needles, especially during years of poor forb and berry production. Chicks and poults, as expected, took a high volume of ants and grasshoppers. Although chicks may require free water, no birds were ever observed drinking. Apparently, the early morning dew and droplets from rain showers supply all the needed moisture.

With the advent of winter the poults disperse and the grouse retreat to dense stands of conifers to take up winter quarters. Here each bird will take up a preferred roost, usually at the base of a large branch of an old conifer, where it may return night after night. Almost nothing is known of the winter habitats of Arizona grouse, but it is likely that, like Blue Grouse farther north, they spend the days feeding on Douglas-fir needles while snow covers the ground.

MANAGEMENT HISTORY

Although the Blue Grouse was recognized as an upland game bird in the state game code of 1929, there was no open season on the species until 1964. In September of that year a three-day grouse season was opened for the White Mountains and Escudilla Mountain with a three-bird bag and possession limit. Thirty-three hunters reported bagging forty-four grouse (White 1965).

The following August sixty grouse were observed during brood counts, and a similar hunt was authorized for September. Most of the fifty-one birds reported harvested in 1965 were taken on Greens Peak, but during the next two years grouse hunting became more general, and seventy-four hunters reported bagging more than one hundred grouse in 1968 (LeCount 1969).

In 1969 the Fort Apache Indian Reservation was opened to grouse hunting, and a statewide harvest of more than four hundred birds was estimated (LeCount 1970a). The next year the North Kaibab was included in an earlier season, and hunters were required to obtain a free permit to provide a sample frame for postseason hunt questionnaires. Five hundred thirty-eight hunters reported taking 370 grouse. The harvest might have been higher except for a torrential Labor Day rainstorm that severely dampened hunters, dogs, and enthusiam (D. Brown and White 1971).

Brood surveys indicated a poor hatch in 1971, and the nine-day season authorized that year failed to increase the harvest. Because of the paucity of two-year-old birds, only 133 grouse were reported bagged in 1972, but increased populations and expanded seasons in the following years resulted in annual harvests approaching or exceeding four hundred birds (Table 4.1).

In 1983 a traditional season was established, opening the first Friday after the first Saturday in September and closing the third Sunday in November. The number of hunters increased in 1984, and future interest is expected to fluctuate with grouse population levels and the weather. Grouse hunting will remain a specialty sport for a small but select group willing to tramp for hours at high altitudes for a chance encounter with this fine game bird.

TABLE 4.1
Grouse Hunt Information in Arizona, 1970–86

Year	Number of Hunters	Number of Hunter Days	Reported Grouse Bagged	Grouse per Hunter per Season
1970	538	984	370	0.7
1971	609	1,349	397	0.7
1972	265	510	133	0.5
1973	399	914	361	0.9
1974	446	1,030	354	0.8
1975	386	845	359	0.9
1976	502	1,215	421	0.8
1977	593	1,379	462	0.8
1978	638	1,621	670	1.1
1979	634	1,590	527	0.8
1980	408	1,054	259	0.6
1981	649	1,594	336	0.5
1982	481	1,512	303	0.6
1983	310	975	304	1.0
1984	665	2,192	635	0.9
1985	756	2,357	678	0.9
1986	732	2,363	590	0.8

SOURCE: Questionnaire data received from special bird-permit holders

The Transplant of Blue Grouse to the San Francisco Peaks

Successful transplants of Tassel-eared Squirrels to unoccupied, mountaintop pine forests was the inspiration for transplanting Blue Grouse to isolated and unoccupied spruce-fir communities on the San Francisco Peaks north of Flagstaff in the early 1970s. The success of such a transplant could be a significant benefit to grouse hunters in the Flagstaff area, and either success or failure would be of scientific interest. The disappearance of grouse bones from the Peaks after A.D. 600 coincided with a general drought (Hargrave, pers. comm.). If conditions for subalpine and montane species have improved since this time, but some animals are unable to reoccupy these habitats because of their isolation, their reestablishment through man's intervention would strongly suggest that wetter conditions have returned (see, e.g., Moore 1965).

Suitable stands of subalpine forest intermingled with aspens, Douglas fir, and small subalpine meadows were located on the San Francisco Peaks where there was also evidence of recent burns and seral communities. Two release areas were recommended, the Inner Basin and the vicinity of the

Snow Bowl ski lift (D. Brown 1972a), but the releases were delayed for two years pending approval by the U.S. Forest Service.

On August 8, 1975, a hen grouse and her three chicks were captured in a drive net in the White Mountains and released near Bismark Lake (D. Brown 1976a). Each bird was banded, and the release appeared promising. However, on October 6, 1975, the hen was reported to have been shot from a flock of what was erroneously believed to be Wild Turkeys.

The following year twenty grouse, five hens, and fifteen juveniles were captured and released in the same area (Britt and Brown 1977). These releases were supplemented in the summer of 1977 with an additional hen and chick and two parentless poults. Postrelease surveys resulted in a sighting of the two immatures and the finding of the remains of a grouse wing (Britt 1978). Later that year a raptor-killed hen was found on State Highway 180. The decapitated bird had been banded as an immature in August 1976.

In 1978 eleven more grouse (one male, two females, and eight chicks) were trapped and released at Bismark Lake and at Raspberry Spring in the Inner Basin (Britt 1979). No grouse were observed on postrelease surveys by the Arizona Game and Fish Department, but four birds were reported by nondepartment personnel, including a banded road kill and a female captured in the backyard of a Flagstaff resident. The finding of the released grouse meant that they were able to survive in their new home. What was questionable was whether enough birds would live long enough to find mates and reproduce. Few reports of grouse were received after 1979; trapping ceased and no further releases were planned.

Then, in November 1982, a road-killed hen was found on Highway 180 near the Snow Bowl turnoff. The bird was an unbanded adult and, because all of the released birds were banded, proof that a transplanted grouse had successfully nested and produced progeny that had survived to maturity. Reports of grouse observations have since increased, and several were taken during the 1986 statewide season, so that it appears that the transplant effort was successful.

POPULATION DYNAMICS

A significant positive correlation was found between winter precipitation and subsequent autumn population levels of Blue Grouse as measured by hunting success determined from mail questionnaires (Table 4.2; D. Brown and Smith 1980). Hunting success was reported to increase only

TABLE 4.2

October–March Precipitation and Blue Grouse Reproduction, Hunt,
and Survival Information in Arizona, 1964–78

| Year | Previous Oct.–May Precipitation (inches) | % Young Observed in August (N) | Grouse per Hunter per Season | | Calculated Adults (%) | Estimated Survival Rate[a] |
			All Grouse	% Change from Previous Year		
1965	12.21	55.3(47)	0.95	−0.29	0.43	0.323
1966	14.60	66.7(57)	1.25	+0.32	0.42	0.442
1967	8.14	70.5(61)	1.13	−0.10	0.33	0.264
1968	14.10	75.0(56)	1.45	+0.28	0.36	0.319
1969	12.20	75.5(98)	1.31	−0.10	0.32	0.221
1970	9.29	65.5(243)	0.69		0.24	
1971	7.92	33.2(53)	0.65	−0.06	0.44	0.638
1972	12.45	58.8(61)	0.50	−0.23	0.21	0.323
1973	21.21	57.8(85)	0.90	+0.80	0.38	0.760
1974	9.14	68.0(25)	0.79	−0.12	0.25	0.277
1975	19.47	74.2(120)	0.97	+0.23	0.25	0.316
1976	13.90	68.7(67)	0.84	−0.13	0.26	0.268
1977	8.13	69.7(84)	0.74	−0.12	0.22	0.262
1978	18.51	71.0(38)	0.99	+0.34	0.29	0.391
$\bar{x}$	12.52	65.4(1,047)	0.97		0.31	0.356

SOURCE: D. Brown and Smith 1980
[a]All grouse from September to September

after years of abundant winter precipitation. There was no correlation between reproductive success and the preceding season's precipitation. It is worth noting, however, that the lowest percentage of young grouse observed was in 1971, the year preceded by the driest winter–spring period for which data were available.

The percentage of juvenile grouse observed in August surveys was, with the exception of 1971, consistently high and reasonably close to the mean of 65 percent reported in other states (Zwickel 1958; Bendell and Elliot 1967; Bunnell and Olson 1978; Zwickel et al. 1975; Hoffman 1978). Largely because of the low juvenile:adult ratio observed in 1971, there was a significant variation in the percentages of young grouse observed in the population. If 1971 is excluded, the variation is greatly reduced and not significant. Examination of climatic data (freezing temperatures, snow depth, etc.) failed to show any peculiar weather factors other than low winter–spring precipitation to explain the low reproductive success in Arizona in 1971.

Observed reproductive success was associated with hunting success but accounted for only 30 percent of the variation (Table 4.2). Good reproductive success occurred in most years, and variations in Blue Grouse population levels in Arizona, as elsewhere, are probably attributable to changes in survival rates more than nesting success (Bendell and Elliot 1967:54; Zwickel 1975).

The mean estimated annual survival rate for all grouse as determined from data collected between 1964 and 1978 was 36 percent (Table 4.2). It approximates the mean annual survival rate of 31 percent reported for grouse of all age classes in an area in Washington close to the center of the bird's range (Zwickel et al. 1968).

Estimated annual survival rates in Arizona were inversely related to density as indexed by the previous year's hunting success—that is, the higher the population level, the lower the following year's estimated survival rate. There was also a negative relationship between the percentage of young grouse observed in August (reproductive success) and that year's survival rate. An inverse relationship between survival and density and/or reproductive success has been noted for numerous wildlife species.

A multiple-regression analysis found that October–March precipitation was also significantly associated with grouse survival rates in Arizona (D. Brown and Smith 1980). How does winter–spring precipitation influence changes in survival and hunting success? Bendell and Elliot (1967) and Zwickel et al. (1968) concluded that spring densities on Vancouver Island in British Columbia and in Washington were related to conditions on the breeding range rather than on the winter range. The effects of winter precipitation on changes in population levels and the apparent unimportance of freezing days and length of snow cover suggest that most mortality in Arizona also occurs between spring and autumn. Mussehl (1963) found that Blue Grouse hens required herbaceous cover—principally native bunchgrasses, grasslike plants, and forbs—to raise their broods successfully. This description of summer brood habitat also applies to Arizona's White Mountains (LeCount 1970b). Zwickel (1973) and Zwickel et al. (1968) found that hens preferred ungrazed meadows in spring and summer and suspected that clumped hen distribution in July and August was due to the drying of grasses and/or heavy grazing and was detrimental to survival. It seems reasonable to assume, then, that mortality is greatest during spring and summer, particularly for nesting hens.

Subalpine bunchgrasses and other cold-tolerant herbaceous plants in the Rocky Mountain region begin growth with snowmelt, and their rate and amount of growth is directly related to available spring moisture (Blaisdell 1958; Turner and Paulsen 1976). This growth is essential for successful concealment of hens and broods. Because hens and their broods account for most of the harvest, variation in their survival is an important factor determining grouse-hunting success (if hen mortality is high, brood mortality is high, too). Survival rates therefore depend on grouse density, reproductive success, and changes in available spring moisture.

Hunting success data indicate that Blue Grouse population levels in Arizona increased in only five of fourteen years (Table 4.2). The winter–spring precipitation amounts prior to these increases in fall population levels were always at least 13 percent greater than the annual mean of 12.5 inches. This finding accounts for the restriction of the species to subalpine environments in the Southwest: the lower, montane habitats are not wet enough for grouse.

GROUSE HUNTING

No other game bird is as pleasing to the palate yet as difficult to come by as the Blue Grouse. These birds are not especially wary or secretive, but unless they are concentrated on a preferred food source such as raspberries, they are thinly scattered in the fastness of their forest home. Furthermore, the high elevations of their habitats call for puffing up steep slopes and enduring more than an occasional rain shower. Blue Grouse have to be earned. More unsuccessful hours are expended in search of this game bird than any other small-game species.

My strategy for finding grouse is to work the edges between the subalpine forest and the meadows and to concentrate in those areas having dense ground cover about the level of my knees—grass, forbs, or shrubs will do. Thickets of ripe raspberries, currants, or gooseberries are ideal. So fond of raspberries are these birds that many hunters confine their grouse-hunting forays to early September, when the birds are gorging themselves on the ripe fruit.

Overgrown logging roads are always a likely spot. Grouse are a successional species and select areas of past forest disturbance. Burns, blowdowns, small clearcuts, and aspen thickets are all good possibilities—anywhere the forest has been temporarily replaced by herbaceous plants. Ground cover is essential, and heavily grazed areas are avoided. Adjacent mature timber is also important, however, as escape cover.

The cocks are not associated with hens and poults, nor are they usually found in the same habitats. All grouse favor points and steep ridges that make for a rapid escape, but the old males rarely leave the cover of the trees and are almost never found in meadows. The best place to look for them is aspen-choked ridges hemmed in by mature conifers and interrupted by small openings; hens and poults, at least early in the season, are most often to be found at the edges of meadows and in berry patches. That is why abandoned logging roads that lead from one habitat to another are so promising; a meadow margin might yield a family group, the aspen grove beyond, a big male.

A dog is not necessary to find grouse. Most birds flush between fifteen and thirty yards, and few hold to a point. As a result, a wide ranging "mile-eater" can be a severe handicap, but a trained, close-working dog can be a tremendous help. In heavy cover even a dead grouse can be hard to find, and locating a crippled bird among deadfalls can be an almost impossible task without the help of a good nose. A well-trained retriever, then, not only increases your success, but saves much time searching for downed birds that might otherwise go unfound.

As with many species of game, the best hunting is during the early morning hours and in the late evening. Most grouse are taken while feeding between eight-thirty and ten in the morning and after three-thirty in the afternoon. The time immediately after a thundershower or other bout of inclement weather can also be productive. The trick is to find the birds on the ground, as a grouse roosting in a conifer is almost impossible to see and rarely presents a clear shot when flushed.

My morning hunting is uphill and I plan to get to the summit of my selected knoll or peak early in the day. Likely looking cover is worked as if a grouse *might* be there, but not as slowly as if a bird was *sure* to be present. That takes too much time, and I want to cover a lot of ground. For this reason I'll be carrying a light shotgun with a sling. Because the birds may be in dense woods, it will also have a short barrel, no longer than 26 inches. There is also a good chance that I will be shooting through aspens or other cover and the shots may be hurried. The gun is a modified-bore 12 gauge to maximize my numbers of pellets and range, as some birds may flush at forty yards or more. Although grouse are large birds, they are not particularly hardy; I prefer a high-base 7½ load. Bring a lunch and plan to be out for the entire day: that's what makes grouse hunting a specialty sport.

Chances are that I will miss the first bird up. I may not even get a shot off! A grouse is always a surprise. But there is no time for despair, if the flushed bird was a hen or young of the year, there's a good chance that the remainder of the brood is still present. As often as not, they'll begin taking off in sequence like planes off of an aircraft carrier. More than once I've bagged a limit of three birds on these initial covey rises—even after letting the first one get off scot-free.

Should I bag a bird, I will check the crop and see what it was feeding on. Was it vetch or raspberries? It's a good bet that other grouse are feeding on the same items. If it's gooseberries, I will seek out the gooseberry patches and concentrate my efforts there. Or if I come across another hunter, I will ask him where his grouse, if any, came from. Situations that are producing birds warrant further investigation.

Arizona grouse are getting more sophisticated. Birds that would jump up into the nearest tree twenty years ago now rocket off in a whirr of wings and confusion equal to any eastern "partridge." Indeed, an adult Blue Grouse weaving through aspens is as sporty a target as any game anywhere.

Still, a flushed bird will oftentimes alight in a tree. Contrary to some experiences and many stories, such birds are not always easily had. Although poults may often "freeze" on the ground or hop onto the nearest available branch, such behavior is not typical of the adults. An old male or broodless hen will take to the tall timber and immediately be concealed high up in an old Douglas fir or Engelmann spruce—perched usually in dense foliage near the trunk. Such birds are impossible to see from the ground and will invariably flush on approach, usually at a distance of about forty-five yards, and almost always in the opposite direction of the intruder. By accident or design, the bird will be shielded by the tree and rarely allow for a decent shot. More often than not, the grouse will then disappear down into a canyon—not to be seen again.

Should I be lucky enough to kill a grouse or two, I will pick and clean them immediately. Grouse are too hard to come by and too delectable to risk diminishing their flavor. Besides, the birds are not in good plumage during the hunting season and there is no need to show off feathered trophies. That purpose is best achieved with a camera in the spring, when the mature male Blue Grouse is in his most photogenic garb.

PART III
Turkeys

Turkeys belong to a strictly New World family of Neotropical origin. Of the two extant species, one—the Wild Turkey—extends northward into the United States. Here it has evolved into four subspecies, one or possibly two of which occur in Arizona.

These large galliforms are strongly sexually dimorphic and bimaturistic. Adult males present exaggerated announcement displays and are promiscuous breeders. The smaller hen tends to the nest and broods and raises the precocial poults. Brood sizes may be large, and despite the turkey's potentially long life, population turnover is usually high.

PAUL BOSMAN

CHAPTER 5

Merriam's Wild Turkey

All turkeys in Arizona, with the exception of a few transient individuals of uncertain origin in the southern Peloncillo Mountains, are of the Merriam's race *Meleagris gallopavo merriami*. The type specimen was collected on January 9, 1900, forty-seven miles southwest of Winslow and was named for C. Hart Merriam, first chief of the U.S. Biological Survey.

Although turkeys from several regions in Arizona have been referred to as "Mexican Turkeys," there are no museum specimens to support the contention that the Mexican, or Gould's, Turkey (*M. g. mexicana*) occurs anywhere in Arizona except in the Peloncillo Mountains along the New Mexico–Arizona border (Potter et al. 1984). The only endemic specimen from southern Arizona is a male collected from the Chiricahua Mountains in 1881. Examination of this somewhat worn and "foxed" specimen in the National Museum shows it to be more characteristic of *merriami* than *mexicana*, a conclusion also reached by A. Starker Leopold (Schorger 1966 *in* Hewitt 1967). The body feathers of *merriami* are an iridescent purplish bronze, and the tips of the tail feathers are generally a cinnamon-buff with distinct black and chestnut barring on the middle retrices. The breast feathers of the larger Gould's, or Mexican, Turkey have a darker, more greenish sheen, much like those of a domestic turkey, and the outer margins of the tail feathers range from light cinnamon to pure white.

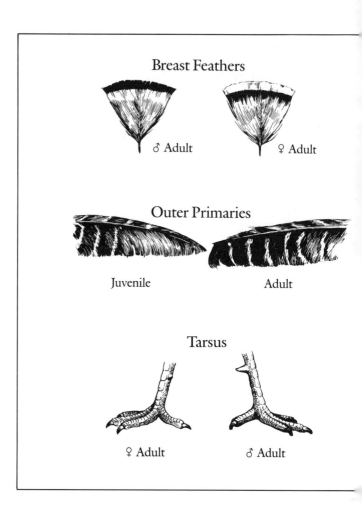

Breast Feathers

♂ Adult   ♀ Adult

Outer Primaries

Juvenile   Adult

Tarsus

♀ Adult   ♂ Adult

The Wild Turkey needs little introduction to students of southwestern game birds. Its gregarious nature and size makes for ready recognition. No other large terrestrial bird has dark, metallic plumage and a nearly naked head.

Once out of their juvenile plumage, the sexes can be differentiated by their breast feathers: the hen's are light buff or white-tipped, whereas the tom's are dark-tipped (Fig. 5.1). Less conclusive characteristics of adult gobblers are pronounced beards, longer legs, and well-developed spurs above the tarsus (20 percent of the hens have beards and not all gobblers have spurs). The droppings of the sexes are also different (Fig. 5.1), and birds having middle-toe tracks exceeding three inches can be assumed to be gobblers. The tarsal length of the leg can also be used to determine the sex of adult birds.

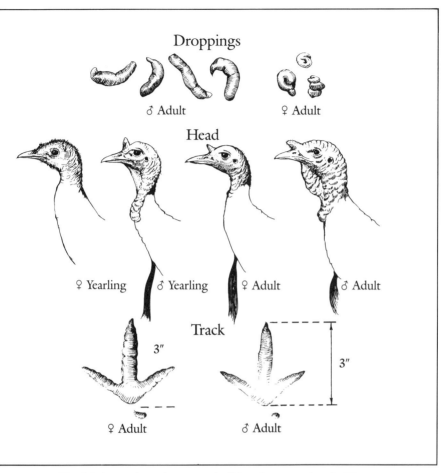

Droppings

♂ Adult   ♀ Adult

Head

♀ Yearling   ♂ Yearling   ♀ Adult   ♂ Adult

Track

3"   3"

♀ Adult   ♂ Adult

Fig. 5.1. Sex and age characters of Wild Turkeys. Drawings by W. L. Freeman.

Juveniles can be differentiated in the field through their first winter by shorter, browner, and less glossy upper secondary wing coverts (Williams 1961; Phillips 1982). Only the two distal-most coverts are replaced in the postjuvenile molt, giving the folded wings of young birds an asymmetrical appearance (Fig. 5.2). Once in the hand, juvenile turkeys can be identified by the nonbarred tips of their pointed, narrow outer primaries (Lewis 1967; Fig. 5.3). The tarsus of juvenile birds is also browner and less scaled than the definitely scaled, purplish red legs of the adult (Fig. 5.1).

Two-year-old and older males, called "toms," or "gobblers," weigh from 12½ to 17 pounds in the fall and between 17½ and 26 pounds in the spring, when they average just over 18 pounds. Yearling males, or "jakes," weigh about 13 pounds in the spring (F. Phillips and H. Shaw, pers. comm.).

Fig. 5.2. Differences in upper secondary coverts (arrows) distinguish juvenile (top) from adult turkeys. Photos by Fred Phillips.

Fig. 5.3. Wings of juvenile (top) and adult Wild Turkey in autumn. Note the rounder, more barred tips of the ninth and tenth primaries on the adult. Photos by Fred Phillips.

Hens more than a year old weigh between 8 and 12 pounds, depending partially on the contents of the crop, which may weigh up to a pound (Mosby and Handley 1943). During hunting season in mid-October, undressed male poults weigh between 6 and 11 pounds; hens, between 3 and 8.

DISTRIBUTION

Rea (1980) has proposed that the Merriam's Turkey is a recent arrival in the Southwest, the result of feral populations of captive birds released by pueblo-dwelling Indians around A.D. 1450. Historically, turkeys were found throughout the ponderosa pine-forested Mogollon and sub-Mogollon region of Arizona from the New Mexico border northwestward to the Aubrey Cliffs and the Hualapai Indian Reservation (Fig. 5.4). The Aubrey cliffs and Hualapai Reservation populations, and those on the Moqui or Coconino Plateau south of the Grand Canyon, represent western extensions of the bird's native range. Historic populations are also still present south of the Mogollon Rim in the Big Lue Mountains, in the Sierra Ancha, and perhaps in the Mazatzal Mountains; introduced birds have replaced extirpated populations in the Juniper (Camp Wood), Bradshaw, Superstition, Catalina, Santa Rita, Huachuca, and Chiricahua mountains. Despite several reintroductions that subsequently resulted in sizable populations, turkeys are no longer present in the Pinaleño (Graham), Galiuro, and Pinal mountains. Outside their native range, turkeys have also been successfully introduced to the North Kaibab Plateau, the Mount Logan–Sawmill Mountain area on the Arizona Strip, and the Defiance Plateau and Lukachukai and Chuska mountains on the Navajo Indian Reservation (Fig. 5.4).

Much of the turkey's former habitat in southern and central Arizona remains depopulated, partly because of the reduction in the quality and extent of riparian gallery forests. Historic turkey areas on the upper Gila, Santa Cruz, and San Pedro rivers have been uninhabited for many years (Davis 1982). The most recent populations known to inhabit the San Pedro River were near Tres Alamos (Jantzen 1955a), and in 1975 a large *merriami* gobbler was collected from a grove of cottonwoods on Tonto Creek near Punkin Center. Mearns's field notes also make mention of turkeys as far west as the Baboquivari Mountains in the 1880s, and several mountain ranges in Cochise, Santa Cruz, and southern Pima counties that formerly supported turkeys no longer do so. The only turkeys in southern Arizona

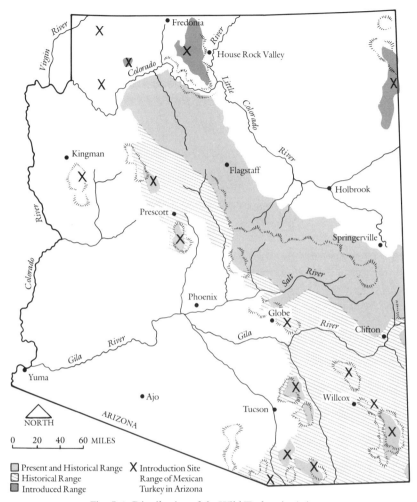

Fig. 5.4. Distribution of the Wild Turkeys in Arizona.

Present and Historical Range   X Introduction Site
Historical Range   Range of Mexican
Introduced Range   Turkey in Arizona

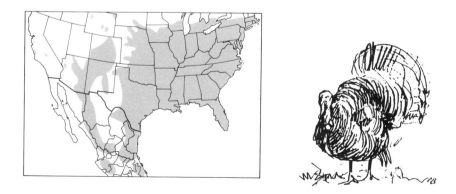

not now inhabiting ponderosa pine-capped mountains are the small population of either Mexican Wild Turkeys or birds of domestic origin that cross over from New Mexico and Sonora into Guadalupe Canyon and the Peloncillo Mountains in extreme southeastern Arizona.

HABITAT

The Wild Turkey in Arizona is most often associated with the ponderosa, or yellow, pine. Although the bird ranges well up into the subalpine forest and meadow home of the Blue Grouse, and a few birds are still found in isolated areas of riparian deciduous forest, most turkeys are usually seen within ponderosa pine forest and adjacent montane meadows.

Turkeys are not found uniformly throughout the forest. Open stands of mature ponderosas, where there is an abundance of forbs and grass cover, are preferred over "dog-hair" thickets of young or stunted pines. Large, stately Gambel oaks are important components of good turkey habitat, and if alligator-bark juniper, Arizona white oak, other evergreen oaks, or quaking aspens are present, so much the better (Fig. 5.5). Aspens, not important in themselves, usually have an understory rich in herbaceous plants that provides a source of greens for turkeys to feed on in the critical period of early spring.

Virgin forests are generally better turkey habitat than logged areas, and ungrazed meadows are more attractive than grazed areas (Reeves 1953a). Higher, wetter elevations make better brood habitat than drier locales. For this reason the most productive habitats are meadows and cienegas bordered by mixed conifer or subalpine forest. Native cool-season grasses are especially desirable, and mixed-forb grasslands populated by pine dropseed, Arizona fescue, wild bromes, and mountain muhly are important for poult survival.

Winter habitat is typically pinyon-juniper woodland at the lower edge of the pine forest; in more southern locales Madrean evergreen woodland is used seasonally and throughout the year. In northwest Arizona in the Aubrey Cliffs, the big birds may even forage in chaparral. The presence of oaks and junipers alone is insufficient, however, and both tall pines and thrifty stands of native grasses are required ingredients for good turkey country. Riparian areas possessing tall broadleaf trees can also provide prime turkey habitat (Fig. 5.6) if sufficient grass seed heads are available nearby to augment periods of poor mast production.

Fig. 5.5. Merriam's Turkey habitat south of Williams in Coconino County—winter aspect. Tall ponderosa pines and Gambel's oak supply roost sites and mast. Note the open ground cover.

LIFE HISTORY

The first stirrings of spring in March and early April find the turkeys working their way as far up onto the summer range as food and snow cover permit. The gobblers arrive first, and small flocks of hens follow them

Fig. 5.6. Riparian deciduous forest used by turkeys in Greenlee County. Now often unoccupied by turkeys, such tall-tree habitats were once favorite turkey-hunting locales of early Arizona settlers.

upslope, scratching through the pine duff for newly emerging blades of bluegrass and forbs. Aspen glens and meadow margins are searched for dandelions, clover, and newly sprouting vetches and mustards. Trickling brooks and streambanks are scoured for snails and watercress. Vitamin A from green vegetation is absorbed into the liver, and the big birds come into reproductive condition.

Depending on the weather and plant phenology, the two-year-old and older gobblers are ready to breed sometime between late March and mid-April, followed by the hens in the latter part of April and first half of May. Mating is promiscuous, the gobbler displaying and mating with any receptive hen that comes into his travel route. Up to several hens may be "acquired" and accompanied on their forays through the forest. Strutting and gobbling serve to stimulate hens into breeding and intimidate potential rivals. The usual arenas for such actions are small openings within the forest, where one or more toms may gather to advertise their wares. Battles are not infrequent, but most competitors soon retreat from the aggressive display of older gobblers laying claim to the most productive areas. Gobblers hatched the previous year are capable of breeding but, except in heavily hunted locales, rarely get the opportunity. After successive matings, most hens, including some hatched the previous year, go off to nest (Lockwood and Sutcliffe 1984), leaving the gobbler to continue his patrols in search of unclaimed hens. The peak of gobbling activity coincides with the time that most nests are initiated, and the gobbler takes no role in nest building, incubation, or poult rearing.

The hen chooses a nest site in spruce-fir forest or other dense vegetation close to herbaceous forage and water (Schemnitz et al. 1984). The nest is secreted among grass, rocks, a deadfall, in a slash pile, or simply at the base of a tree. Dried grass, oak leaves, and pine needles serve as a lining. The eggs number from eight to fifteen and are laid at the rate of one each day and a half, so that a period of almost two weeks is required to lay a clutch (Hewitt 1967). The eggs measure approximately 2½ by 1¾ inches and are of a dull buff color flecked with spots that vary from reddish to purplish brown. Incubation requires twenty-six to twenty-eight days from the time that the last egg is laid, placing the peak of the hatch in late May or early June. A prolonged nesting season is unusual; renesting is significant only in years when the laying season is interrupted by unusually cold temperatures, as occurred in 1953 (Project Personnel 1954).

Because of different food requirements, the sexes tend to remain separated through the summer. Meadows, cienegas, and streamsides are frequented by hens and newly hatched poults in search of greens and such insects as stoneflies, crickets, leaf beetles, and moth caterpillars. Toms are more catholic in their preferences, foraging throughout the forest on left-over pine seed, dandelions, and other leafy forbs such as goosefoot and smartweed. The spikes and florets of native high-elevation grasses—pine dropseed, mountain muhly, Arizona fescue, redtop, junegrass, and mountain brome—are important dietary items for both sexes (Reeves and Swank 1955). Water is taken regularly during early morning or late afternoon at a favorite spring, seep, or stock tank (Scott and Boeker 1975) and has long been thought to be an essential component of turkey habitat in Arizona. Although the birds' actual water requirements have yet to be determined, Cosper (1949a), Spicer (1959), Scott and Boeker (1975), and others have reported few turkeys nesting or roosting more than one and a half miles from water. Reeves (1951) thought that the abundance of turkeys was directly proportional to the amount of water available.

Turkeys spend the middle of the day loafing in the open forest preening and dusting. At no time are the birds more than fifty yards from cover—bracken fern or other herbaceous growth is used to advantage when feeding or traveling—particularly when poults are present. "Brood lanes," feeding areas having an unobstructed view through the tree canopy, appear to be used as a defense against aerial predators. Dense thickets of jackpine and shrubbery are avoided except as escape cover. Feeding resumes again during late afternoon, with the birds going to roost at sundown, often in the same trees as the night before, although more roost sites are used in summer than in winter (H. Shaw, pers. comm).

During midsummer, turkeys form aggregations by sex and age: hens with poults join other hens with poults, nonnesting or unsuccessful hens (mostly yearlings) form similar flocks, as do yearling toms and the older gobblers. Except for hens with young poults, which have to be brooded on the ground for the first week after hatching, turkeys tend to roost as a flock. Roost sites vary by season and flock size but are usually within a mixture of pine age classes and are often on east slopes and ridges, giving the sleeping birds maximum protection from the elements and the advantage of the first light of morning. The actual roost trees are characteristically a group of tall mature pines, a single old "yellow-belly" pine, or less commonly, old cottonwoods or sycamores. The birds perch on horizontal branches in the top half of the tree from thirty to one hundred feet above the ground, sailing down to their choice feeding areas at dawn (Boeker and Scott 1969; Scott and Boeker 1975; Phillips 1980).

Communication takes a variety of forms. The "yelp" call, a *keouwk, keouwk, keouwk,* is given by both sexes and serves as an assembly call. The *put* is a worried call and alerts other birds to the suspicion of danger. A softer *kut* is given by the hen to keep the poults together, and a whistled *kee, kee, kee* or *kee, kee, run* serves to reunite the flock after the danger is over. Like other gallinaceous game birds, the hen may feign being crippled in an effort to lead an intruder away from young chicks.

Summer and early fall is usually a time of food abundance. Grass spikes, florets, and (later) Gambel oak acorns are preferred foods. Manzanita berries, squaw-bush fruits, and Emory and Arizona oak acorns are taken when available. Lacking a mast crop, the turkeys must rely on the seed heads of montane grasses and, on south slopes and lower elevations, the seed heads of grama grasses. Grasshoppers and other insects are still important foods, and overgrazed areas lacking herbaceous vegetation are avoided. Wild grapes, buckwheat seeds, sunflower seeds, smartweeds, dandelions, and sedges round out the early autumn diet.

Water is critical during the dry period of early fall, and turkeys become closely tied to a water source, which they now visit in midday. By mid-September turkeys from the highest elevations begin drifting downslope. Daily movements, formerly encompassing an area within a mile or two of the roost site, increase. The turkeys, especially younger birds, range widely and may travel twenty miles or more (Shaw 1970; Phillips 1982). By November few birds remain above the elevations of pine forest. Although some turkeys are present on the "winter range" throughout the summer, these birds usually winter elsewhere, and few if any populations are sedentary (Reeves 1953c; Scott and Boeker 1975). The turkey is probably best described as seasonally nomadic rather than migratory, as winter ranges are poorly defined. The birds now disperse and reassemble, spending the winter segregated into loose flocks of hens, gobblers, and birds of the year, some containing dozens of birds.

Winter can be hard on turkeys. In those years having a cone crop, pine seed becomes available in November and, if accessible, provides the major food source when acorns are scarce (Jantzen 1957a, b). The turkeys remain as close to the pines as snowfall permits, following the pine and oak stringers downward in canyons to as low as 5,500 feet elevation. During heavy snow cover the birds retreat into dense pinyon-juniper stands, feeding on juniper berries (their principal emergency food), grass seeds, and whatever acorns and pinyon seeds they can find. During severe winters losses due to starvation and predation may be high, especially among poults. Even in the relatively mild climates of Arizona, annual mortality averages between 50 and 75 percent (Reeves 1953b; Scott and Boeker 1975).

MANAGEMENT HISTORY

Unlike several other big-game species in Arizona, turkeys were more widespread and abundant prior to settlement than in modern times. Early explorers frequently reported large numbers of turkeys, not only in the better-watered mountains, but along the upper Santa Cruz, upper Gila, San Francisco, and San Pedro rivers (Davis 1982). Mearns's field notes indicate that turkeys were plentiful in West Clear Creek, along Oak Creek, and on the Mogollon Rim in the mid-1880s. Consider Barnes's (1936) description of a turkey hunt by General George Crook and some of his officers near Fort Apache in November 1880:

> At that time the mountains around Fort Apache were alive with game of all kinds, especially wild turkeys. Great gorgeous fellows they were and with a fine acorn and pinyon nut season they were fat and juicy. Also the mule deer was equally plentiful and fat.
>
> The officers left the post early one morning, rode about twenty miles to a grassy mesa where the oaks and pinyon groves simply swarmed with both the species. The party hunted that evening and early next morning. The evening of the second day saw them back at the post with over a hundred huge gobblers and 20 or 25 bucks; all killed from the one camp and with the regulation army rifle.

Even as late as 1894 the Mogollon Rim country abounded in turkeys:

> Having reached our turkey camp the shotguns being cleaned and shells assorted, we started on our first turkey hunt. Chevelon Creek, where we had decided to hunt, runs through a deep and narrow canon. . . . Our count for the evening was, Messrs. Wood and Carley one deer and four turkeys, Mr. Briggs and the writer seven turkeys. . . . All were well pleased with the evening's work and concluded that one more day, with fair luck would do us, as we were not market-hunting and did not wish to be considered game-hogs.
>
> Next day's hunt added eleven more turkeys to our bunch, and we were all in camp at one o'clock p.m. (Secrist 1896)

Such feats would be difficult to duplicate today, and if these and other accounts are accurate, turkeys were formerly much more abundant than now.

By the mid-1880s turkeys were becoming scarce in the more settled regions of southern Arizona, prompting W. E. D. Scott (1886) to write that

> the bird seems, from what I can learn, to have already greatly decreased in numbers in most localities, and to have become exterminated in others where it was formerly abundant. In the pine woods of the Catalinas at the highest altitudes it was very common late in November, 1885, though snow covered the ground.

The depletion of Arizona's most prized game bird did not go unnoticed. In 1887, in its first game code, the territorial legislature made it unlawful to take or sell turkeys and other game birds between the first day of March and the first day of September. Trapping turkeys was prohibited, even on one's own premises. In 1893 the legislature closed the season from April 1 through September 1, and made quail the only game that could be hunted or sold on a person's enclosed properties. The shipment of game by common carrier was also banned during the closed season, and the market hunting of turkey was greatly curtailed.

Populations of all game species continued to decline, and in 1897 the territorial game laws were again amended. The eggs of game birds were now protected and the sale of Wild Turkeys was prohibited at all times. Wild Turkey hunting was again curtailed in 1905 with an open season set to coincide with the deer season, between September 15 and November 30. There was as yet no bag limit, as the species was still considered to be locally common.

With statehood and the new game code, turkeys were formally declared to be "big game." The season on deer and turkey was set from October 1 through December 15, and a bag limit of three turkeys per season was established. Turkey populations continued to decline, however, and in 1927 the legislature reduced the season to the month of October with a two-bird bag limit. J. Stokely Ligon, the Southwest's foremost conservationist of the time, considered the range of the Merriam's Turkey in 1925 to have been reduced by two-thirds and the remaining populations to be in jeopardy (Ligon 1927, 1946).

What happened to Arizona's turkeys? Nelson (1885) told the tale in his description of conditions in southern Arizona prior to the turn of the century: "the occupation of every permanent spring or creek by ranchmen, and the presence of prospectors at all seasons, has nearly driven the game from these hills." Twenty-five more years of settlement, homesteading, and ranching continued to take a steady toll of wildlife, and the appropriation of permanent waters and the ubiquitous grazing of stock was particularly devastating to turkeys. Homesteading did not begin to decline in Arizona until the late 1920s (Bahre 1977).

In 1930 the new Game and Fish Commission closed the turkey season south of the Gila for an indefinite period. By 1936 the taking of turkeys with shotguns was prohibited even though the supply in northern Arizona had been described as recently as 1933 as "inexhaustible" (Cosper 1949a).

The turkeys' decline in numbers was emphasized by the fact that trapping and transplanting operations in 1938 and 1939 had to be negotiated with the Apache Indian tribes, as no surplus birds could be found in the state's national forests. Concern for turkeys in the 1930s was one of the primary motivations for the establishment of numerous game refuges, many of them specifically set aside for this species.

Turkey management in the 1940s concentrated primarily on restocking southern Arizona ranges. Despite some good turkey hunting on the Apache Indian reservations (Murie 1946), most populations were still thought to be declining. The season was therefore closed in 1945, and when the eastern part of the state was reopened the next year, the bag limit was reduced to one bird per hunter. As in previous years, the turkey season was concurrent with the deer season.

The first systematic turkey surveys were initiated in 1947. Morning and evening survey routes were conducted during July and August to determine relative population densities and hatching success. The number of hunters was monitored by the requirement of a special permit, and hunt check stations collected both biological and hunt data. Hunt success increased from a reported 9.7 percent in 1946 to 20.2 percent in 1947. A separate five-day turkey hunt before the deer season was recommended and continued for many years, thereby allowing the collection of comparable hunt data.

In the late 1940s turkeys were thought to be on the increase, although the entire Coconino National Forest remained closed to hunting to allow for a faster recovery. The state's turkey range was mapped and classified as optimum, fair, and marginal habitat based on vegetative and water criteria (Cosper 1949a, b). Turkey restoration plots, fenced exclosures around springs and in meadows, were established and found to be attractive to hens and poults (Hall 1950a).

In February 1949 the state's first emergency, big-game feeding program was prompted by a severe snowstorm. Oats were brought to wintering concentrations of turkeys by Department of Game and Fish personnel on skis and in war-surplus "weasels" and were dropped in ten-pound paper bags from light planes. Operations were suspended when one of the aircraft crashed south of Williams, killing both occupants. Despite the severity of the storm, few losses were reported and the turkeys came through the winter in good condition. When the turkey harvest and hunt success increased in 1949, it was decided that feeding programs were unnecessary and they have not been attempted since.

Turkey management intensified in 1950 when the Game and Fish Department hired R. H. Reeves as a full-time turkey biologist. Reeves (1951) recommended additional springs and seeps for fencing and development as turkey numbers began to improve. In 1951, check-station data from the Apache National Forest showed a steady increase in hunt success, and for the first time since 1946 the Coconino and western half of the Sitgreaves national forests were open to hunting, as was Mount Graham in the Crook National Forest—the first season on a restocked population. The number of turkey hunters doubled.

Hunt success in 1952 exceeded 26 percent, much higher than that reported in other states. Turkeys were thought to be increasing, and a longer and more general season was recommended (Reeves 1953b). Studies had determined the turkey's statewide distribution (Reeves 1953c), and some conclusions about the influences of habitat and climate on reproduction and population levels could be postulated (Reeves 1953d). Predation was now considered to be a relatively unimportant factor affecting turkey numbers (Reeves 1953c). The major detriments to turkey populations were now thought to be logging, grazing, recreational development, and poaching (Reeves 1953a). Unfortunately, Reeves resigned in 1954 and his banding studies to determine variations in annual mortality rates were discontinued along with the check stations.

Reported hunt success in 1954 climbed to 29.7 percent, but because of the low number of poults observed during the 1955 summer surveys, permit numbers in 1955 were greatly restricted and shooting hours shortened. Despite these changes and the lowest percentage of poults in the harvest yet recorded, hunt success was a record 32 percent (Jantzen 1956b). Prescribed shooting hours proved unpopular and were abandoned in 1956. Because of prolonged drought and increased logging activity, the season was reduced to four days, but for the first time the North Kaibab and the Catalina Mountains were opened to hunting, and a second season was authorized for the Pinaleños (= Mt. Graham). Statewide hunting success matched the previous year's record.

Although the number of permits was again reduced in 1957 owing to low poult:hen ratios, the trend was for less intensive management and more liberal hunt regulations. The Chiricahua Mountains were opened to hunting in 1958, and in 1960 an early September season was finally initiated in the Apache National Forest. The Kaibab was opened to unlimited hunting during the regular early October season, and 6,897 hunters reported a record statewide kill of 1,402 turkeys (Project Personnel 1961).

Hunt regulations continued to be liberalized through the 1960s. Shotguns were again legalized in 1961 and a nine-day season was authorized. In 1962 four game-management units were open to unlimited hunting, and

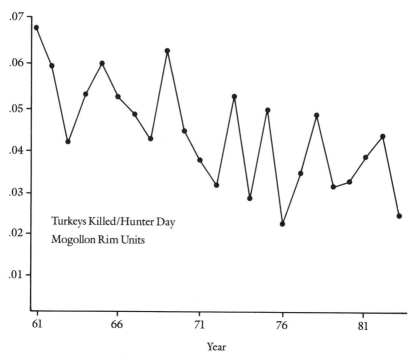

Fig. 5.7. Turkey hunt success, 1961–83, for Mogollon Rim and White Mountain game-management units. Data from Harley Shaw.

the following year the permit limitations were dropped entirely. An eleven-day season became the standard and hunter numbers increased more than 70 percent. By 1963 hunt success had dropped to 9.2 percent—the seventh year in a row of decline.

A spring gobbler hunt, first recommended in 1963, was finally approved for one White Mountain area in 1965. One hundred permits were issued, and seventy-nine hunters took thirty birds. Hen:poult ratios, turkey numbers, and fall hunt success were again improving, and more than two thousand turkeys were harvested during the fall of 1965. The next year more areas were opened to spring gobbler hunting by permit, and an unlimited fall season was authorized statewide. After a prolonged decline in turkey populations through the dry years of the late 1960s and early 1970s, management emphasis shifted toward gobbler-only spring seasons and away from unlimited fall hunting. Several areas were closed to fall hunting in 1969, and in 1973 the Galiuro and Pinaleño mountains, where turkeys had been reduced to remnant status, were closed to turkey hunting entirely. In spite of a series of wet years beginning in 1979, turkey numbers failed to recover, and in 1986 the fall season was shortened to seven days.

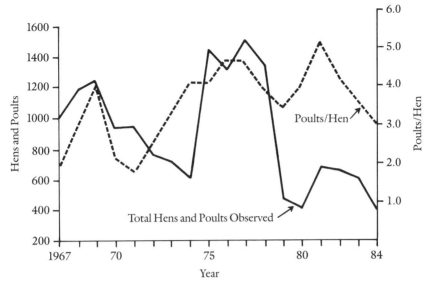

Fig. 5.8. Turkey survey data, 1967–84, from Mogollon Rim and White Mountain game-management units. Data from Harley Shaw.

Turkey populations in Arizona remain below former levels. Although subject to annual fluctuations imposed by climatic variations, hunt-success estimates for the main turkey range show a distinct downward trend since the 1960s (Fig. 5.7). The cause of this decline is unknown, but as there is no corresponding downward trend in poult:adult ratios (Fig. 5.8), it must be due to increased mortality. Fall hunting and disturbance, logging, grazing, and summer recreational use (e.g., Phillips 1982) have been suggested as reasons for an increased mortality rate.

Increased logging and U.S. Forest Service practices geared toward even-aged timber management have adversely affected almost all of the turkey's range in Arizona. Pine seed, when produced, is an important food source for turkeys beginning in November and continuing through the following year (Reeves and Swank 1955). The best cone-producing trees are large "overmature" and "decadent" age classes targeted for removal in timber management plans. Old "yellow-belly" trees are also essential roost sites (Phillips 1982), as well as an important winter food source in the pine stringers at lower elevations. The increased harvest of mature trees at all elevations could therefore force turkeys in years of moderate cone production to rely more on seed heads and other grass parts than formerly (Murie 1946; Reeves and Swank 1955).

Native cool-season grasses, where not replaced by seeded exotic grasses less valuable to turkeys, are increasingly grazed by cattle and elk. It is interesting that the growth in elk numbers since the 1970s closely parallels the decline in turkey populations noted in the Sitgreaves, Coconino, and South Kaibab national forests. Turkey populations on the higher, wetter, and elk-free North Kaibab have not shown a long-term decrease, and their numbers in the even better-watered Apache National Forest (where elk populations were suppressed from the late 1960s through the mid-1980s) do not appear to have experienced as marked a decline as those on the drier turkey ranges farther west.

Recreational use of turkey habitat has dramatically increased since the 1960s. Key streamside and meadow habitats are affected more and more by visitor use. Such activity tends to force turkeys into less favorable areas, thus exposing the birds to food shortages related to grazing and logging. Better resource management and allocation may be required if turkeys are to regain their former numbers in Arizona.

No satisfactory explanation has been put forward, however, for the reduced numbers of turkeys in parts of southern Arizona, and the bird's almost total disappearance from the Pinaleño and Galiuro mountains since 1968 is a mystery. Although the resumption of logging in the Pinaleños between 1958 and 1973 coincides with the disappearance of turkeys from that range (see, e.g., Knopp 1956), such activity would not explain their absence in the Galiuros. Heavy snow cover at high elevations and heavy grazing at lower elevations, though possible explanations, are not entirely plausible either, given the wide array of low habitats available. The potential for the transmission of disease from domestic poultry may be worthy of investigation. Although Hall (1952) reported Arizona turkeys to be free of disease and parasites, a sample of birds from the Kaibab National Forest in 1986 showed a high incidence of *Mycoplasma* spp. Subsequent tests for this pathogen were inconclusive, but studies elsewhere have shown poultry-borne disease to be capable of thwarting Wild Turkey restoration efforts (Amundson 1985).

Restocking

Attempts to restock Arizona's depleted turkey ranges began at least as early as 1919. During the fall of 1919 and the spring of 1920, eighty-one Wild Turkeys were trapped south of Escudilla Mountain and transplanted to the Catalina, Chiricahua, and Pinal mountains, and to the Camp Wood and Hualapai Mountain areas. As of 1921, the transplants were thought to be doing well in all but the Catalina Mountains, and conditions in the state's

turkey range were considered to be improving (Arizona State Game Warden Report, 1917–21). Restocking pen-reared turkeys was emphasized as a
game-restoration technique throughout the 1920s but it was not until the
initiation of a federally funded restocking program in October 1939 that a
coordinated attempt was made to reestablish turkeys and maintain records
of the results.

By the late 1930s the only "trappable" populations of Wild Turkeys remaining were on the Fort Apache and San Carlos Indian reservations,
which were closed to public hunting and not yet subject to heavy timber
cutting. During the winter of 1938–39, twenty-six birds were trapped at
Malay Gap on the San Carlos Indian Reservation and released at Alder
Springs in the Catalina Mountains and in Greenhouse Canyon in the Chiricahua Mountains (Gambrell 1940a, b). Only eight hens were released into
the Chiricahuas, so the following summer this plant was bolstered with
twelve semitame turkeys from Chihuahua, Mexico.

The Catalina birds spread widely, but the following summer, hens with
poults were observed at the head of Romero Canyon and on Mount Lem-
mon. The transplants to the Chiricahuas were less encouraging, and the
twelve Mexican turkeys had dwindled to one gobbler and five hens by
March 1, 1940. That month another twenty-six birds were captured at Malay
Gap and transplanted to the Catalinas and to Tripp Canyon in the Pinaleño
Mountains. Difficulties with the White Mountain Apaches were resolved,
and four gobblers and a hen, trapped in Post Office Canyon, were released
into the Catalinas; an additional two gobblers and five hens from Big
Springs were taken to the northwest slopes of Mount Union in the Brad-
shaw Mountains. Another seven gobblers were captured on Dry Prong
Creek in the Crook National Forest and released on the west side of the
Chiricahuas. Predator control, then deemed essential for all transplant efforts, was conducted at all capture and release sites (Gambrell 1940b).

Another thirty-one birds were trapped and released in the spring of 1941,
all from the Fort Apache Indian Reservation. Thirteen were released on
Mount Union, one gobbler and ten hens were released in Tripp Canyon,
and seven hens were transplanted to Barfoot Park in the Chiricahuas (Gambrell 1941). No turkeys were transplanted in 1942, but follow-up investigations resulted in several sightings of poults in both the Catalina and
Pinaleño mountains. A large number of observations in the Pinaleños—
some as far as twenty-six miles from the release site—were thought to be
the result of reintroductions prior to the 1940 and 1941 releases as the Forest
Supervisor was certain that turkeys were still present on West Peak in 1940.

The population on Mount Graham was estimated to be between two hundred fifty and one thousand birds (Arrington 1942d).

By 1943 turkeys were thought to be established in all four of the release areas and the restocking program was considered a phenomenal success (Arrington 1943). Although trapping efforts failed in 1943, 1944 was the biggest year yet for turkey transplants. Another one hundred forty turkeys were transplanted to Turkey Flat in the Pinaleño Mountains, Sweetwater Spring in the Santa Rita Mountains, the head of Hassayampa Creek in the Bradshaw Mountains, the Pinal Mountains between Sulphide and Pinal Peak, the Miles Ranch in the Superstition Mountains, Walpine Lodge in the Hualapai Mountains, and to an area near Walnut Creek Ranger Station in the Juniper Mountains. All of these sites except the Hualapai Mountains were within the turkey's known historical range.

In 1946 another thirteen turkeys were transplanted to the Santa Rita Mountains and all of the release areas were visited. The outlook was encouraging. The population in the Pinaleños was described as "large" and in the Bradshaws as "booming"; turkeys in the Santa Ritas were thought to be on the way to "becoming established"; prospects were deemed "good" in the Pinal Mountains (where a few pen-reared birds were present prior to the release). Turkeys were already considered established in the Catalina and Chiricahua mountains, and only the Walnut Creek, Superstition, and Hualapai releases were thought to be in need of further evaluation. The populations in the Chiricahua and Pinaleño mountains were thought to be so large as to be in danger of overtaxing their food resources, and a limited number of hunting permits was suggested but not approved for these areas (Arrington 1946).

By 1949 the state's turkey populations had recovered to the extent that trapping off the reservations was practical. Twenty-three turkeys were captured in the White Mountains and released on Fort Huachuca in January 1950. The next month sixty-six turkeys were trapped and released, twenty-seven of them going to Pine Flat on the North Kaibab. This release of eight toms and nineteen hens to nonhistoric but obviously suitable habitat was destined to be one of the most successful transplants of turkeys anywhere. Another twenty-three birds were transported to Fort Huachuca, and four gobblers were released on the South Rim of Grand Canyon National Park to supplement some hens regularly seen there.

No turkeys were again transplanted until the winter of 1954–55 when twenty-nine were released into the Dos Cabezas Mountains (Webb 1955). The following year twelve additional birds were sent to the Dos Cabezas

Mountains and hauled by horseback to Mexican Springs, a transporting method that proved impractical (Webb 1956b). In 1961 another thirteen turkeys were dropped from an airplane over the Dos Cabezas Mountains, a technique that did prove promising—all birds but one opening their wings and gliding down to a "soft" landing (Webb 1960, 1961b). Nonetheless, the Dos Cabezas Mountains transplant failed.

The Mount Trumbull and Mount Dellenbaugh areas on the Arizona Strip were recommended as the next release sites, and thirty-seven turkeys were released at Nixon Springs, near Mount Trumbull, in February 1961. Also that year, thirty-nine Rio Grande Turkeys (*M. g. intermedia*) from the King Ranch in Texas were released at Corral Nuevo in the Atascosa Mountains. Although the Mount Trumbull transplant appeared promising, subsequent observations of the Rio Grande birds were few and scattered. Comparison of climatographs showed that the Arizona site was drier and cooler than the Rio Grande birds' original home. Perhaps for that reason, only one unverified report of reproduction was received (Webb 1962).

In the late winter of 1962, turkeys were again trapped near Flagstaff, and twenty-five were air-dropped in the vicinity of Mount Dellenbaugh. The same year another thirty Rio Grande turkeys were released at Corral Nuevo.

Mingus Mountain was surveyed as the next potential transplant site (Webb and Robeck 1962), and in 1963 twenty-seven turkeys from areas south of Williams and Flagstaff were transplanted to the Methodist Camp and Potato Patch on Mingus Mountain. That was the last year for the restocking project. Although three more plants would be made by regional personnel—to Black Rock Mountain on the Arizona Strip, to the Bradshaw Mountains, and to the Mount Dellenbaugh area—there was little potential for additional transplants. The only pine-forested, montane region not occupied by turkeys and not selected for a turkey transplant was the small summit area on Pine Mountain in the Pine Mountain Wilderness Area. Transplants to areas of oak woodland where pines were absent proved unsuccessful, and until there is a resurgence in the quality of riparian deciduous forests along the state's streamways, there appears to be little opportunity to expand turkey populations through further restocking.

As of 1988, the turkey transplant efforts can best be described as a qualified success. The disappointing and mysterious loss of good turkey populations in the Pinaleño and connected Galiuro mountains is offset by a thriving population on the North Kaibab. Turkeys are present in moderate numbers in the Catalina Mountains, in the Chiricahua Mountains, and in the Mount Trumbull area. Small populations persist in the Santa Rita,

Huachuca, and Bradshaw mountains, but turkeys are now absent from the Pinal and Superstition mountains and, after a promising beginning, have disappeared from the Mount Dellenbaugh area. The transplants to the Dos Cabezas and Atascosa mountains failed entirely, as did the release at Black Rock on the Arizona Strip. No Mexican turkeys are known to be present on Fort Huachuca, where a few were introduced by military personnel in 1979.

POPULATION DYNAMICS

The vagaries of both annual and long-term turkey population levels have long intrigued biologists. Reproductive success and overwinter survival dictate the numbers of any temperate species, and one of the first federally funded investigations in Arizona was designed to measure poult production and predict overwinter carryover prior to establishing annual hunt regulations. Poult production was suspected to be related to climatic factors, and overwinter survival was thought to be determined by food availability. Predation was considered a key factor also (Hargrave 1939; Ligon 1946).

Although predation per se was discounted as important to either poult production or adult survival (Reeves 1953e; Spicer 1959), several years of study showed the other assumptions to be essentially correct. As determined from midsummer surveys, poult production ranges from 0.6 to 5.9 poults per hen, with subsequent percentages of juveniles in the bag ranging from 20 to 75 (Jantzen 1958b; Phillips 1982). Reeves (1953d) determined that reproductive success was negatively correlated with the number of days below 25°F during the April–May nesting period. However, fall population size and hunt success was more dependent on the number of adults available than on poult production (Shaw 1968a). Working with a western population in the arid Moqui area south of the Grand Canyon, Shaw (1977) found turkey numbers and hunt success to be strongly correlated with the amount of precipitation received the previous winter and spring, but population size was only weakly related to reproductive success.

Overwinter carryover depends on food availability and varies with mast production, grass growth, and snow cover (Reeves 1953a–g; Phillips 1982). Attempts to measure annual variations in survival with band recoveries were frustrated by the need to obtain large numbers of birds for adequate samples and by the long distances traveled by turkeys (Reeves 1954; Shaw 1977; Phillips 1982). Relative survival rates can be obtained, however, from

TABLE 5.1

Spring Drought and Turkey Survey and Hunt Information from the Williams Area
of the South Kaibab National Forest, Arizona, 1964–83

Year	Hunt Success (Fall Population Level) (%)	Base Population (= Hunt Success Previous Year) (%)	Estimated Survival Rate[a] (%)	Poults Observed on Summer Surveys	April PDSI[b]
1964	3.3	2.9	69	41.0	−24
1965	8.8	3.3	100	50.7	14
1966	5.9	8.8	42	37.0	−8
1967	4.2	5.9	54	24.0	−25
1968	4.9	4.2	36	69.0	−4
1969	6.3	4.9	33	74.0	−4
1970	6.1	6.3	49	50.0	−8
1971	4.2	6.1	43	38.0	−33
1972	3.1	4.2	31	58.0	−32
1973	6.1	3.1	58	71.0	59
1974	3.4	6.1	21	62.0	−22
1975	7.4	3.4	71	68.0	13
1976	1.2	7.4	8	51.0	5
1977	4.3	1.2	100	57.0	−18
1978	7.9	4.3	54	71.0	23
1979	3.4	7.9	18	59.0	55
1980	4.4	3.4	38	71.0	54
1981	2.4	4.4	23	57.0	−2
1982	4.1	2.4	100	0.0	13
1983	1.0	4.1	10	59.0	44

[a] Extrapolated adult turkeys per hunter divided by all turkeys per hunter previous year
[b] Palmer (1965) Drought Severity Index for Northwest Arizona

hunt data, assuming that hunt success reflects population levels and that the number of juveniles in the harvest reflects annual variations in poult production.

The most consistent, long-term survey information on Arizona turkeys has been collected from the Williams area (Phillips 1982; Table 5.1). Seventeen years of data show the relative importance of base population size, overwinter survival, and reproductive success. Multiple-regression analysis of these three variables explains 72 percent of the variation in fall hunt success.

Base population alone explains about 37 percent of the variation in fall hunt success, not a surprising statistic given the relatively long life span and single annual nesting of this species. Base population was negatively correlated with the following year's reproductive success and survival, probably because yearling hens achieve lower reproductive success than adults and survival is dependent on density. Early beliefs that large turkey populations should be heavily harvested to reduce winter loss may have been justified (e.g., Hall 1952).

The percentage of poults observed on summer surveys was strongly correlated with spring moisture. Spring temperatures probably explain much of the remaining variation, as reported by Reeves (1953b) and Project Personnel (1954). Variations in ratios of poults to hens, however, explained only about 7 percent of the variation in hunt success.

Annual survival explained about a third of the variation in hunt success and was almost five times more important than reproductive success in determining fall population levels. Unfortunately, factors governing survival are difficult to isolate. Mast production is not predictable on the basis of climatic data, and the effects of heavy snows like those that decimated turkey populations on the North Kaibab during the winter of 1978–79 are difficult to quantify. Spring and/or summer precipitation, respectively, affect cool- and warm-season grass growth. Production of grass seed heads could influence survival rates in some years, as good grass growth can make up for mast shortages (Reeves and Swank 1955). The remaining variation in hunt success is thought to be due to sampling error and such fluctuating factors as water availability, unseasonable weather, and access restrictions.

TALKING TURKEY

Three North American birds are worthy of big-game status—the Canada Goose, Sandhill Crane, and Wild Turkey. To bag all three has taken me more than twenty-five years of hunting. My most memorable hunts have been after the Wild Turkey. No other game is as fine a prize. It was not until a spring gobbler season was opened in Arizona and Fred Phillips, wildlife manager in Williams, taught me some fine points about turkeys that I learned how to hunt this fine bird.

The eight turkeys I have since had the good fortune to bag have all been gobblers, called in during the spring season. For me, there is no other way to hunt these birds. The heart-pounding approach of an excited gobbler twirling in full strut; that moment of truth as he finally comes to within twenty yards; the momentary extension of his red, white, and blue head as he perceives the movement of the gun barrel—all are preludes as essential to the kill as the "moment of truth" is to bullfighting.

The hunt is a series of rituals. The spring air before first light is decidedly chilly, making the early arising as uncomfortable as it is necessary. The predawn tramp through the dark forest up to the distant ridgeline is taxing and brings on a sweat despite the cold. The green light in the east does little to diminish the chill and the gloom. But with the proper scouting and a little luck, you will hear a tom gobble from his roost sometime around 5:10 A.M.

You have twenty, maybe thirty minutes before he leaves the big pine that is his nighttime bed. Quietness is crucial. The game is to get close without being detected; if the turkey hears you, he will flush. A spooked turkey is an almost hopeless proposition.

One problem is that the roost tree invariably extends above the ridge-line, allowing the bird the advantage of first light. The first *cheer-up*s of robins are already awakening the forest. Fifteen minutes have gone by since the first gobble. Great care must be taken not to startle the quarry. He will soon give a farewell gobble and be off the roost. Time is of the essence.

The light in the east has turned a yellow and gold; the outlines of the pines are dim but visible. The still-bare skeletons of Gambel oaks are barely discernible in the receding darkness. Their last-year's leaves crunch under-foot. A good turkey ridge always has oaks. It is time to select a stand.

Selecting the initial stand is urgent business, yet one that requires great care and foresight. Keep in mind that everything will look a lot different twenty minutes later, and if you get a turkey "on the string," you will not be able to leave your chosen position for a better one. The tree, log, or rock selected as a blind must provide both visibility and concealment. Your out-line should be broken but you must be able to swing the gun barrel unim-peded. The caller should also be shaded from the coming sun. For this reason, a standing tree is usually better than a fallen one. Another impor-tant consideration is that turkeys are easier to call uphill than down; ridges and small rises are the best sites.

Be as silent and inconspicuous as possible when settling in. For this reason, if no other, it pays to hunt alone. That way there is no talking and all noise is reduced. Once in position, begin calling. If the gobbler is still in the tree or somewhere on the ridge, he is available to be enticed in by your call.

I prefer the Lynch 101 box call. The diaphragm call is actually better, as it allows a greater repertoire of calls and does not require telltale move-ments of the hands. But try as I might, I cannot master this device without gagging.

Start with the hen "yelp," calling slowly and persistently: *chew-chew-chew*. Keep the cedar paddle and rim of the box well chalked and strive for the proper resonance. Once the right pitch is obtained, increase the volume and call with greater frequency for a number of interrupted series. With luck, you will hear a responding gobble at the end of each pause. If so, do not worry about overcalling—you cannot call too much unless, or until, your turkey is in sight. Most Merriam's Turkeys are still relatively unsophisticated and forgive out-of-tone notes that would panic an experienced southeastern gobbler.

A bird "en route" requires care and patience. At the close of each gobble, keep enticing him with additional yelps. Remember to sit motionless, hands out of sight. Some turkeys will rush right in; others will coyly circle and sneak in only after you have all but given up. Some will keep you waiting for an hour or more before making their commitment—if indeed they ever do. Still others, especially gobblers accompanying hens, may be almost impossible to call in.

Turkeys are loath to cross fences or pass through dense underbrush. They usually skirt locust thickets and stands of aspen. They come downhill reluctantly, and open clearings are formidable barriers. Your bird may come without ever gobbling! If so, the first announcement of his presence is likely to be the sound of his wings strutting against the ground—an odd, unforgettable sound not unlike that of a locomotive gathering steam.

I have had several gobblers come in full strut, twirling like tops and looking like moving stumps. More than a few have sneaked in from the least expected quarter, startling me with a gobble twenty feet behind my back. Whether gobbling or silent, his approach is always a heart stopper.

Keep calling. If thirty minutes go by without a response, move quietly through the forest, following the ridgeline. Stop every twenty minutes or so and call from stands at appropriate sites. You may hear a gobble from the location of your last stand. If so, sit down, call, and wait for the turkey to find you. Do not get impatient and stand up too quickly. If he sees you, he will be gone for good. Give the bird time to get to you. He may have to come a long way—or he may be spending so much time in strut that his progress is slow.

After 8:30 A.M. your chances fade. If you have not got a bird working by 9:00 A.M., you are in trouble. However, a turkey heard after 9:30 A.M. is a sure bet if you play him right. These late-calling gobblers are invariably sexually active birds without hens.

Wind is an even greater enemy than time. Strong, gusty breezes make calling hopeless, especially after the first hour or so. The afternoons are never as productive as the mornings; a spring turkey hunter *has* to be an early riser. And do not expect to call in a gobbler after 4:00 P.M., when he is on his way to roost. Unless you just happen to be in his way you will be unsuccessful at bringing him in no matter how many times he answers. Your best bet is to follow him to bed and be ready for him tomorrow.

If you have not located a turkey, check dusty roads and around stock tanks for gobbler tracks. Look for his long, curved droppings and note where you find them. Keep an eye out for scratchings in the pine litter and for shed feathers. Above all, make sure you are in the woods each morning before 5:00 A.M. and listening for gobbles. Once located, most gobblers can be worked. For some birds you may need several days to come up with the right approach.

There are always exceptions. I once called in and killed a gobbler at 3:00 P.M. during a driving snowstorm. It just so happened that he was "hot" and I was in the right place in his home territory. Keep in mind that each gobbler is an individual, and for every stereotype, there is another one that breaks the mold. Try not to place all of your efforts on one turkey. I am convinced that some birds just cannot be had.

Once he is in, keep your head and keep it down. Do not let him see any movement. Let him get to within twenty yards. Twenty-five yards is maximum range. Pull the gun up ever so slowly. Hold on his head. He has probably seen you by now and is craning his neck for a better look. Now is the time. Fire! A load of magnum 4s should kill him instantly.

Never shoot a gobbler in full strut. His fluffed-out feathers form a for-midable shield, and the primary target—his head—is tucked back and hard to draw a bead on. A wounded turkey is a heartbreaker and will ruin any hunt no matter how successful it later turns out. Get a second shell into the chamber immediately after shooting. If he gets up, no matter how wobbly, shoot him again—*immediately.*

You have bagged North America's greatest game bird and a highly edible prize as well. As you sit back and admire the spectacular plumage of your trophy, you know you will be talking turkey again.

PART IV

New World Quails

New World quails originated in the Neotropics and are birds of tropical and warm temperate regions. Of the six species found in the United States, four are (or were) present in Arizona. One other, the California Quail, has become established in the state since the 1960s. Only the state of Texas can claim as many native quail, and if the Mountain Quail were to be successfully established in Arizona, as suggested by Gutiérrez (1977a), Arizona could claim all six species.

Quails display varying amounts of sexual dimorphism but all are seasonally monogamous. Both sexes care for the young, and clutch sizes may be large. Individuals have short life spans, and populations tend to fluctuate widely. With the marginal exception of annual altitudinal movements by the ambulatory Mountain Quail, New World quails are nonmigratory.

SEX RATIOS, SEXUAL SELECTION, & SEXUAL DIMORPHISM

The preponderance of males in populations of New World quails is of special interest (D. Brown and Gutiérrez 1980). Unbalanced sex ratios cannot be explained through sample bias and differential vulnerability because they occur in areas where almost the entire population is collected or trapped (Kabat and Thompson 1963; Gallizioli 1967). Disparate sex ratios in trapped and hunted samples also appear to be closely related to those observed in the field (Emlen 1940:92). As first noted by Wallmo (1956a) for Scaled Quail, the preponderance of males is greatest in years of high population levels, presumably because of a high carryover of adults.

The usual explanation for the disparate number of males is that although the sex ratio is essentially 50:50 at hatching, higher female mortality results from predation and stress during nesting (Stoddard 1931; Wallmo 1956a; Rosene 1969; Anthony 1970; Leopold 1977). However, this hypothesis is only partially satisfactory as it does not explain the evolutionary reason for this phenomenon.

Since Darwin's (1871) discussion of sexual selection, biologists have attempted to explain unbalanced sex ratios as a feature operating primarily in polygamous species (Trivers 1972; Emlen and

TABLE IV.1

Sexual Dimorphism and Sex Ratios in Some North American Quails

Species[a]	Males (%)			N	Source
	First Year	Adults	All Birds		
Mearns' (Montezuma) Quail	57.8	62.9	59.3	3,263	D. Brown, unpubl. data, Arizona[b]
Gambel's Quail	51.9	57.1	54.2	69,719	S. Gallizioli, unpubl. data, Arizona[b]
	53.1	56.5	54.9	3,628	Sowls 1960[b]
California Quail	49.9	58.3	53.1	1,325	Emlen 1940[b]
	48.5	59.6	51.8	847	Raitt and Genelly 1964[c, d]
	50.7	57.9	53.6	29,694	Leopold 1977[b]
Bobwhite Quail	50.5	61.7	53.2	1,633	Leopold 1945[b]
	50.4	59.1	52.0	42,492	Bennitt 1951[b]
	51.1	61.1	57.2	2,865	Kabat and Thompson 1963[b]
	50.8	62.9	52.7	381	Kabat and Thompson 1963[c]
	51.2	56.7	52.2	54,314	Sinn 1978[b]
Scaled Quail	44.0	56.6	47.3	2,842	Campbell et al. 1973[c]
	40.6	52.8	45.6	1,035	S. Gallizioli, unpubl. data, Arizona[b]
	48.7	60.2	52.6	1,244	Campbell and Lee, 1956; Wallmo 1956b; Schemnitz 1961[b]

[a] Arranged in order of decreasing sexual dimorphism
[b] Shot samples
[c] Trapped samples
[d] Trapped throughout the year

Oring 1977; and others). Scant attention has been paid to sexual selection in monogamous species, although Fisher (1958:146–56) showed that conditions for sexual selection, that is, female preference for certain male traits (especially plumage differences) and variation in male mating success, are also present in monogamous species.

Large fall–winter samples of several species of North American quail are roughly arranged in order of decreasing sexual dimorphism in Table IV.1. These data indicate that in the most dimorphic species skewed sex ratios begin to appear in the first-year age class, *before* pair-bond formation and nesting. Thus, differential mortality occurs within the first year of life. With the rigors of nesting, the sex ratio presumably becomes even more disparate.

The percentage of males is larger than females in the adult cohorts of all species than among first-year birds (Table IV.1).

Juvenile males nonetheless predominate in all species except Scaled Quail (which are difficult to sex) and California Quail. Williams (1957) observed an early opposite differential mortality for California Quail, with males having higher mortality during the initial weeks of life. By fourteen weeks of age the trend had reversed and males outnumbered females. Raitt and Genelly (1964) reported a similar pattern in California Quail except that the mortality reversal shifted later in the life cycle. Emlen (1940) observed not only a later trend toward disparate sex ratios in this species but also a variation in sex ratios by area.

Assuming that in a primitive predimorphism stage females suffer greater nesting mortality than males, the adult sex ratio therefore begins to favor males. Because quail are monogamous, not all males obtain mates: thus one of two necessary conditions for sexual selection is met, that is, there is a "differential ability in finding mates" (Wilson 1975:322). The second condition is a variation in male quality that is detectable by the female. Among most quails, male fitness is manifest in plumage characters and mate selection is renewed each year.

At the next evolutionary level, the "runaway" phase, spectacular plumage continues to develop even though it may be a disadvantage in natural selection simply because females now have a strong preference for dimorphic plumage. When female preference for the plumage advertisement is favored, sexual selection occurs. The greater the advantage of being a preferred male, the longer it takes for natural selection to overtake sexual selection. It follows, then, that the more the sex ratio is skewed, the greater the intrasexual competition. The greater the intrasexual competition, the greater the tendency for males to outnumber females. Greater male survival assures greater female selection. Thus, there is a correlation between sex ratios and sexual dimorphism (Table IV.1).

At some point the decrease in fitness owing to lowered advantage in natural selection catches up with the increase in fitness owing to success in mating, and an equilibrium is reached. The cryptically colored Scaled Quail is the least dimorphic of the quails and appears to have the lowest ratio of males to females. The benefits of protective coloration may be relatively more important than sexual dimorphism to this and other species found in grasslands and other open habitats.

PAUL BOSMAN

CHAPTER 6

Mearns' (Montezuma) Quail

When strolling through southern Arizona's grass covered mountains, you may be startled by an explosion of birds underfoot. One or several take off, then another and another, some making soft, startled cheeps. The birds fly like quail and, after arching over and through the trees, tumble down into clumps of bunchgrass. Some give the impression of being tawny colored; others display much black, some white, and even flashes of rich chestnut. You have encountered a covey of Mearns' Quail (*Cyrtonyx montezumae*), also known as Montezuma or Harlequin Quail.

Male Mearns' have white and black harlequin-marked heads, capped by a russet shock of feathers to form an ill-fitting crest. As if their heads were not striking enough, the males also possess handsome brown and black checkered backs interlaced with white darts. The breasts and underparts are a rich mahogany turning to black at a rump that terminates in a stubby, almost nonexistent tail. The flanks, too, are black, but spotted white like a guineafowl's. Dark, soulful eyes and a heavyset, pale blue beak complete an extraordinary appearance.

The hens, markedly different from the cocks, are cinnamon color with brown, black, and buff markings. Most females have an overall pinkish tinge grading in some individuals to patches of a burnt orange-yellow. The gray-blue feet of both sexes are equipped with long, scythe-shaped claws that facilitate scratching and digging but make perching impossible.

Mearns' are the largest of Arizona's quails. In winter adult males average about 6.9 ounces, females about 6.2 ounces. Arizona birds, like those in New Mexico, Texas, and northern Mexico, are of the *mearnsi* subspecies named after E. A. Mearns, who conducted an intensive biological survey of the United States–Mexico border region in 1892. Two other races and a closely related species are found in central and southern Mexico.

DISTRIBUTION

Essentially a Mexican species, Mearns' Quail extend northward into the United States to the mountains of southwest Texas, southwest New Mexico, and southeast Arizona. Arizona birds are accordingly most numerous in the border region in the Baboquivari, San Luis, Pajarito, Atascosa, Tumacacori, Santa Rita, Patagonia, Huachuca, Chiricahua, and Peloncillo mountains, with lesser numbers in the Mule and Whetstone mountains and in portions of the Rincon, Catalina, Galiuro, Pinaleño, and Pinal mountains (Fig. 6.1). These quail can also be found with some regularity below the Mogollon Rim in the watersheds of Eagle Creek and the Blue, San Francisco, Black, and White rivers. Above the Mogollon Rim the distribution of Mearns' Quail becomes sporadic and unpredictable. They have been found up to elevations of 10,000 feet on Escudilla Mountain, Green's Peak, and Mount Baldy (e.g., Phillips et al. 1964). Only rarely and only in the most favorable years are observations recorded from Sulphur Springs Valley, Altar Valley, and other valley locations below the limit of oaks.

Mearns' Quail have retreated from the northwestern portions of their historical range during the last century and can no longer be found around Fort Whipple, where Elliot Coues (1866) collected two, nor on San Francisco Mountain, where Beale's (1858) party encountered them. The birds are rare in the Tonto National Forest, where "fool quail" were formerly reported as common in such areas as Buzzard Roost Mesa, Pleasant Valley, and near Payson (Hargrave 1940). Relict populations are still present at several of these sites, and some observations of Mearns' Quail outside of their "normal" range have been reported by Yeager (1966, 1967) and D. Brown (1973b) and are shown in Figure 6.2. Given adequate summer precipitation and the relaxation of grazing pressures, this species might regain its former range and numbers.

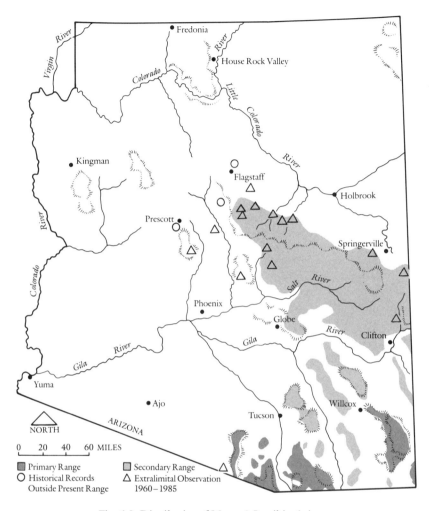

Fredonia

House Rock Valley

River

Colorado

Little

Colorado

River

Kingman

Flagstaff

Holbrook

Prescott

Springerville

Salt River

Phoenix

Globe

River

Clifton

Gila

River

Gila River

Yuma

Ajo

Willcox

Tucson

ARIZONA

NORTH

0   20   40   60 MILES

■ Primary Range   ■ Secondary Range
○ Historical Records   △ Extralimital Observation
  Outside Present Range   1960–1985

Fig. 6.1. Distribution of Mearns' Quail in Arizona.

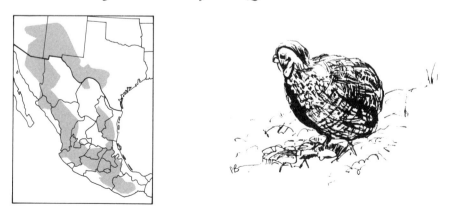

*Fig. 6.2. Mearns' Quail habitat of Emory oaks and blue oaks in
the Pajarito Mountains along the Arizona–Sonora border.*

HABITAT

Nearly all of the Mearns' Quail in Arizona are found in Madrean evergreen woodlands of oaks and pines (D. Brown 1982a; Fig. 6.2). A grass
understory is essential, however, and without this element the birds are
lacking. The typical Mearns' Quail landscape in Arizona is an open woodland populated by such evergreen oaks as Emory oak, Mexican blue oak,
Arizona oak, and less commonly, gray oak and Toumey oak. Alligator-bark
and one-seed junipers are not infrequent, and a few mesquites may even be
present. At higher elevations (5,500 to 6,800 feet) participants of the Mexican pine-oak woodland community appear, and silverleaf oak, Mexican
pinyon, Chihuahua pine, Apache pine, ponderosa pine, and madroño are
typically present. In the most favorable Mearns' Quail habitats the crown
cover of the trees is greater than 20 percent and is optimally about 30 percent (R. Brown 1982).

The species composition of the bunchgrasses varies with locality and
site but always consists of summer-growing perennials. Typical species are
sideoats grama, cane beardgrass, wolftail, sprangletop, and Texas bluestem.

Poorer sites are characterized by blue grama, hairy grama, and three-awn. On steep north slopes within the woodland, the most prevalent species is often bullgrass (*Muhlenbergia emersleyi*). Other, more localized species include pinyon ricegrass and vine mesquite-grass.

Mearns' Quail are loath to leave their woods and rarely make forays into pure grassland beyond a few dozen yards. Chaparral and shrub species are relatively unimportant as cover and detract from the sedges, forbs, and grass cover on which the birds depend. A possible exception is the catclaw mimosa, in which thickets the quail are often associated. Whether this is because the plants serve as protective cover or because the thorny branches discourage grazing is uncertain. Otherwise, the occurrence of such shrubs as pointleaf manzanita, cliffrose, and Mearns' sumac contributes little to the birds' welfare other than to provide incidental food items during poor food years (Bishop and Hungerford 1965; R. Brown 1978).

Summer precipitation is an essential component of Mearns' Quail habitat. Without adequate summer rainfall, the birds cannot exist; mean July–September precipitation must exceed ten inches. This summer rainfall pattern is what drives the phenology of the grasses and forbs that provide the Mearns' Quail's food and cover.

Most Mearns' Quail country is also warm temperate, and freezing temperatures do not normally occur more than 125 to 150 nights during the year. Temperatures almost always rise above freezing during the day, and although snowfall during winter months is not uncommon, any snow cover can be expected to melt in a day or two.

Mearns' Quail are also found in riparian communities, occasionally in ponderosa pine forest, and more rarely in subalpine forests and meadows. In each of these situations bunchgrasses (for example, mountain muhly) are present along with the sedges and bulbs on which the birds depend for food. How these populations survive the rigorous winters at high elevations is a mystery, and Ligon (1927) thought that the birds must make altitudinal migrations.

Mearns' Quail may also sometimes be seen in drier habitats such as semidesert grasslands or pinyon-juniper woodlands, especially after successive years of above-average summer precipitation. Such situations are uncommon and temporary, and the normal lower elevational limit of Mearns' Quail in Arizona is about 4,100 feet, with most birds found between 4,800 and 5,100 feet. They are birds of the mountains, bajadas, and high canyons, with primary residence in Mexico and southeast Arizona.

LIFE HISTORY

Like other southwestern quails, Mearns' begin pairing in late February and March (Yeager 1966, 1967). Males greatly outnumber hens and are presumably selected on the basis of advertised "buzz" calls. Some fighting occurs between males, and territories may not be finalized until May or June, as Bishop (1964) noted that pairs removed in March or April were soon replaced by other pairs. Pairs collected in May and June were not replaced, indicating that surplus birds were no longer available and that nesting territories were firmly established.

Actual nesting does not begin until late June, July, or even August and closely coincides with the advent of the summer rains. The factors that trigger nesting have yet to be determined, but this activity appears to be related to increasing humidity, the emergence of new vegetative growth (green feed) and insects, and the intake of these items into the bird's diet. It is not related to photoperiod, as most nests are initiated after the summer solstice, when daylight hours are declining.

The nest is on the ground and is constructed with some care. Great effort is made to keep it concealed from intruders, and the female covers the entrance with grass or leaves when leaving (see, e.g., Wallmo 1954). Wallmo (1954) described the nests as tunnels in leaf litter or in clumps of residual grass, with chambers measuring approximately four by six inches. Most were lined with leaves, grass parts, and down; all were protected from the elements by either an overstory of broadleafed trees, overhanging grasses, or a carefully woven canopy of residual grass or other small-stemmed plant parts. Nest sites ranged from cool, moist canyon bottoms to hot, arid slopes.

Nest-building has not been observed in the wild, and the male's role is uncertain. The eggs measure about 1.19 by 0.98 inches and are chalk white if not stained by moisture (Bent 1932; Wallmo 1954; Leopold and McCabe 1957). Clutch size varies from six to sixteen but averages about eleven. The male probably does not assist with incubation although he is in attendance nearby. If the nest is unmolested, the eggs hatch in about twenty-five days—a day or two longer than for other southwestern quails (Leopold and McCabe 1957). The hen may attempt to renest if the first clutch is destroyed, but there is no second hatch. By backdating the replaced wing feathers of juvenile birds, Yeager (1966, 1967) determined that the hatching dates in 1965 and 1966 were between July 22 and September 26, with a peak in early to mid-August.

The chicks immediately leave the nest to forage with their parents, and the brood is reared by both sexes. Should danger threaten, either or both parents may feign injury, fluttering on the ground to distract the intruder. If anything, the male is even more protective than the hen, and he may cover the chicks with his wings or "attack" a real or perceived enemy (Leopold and McCabe 1957).

From October through January the size of the family (that is, the covey) is relatively stable unless there is inadequate food or a reduction in ground cover. Daily activities are usually limited to foraging and roosting in a sedentary home range of about fourteen or fifteen acres that overlaps the range of the original pair (R. Brown 1978). The size of these oblong territories depends on food availability, covey size, and overall quality of the habitat. In years of large populations and/or food shortages, many of the birds may be forced to forage away from their traditional territories. Such emigrations are uncommon, and R. Brown (1982) noted only one such year in the eight years of his study.

In winter there is some intermixing of adults, as more than one adult male has been found in coveys in January and February. Whether these are excess males or unsuccessful parents is unknown. Some dispersal method must ensure sexual selection outside the family covey to prevent inbreeding, although it is possible that some pairs remain mated for more than one season.

Behavior

Mearns' Quail behavior is appropriate for the dense grass cover that the birds need to survive. Their response to a threat is to squat down and depend on the tall residual grass growth to conceal them. So ingrained is this response behavior that it is often employed when the birds are caught out in short grass, bare ground, or even on pavement. Even when so exposed, the quail may allow someone to approach to within a few feet, hence their common name of "fool quail" among settlers. Nonetheless, under natural conditions this defense works quite well, and most Mearns' Quail remain unseen unless they are almost stepped on and forced to flush.

Mearns' Quail, like other quails, burst into flight and attain a maximum speed in excess of twenty miles per hour in a couple of seconds. This rapid flight is not sustained over long distances, however, and many birds alight after only forty to sixty yards, although occasional flights may exceed one hundred yards. Although Mearns' Quail can be strong runners (Yeager

1966), and most of the bird's normal travel is on foot, pursued birds usually run only a few yards before hiding in grass or flushing.

Like other grassland-dwelling birds, Mearns' Quail roost on the ground. Nightfall finds these strictly diurnal birds huddled together facing outward similar to bobwhites. The roost site varies each evening but is always in tall grass and commonly in or near a canyon bottom or other small drainage. During fall and winter the roosts may be on open, grassy hillsides with a southern or western exposure. The sleeping quarters of the previous night are identifiable by the pressed form of the covey in the grass and a small ring of feces deposited in the center.

Feeding Habits

Mearns' Quail feed exclusively on the ground, where their stout legs and long claws are adept at scratching and digging. Investigators have found that two items—the bulbs of wood sorrels (*Oxalis spp.*) and the bulbs and tubers of flat sedges (*Cyperus esculentus, C. rusbyi,* etc.)—are the predominant foods from October through June (Leopold and McCabe 1957; Bishop and Hungerford 1965; R. Brown 1978). Acorns of Emory and blue oaks are important dietary items in those years that a mast crop is produced.

With the advent of the summer rains, insect emergence brings about the only major alteration of food habits. Although some grasshoppers and other insects are taken throughout the year, during the two to three months when the quail are nesting and raising chicks, insects, especially beetles, are the principal dietary items for adults and young alike. Otherwise, the predominant foods are *Oxalis* bulbs and sedge tubers supplemented by a great variety of forb and grass seeds, including those of the tepary bean (*Phaseolus acutifolius*), spurge, lupine, milk pea, and paspalum. All of these plants grow and set seed after the summer rains, on which the quail's yearlong food supply depends. Only rarely are cultivated grains eaten (Leopold and McCabe 1957).

When feeding, Mearns' Quail scratch with one foot and then another, frequently pausing to inspect for food items (Bishop 1964). The birds search for seeds and tubers by raking the duff and topsoil under bushes and trees and at the base of rocks to a depth of about one-eighth of an inch. These fan-shaped "scratchings" may cover several yards and can be confused with marks made by feeding javelina, turkeys, coatis, and skunks. The "diggings" for *Oxalis* bulbs are more distinctive. These cone-shaped depressions are about two inches long, one inch across, and two to three inches deep. One side of the cone is dug away and the excavated dirt deposited next to the hole. Inside the pit are shucks of consumed bulbs, for the quail removes the outer shell of both bulbs and acorns (Leopold and McCabe 1957).

While feeding, the birds may travel so close together as to be touching one another (Bishop and Hungerford 1965). Foraging begins late in the morning (after sunrise), is generally uphill, and continues at least intermittently throughout the day with pauses during midday. Crops are usually filled by about three o'clock in the afternoon, and the quail begin working their way downhill toward a roost site. Although Mearns' Quail occasionally drink, they do not seek out water but subsist on moisture provided by their food.

Vocalizations

At least four types of calls have been identified from these commonly silent birds. The most noticeable vocalization is an assembly call of seven to eleven descending whistles given by adult or juvenile birds of either sex (R. Brown 1976). These quavering whistles, which sound somewhat like a Canyon Wren's, are given throughout the year and serve to reunite separated coveys and pairs. The shriller notes can be heard by the human ear at a distance of up to three hundred yards (R. Brown 1976). These gathering calls are most often given by females and are usually heard after a covey has been broken up and the birds scattered. The notes have a ventriloquial quality, and the caller is located with difficulty. Better success at locating the caller can often be had by imitating the whistles and "calling" the birds in.

Another call is a low moan or owl-like whine, only heard when the birds are within a few feet. These *ough, ough, ough* calls, which also descend in scale, appear to serve to keep the covey together as the birds forage and travel. Similar reassurance calls are given when the quail are pressed and sense a disturbing influence, and are probably analogous to the *pit-pit* calls of Gambel's Quail. When disturbed to the point of flushing, Mearns' Quail may also give excited cheeps and chirps.

The male's announcement call is an almost insectlike buzz that begins at a relatively high pitch and rapidly ascends to an inaudible level. This buzz call is accompanied by a rapid gular flutter that produces an oscillating timbre, or "gargle" (R. Brown 1976). Unlike the advertisement calls of other quails, buzz calls are not given from a prominent vantage point, but are emitted from the ground. The call is audible to about two hundred yards (Bishop 1964; R. Brown 1976).

Buzzing occurs during two periods of the year: from late February through early April during initial mate selection and pairing, and in late June and July at the onset of incubation (R. Brown 1976). Unattended males are especially vocal, and the call is probably most often given by unmated males and those whose hens have initiated nesting. Buzzing by one bird frequently elicits a similar response from neighboring males. Most calling is in the morning with a lesser peak in the evening (R. Brown 1976) but is irregular from one day to the next and does not, as with other quails, provide a reliable census technique.

MANAGEMENT HISTORY

There is little question that Mearns' Quail, or as they were formerly known, Messena quail, were more widespread in Arizona at the time of settlement than they are today. In his field notes for January 1885, E. A. Mearns (1884–86) made several references to Messena quail below the Mogollon Rim, including a covey flushed at Indian Gardens along Oak Creek Canyon, where this species no longer occurs. Kennerly (1856) noted that "in the valley of the Santa Cruz river and among the adjacent hills, it [Messena quail] was extremely abundant."

The unregulated herds of livestock that arrived in the 1880s and the summer droughts that began in 1884 boded ill for Mearns' Quail in southern Arizona. By the 1890s Arizona's rangelands were in desperate shape, as described by early ornithologist Herbert Brown (1900):

> During the years 1892 and 1893 Arizona suffered an almost continuous drouth, and cattle died by the tens of thousands. From 50 to 90 per cent of every herd lay dead on the ranges. The hot sun, dry winds and famishing brutes were fatal as fire to nearly all forms of vegetable life. Even the cactus, although girdled by its millions of spines, was broken down and eaten by cattle in their mad frenzy for food. This destruction of desert herbage drove out or killed off many forms of animal life hitherto common to the great plains and mesa lands of the Territory. Cattle climbed to the tops of the highest mountains and denuded them of every living thing within reach.

Nonetheless, Brown (1900) went on to state that

> the Messena, occupying the highest ranges, were naturally better protected and thus escaped the general doom. They were, however, never very numerous and

soon became exceedingly rare, but when conditions again became favorable they seemed to recover from their losses more readily than did their congeners, and in a few more years were again to be found in their old time numbers.

Overgrazing continued and the periodicities of summer drought came and went. Swarth (1904, 1909) considered the birds uncommon in the Huachuca Mountains in 1896, abundant in 1898, but extremely scarce in 1902 and 1903. Long-time resident ranchers have told me that "fool quail" were generally more abundant, particularly in the Tonto National Forest, before the 1920s than after. Because of this scarcity, Section 34 of the game code of 1929 stated that "Bobwhites, mearns (or fool) quail may not be taken at any time," and the protected status was to continue for more than thirty years. The mid-1930s saw more drought and continued diminishment of quail populations. By the 1940s some considered Mearns' Quail to be exceedingly rare even on ungrazed areas such as Fort Huachuca (Brandt 1951).

With a general recovery of Arizona rangelands after World War II, large numbers of Mearns' Quail were again reported (Wallmo 1954). Many Arizona newcomers were intrigued by the state's borderland birds, and interest in Mearns' Quail accelerated. A controversy developed between those who thought Mearns' Quail might provide a great sporting resource and those who believed that hunting might jeopardize an uncommon bird attractive to tourists. In 1960 the Arizona Game and Fish Commission authorized an experimental two-day Mearns' Quail season in December. One hundred seventeen hunters passed through three check stations in the Santa Rita Mountains. Forty-five quail were bagged, but not one of the hunters had come close to taking the ten-bird limit. Mearns' Quail were hard to come by.

In 1961 a nine-day December season was authorized. The lateness of the season was necessitated by the bird's late nesting habits, and inclement weather prevailed during most of the hunt. Only nineteen hunters and 8 quail were checked. After some debate the commission authorized a nine-day season for the following year. Thirty-nine hunters reported in with 50 quail, and in 1963 the season was statewide and extended to twenty-five days. That year fifty-two hunters bagged 128 Mearns' Quail.

The early 1960s were years of above-average summer precipitation, and Mearns' Quail and hunter interest gradually increased. In 1965 the months of December and January were opened to Mearns' Quail hunting, and 226 hunters took 875 of these novel game birds. Almost all of the successful hunters used pointing dogs, and a new clientele was established, a cadre that now harvested several thousand Mearns' Quail a year.

POPULATION DYNAMICS

The effects of grazing on Mearns' Quail populations has long been recognized but not understood (e.g., Brown 1900; Ligon 1927; O'Connor 1939). Investigators agreed that livestock grazing importantly affected the distribution and density of Mearns' Quail and that the quail disappeared from heavily grazed areas (O'Connor 1939; Miller 1943). Leopold and McCabe (1957), in the first life-history study of this species, concluded that grazing destroyed the bird's food sources. Wallmo (1954), however, noted Mearns' Quail populations in 1950 and 1951 to be lower on Fort Huachuca Military Reservation, which was closed to grazing, than in adjacent grazed areas.

Grazing intensities on many ranges tend to be relatively constant from year to year, with portions of individual allotments chronically overused, in generally good condition, or ungrazed. Wallmo (1954) found that Mearns' Quail populations fluctuated markedly whether on lightly grazed or protected ranges, and he assumed that these fluctuations were at least partially dependent on climatic factors. Both Leopold and McCabe (1957) and Bishop and Hungerford (1965) stressed the importance of summer precipitation on nesting and food production.

Mearns' Quail wings can be differentiated by sex and age (Leopold and McCabe 1957; Yeager 1966; Fig. 6.3). Information was obtained on annual variations in age ratios and hunt success over a thirteen-year period by sending wing-envelope questionnaires to known Mearns' Quail hunters. These data and calculated survival rates were then compared to precipitation amounts received the previous summer (D. Brown 1979; Table 6.1).

Mearns' Quail reproductive success, though variable, was consistently higher than that of other southwestern quails. The percentage of first-year quail in the bag ranged only from 57 to 88 percent (Table 6.1) and was positively correlated with the preceding summer's precipitation. The maximum percentage of juveniles in the harvest was 78 percent (with the extraordinary exception of 1977–78), and it appears that summer precipitation in excess of about nine inches is superfluous and contributes little to nesting success. It is interesting to note that reproductive success was negatively correlated with the previous year's winter precipitation (October through March). Also, unlike Gambel's Quail, there was no correlation between Mearns' Quail nesting success and hunting success. Summer precipitation therefore has little immediate effect on the following fall's population levels.

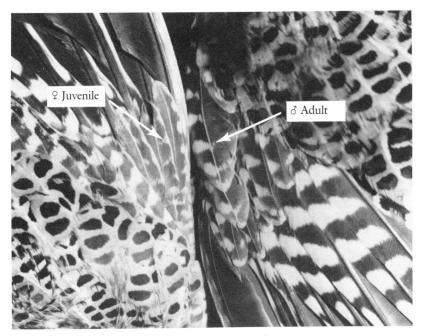

Fig. 6.3. Adult male Mearns' Quail wing (left) compared to that of a juvenile female. Note the distinct barring on the adult wing coverts as compared to the irregular barring on the juvenile's.

TABLE 6.1
June–August Precipitation and
Mearns' Quail Hunt Information in Arizona, 1965–78

Year	June–August Precipitation Preceding Hunt (inches)	Birds Per Successful Hunt[a]	Harvest of First-year Quail[a] (%)	Adult Quail per Successful Hunter	June–August Precipitation, Previous Year (inches)	Estimated Survival Rate (%)
1965–66	7.81	3.9 (226)	66 (875)	1.3	11.34	
1966–67	10.85	2.7 (146)	74 (388)	0.7	7.81	0.18
1967–68	11.03	6.9 (246)	77 (1,650)	1.6	10.85	0.59
1968–69	7.51	7.4 (130)	66 (953)	2.5	11.03	0.36
1969–70	10.57	5.3 (43)	71 (229)	1.5	7.51	0.20
1970–71	8.99	6.0 (91)	78 (543)	1.3	10.57	0.25
1971–72	9.96	6.3 (139)	77 (877)	1.4	8.99	0.23
1972–73	8.07	6.8 (168)	71 (1,146)	2.0	9.96	0.32
1973–74	6.17	5.6 (52)	57 (290)	2.4	8.07	0.35
1974–75	9.21	6.3 (97)	78 (608)	1.4	6.17	0.25
1975–76	7.58	6.4 (75)	67 (407)	2.1	9.21	0.33
1976–77	8.62	4.8 (43)	76 (238)	1.2	7.58	0.19
1977–78	8.34	6.5 (142)	88 (752)	0.8	8.62	0.17

[a] Sample size in parentheses

The data in Table 6.1, however, show a positive linear relationship between summer precipitation and the following year's hunt success, with the *succeeding* year's hunt success. Overwinter survival of coveys is thus more important in determining a given year's population level than that year's reproductive success. This conclusion is also supported by the positive correlation between summer precipitation and the following year's estimated survival rate. Lack of food and/or reduced grass growth brought on by inadequate summer precipitation decrease Mearns' Quail survival rates and subsequent population levels. It follows that reduced grass cover brought on by livestock grazing would also lower the survival rates.

R. Brown (1978) showed a strong positive correlation between June–August precipitation and the production of two key foods: wood sorrel and tepary bean. In contrast to the conclusions of Leopold and McCabe (1957), R. Brown (1982) found the best food-producing pastures to be heavily grazed. Severely grazed pastures produced almost twice as much food as moderately grazed ones. Heavily grazed pastures held no quail, however; nor did any birds attempt to nest there. Food production was not the main factor determining their abundance.

These studies show that Mearns' Quail abundance is determined by variations in survival, and that survival is related to grass growth the previous summer and to grazing intensity. In R. Brown's (1982) study 95 percent of the Mearns' Quail were on pastures having less than 45 percent of the annual growth eaten by cattle, and he concluded that utilization rates approaching 50 percent were detrimental to Mearns' Quail and that utilization rates between 35 and 40 percent were ideal.

Most mortality is the result of birds' being exposed to predation due to lack of hiding cover caused by inadequate summer rains and/or heavy grazing, or being forced into unsuitable habitat because of inadequate food production—also a function of below-average summer precipitation. Deep snows and extended periods of frozen ground have periodically also caused high mortality, both locally and generally (see, e.g., Leopold and McCabe 1957). After a three-day storm in February 1966, snow cover remained on south- and west-facing slopes of the Santa Rita Mountains for four to six days. Yeager (1966) later found several dead and emaciated Mearns' Quail and noted others capable only of weak flight. Both Yeager (1966) and others noted a measurable decline in winter coveys of Mearns' Quail after this episode, and hunters bagged significantly fewer adult birds the following season.

HUNTING MEARNS' QUAIL

Of all the game birds found in the Southwest, none surpasses the Mearns' Quail in sporting qualities. Not only does the bird hold well for a dog, it provides the trickiest kind of shooting and is excellent table fare. Its bizarre appearance and exotic distribution make it unique. As if these qualities were not enough, the birds are often to be found in good numbers. Some call it Arizona's greatest game bird.

A good pointing dog is a must to successfully hunt Mearns' Quail. One can occasionally stumble into a covey, particularly when populations are high, but such encounters are too irregular and inefficient for serious aficionados of these clown-faced bombshells. The quail are just too well hidden and hold too close to be "walked up." The bird's penchant for tall grass cover also requires the gifts of a retriever. Otherwise, too much time will be spent looking for downed birds that are easily lost.

To me, the ideal partner is a Brittany Spaniel. These pointing dogs range close and work well in close quarters. Other excellent breeds, such as the English pointer and German Shorthair, tend to cover too much country and are often out of sight when on point. However, the selection of a hunting dog is a personal opinion. I have seen labradors work well.

It is not necessary to get up early to hunt Mearns' Quail. During winter months the birds are rarely off the roost before eight-thirty, and on cold mornings they may "sleep in" until ten o'clock. Before then there is no fresh scent and no birds to work unless one stumbles onto a roosting covey. Also, the steep country is likely to tire you and your dogs before the best hunting begins in the afternoon.

The quails' morning forage is usually up the more heavily wooded side of a canyon or draw. The birds gradually work their way uphill until midday or until they come to a ridge. Mearns' Quail normally spend little time on ridgetops and rarely cross treeless areas. Afternoon feeding is usually downhill, and evening often finds the birds in the same canyon bottom they occupied the night before.

Working this pattern to advantage, try to get your dogs to follow up where the quail have been. Look for scratchings and diggings, the telltale evidence of feeding quail. The behavior of your dog should tell you if they are fresh or not. Great interest, much tail-wagging and sniffing, and short points mean the birds are close. If so, be ready and keep your dog in sight. He or she should be able to trail them up.

A locked-on point means birds—if not immediately in front of the dog, usually within a few yards. Although Mearns' Quail can and do move ahead of a dog, their usual reaction is to freeze and hold tight. If you are not careful, you or the dog may walk through them and flush them prematurely. With the dog on point you are ready for the covey to rise. Try to get a clear view and maneuver yourself and your companion into as good a position as possible. Two hunters are an effective team. More than that makes for complicated shooting and can be dangerous.

Shooting at an exploding covey of Mearns' Quail in oak timber is tricky and for this reason I prefer an ounce load of #8s. You must pick individual birds and shoot fast. Even a crack shot will knock down as many oak leaves as feathers. Keep an eye both on where downed birds fall and which direction most of the others go. Few birds will fly more than a hundred yards, and some, after arching over a few trees, may even plop down within sight. If the covey is large you will want to follow them up and have another go at the singles. Chances are that even after the most well-planned covey rise you will not have more than two quail apiece.

Mearns' Quail are not noted for running. If the grass cover is adequate, crippled birds, if properly marked, can usually be found by even a novice dog. Stand where the bird fell and make the dog keep coming back to try anew. Use a leash if you have to. Sometimes it takes several minutes for enough scent to build up for the dog to nose it out.

Single birds are the same. If you saw a bird go down, it's there somewhere. At least they used to be. Of late, it seems that Mearns' Quail have adapted to moving out ahead of the dogs. Some hunters believe that the birds with a tendency to run and hide after landing rather than landing and holding may be leaving more descendants.

It is not usually worthwhile to spend much time chasing after small coveys or those that are badly scattered. However, if coveys are scarce, it may pay to wait out a broken covey of seven or more. This is the time to relax and eat a sandwich; let the dogs rest. Often, after a wait of about thirty minutes, the descending whistles of the separated birds can be heard. The source of these quavering calls may be difficult to locate, and an interesting game is to imitate the calls with a hollow reed. The answering bird can then be pinpointed or, in some instances, lured to within a few feet of the caller.

Generally, however, your time is best spent looking for another covey. This may take only a few minutes or the rest of the day, depending on the quality of the habitat and the density of birds. In a normal year two hunters and a good dog can expect to locate five to six coveys in a day's hunt—not unlike bobwhite hunting in the South. Given an average bag of one or two birds per covey, that is satisfactory quail hunting, even by Southwest standards. And these are the exotic Mearns' Quail—a species that can be hunted in the United States only in Arizona or New Mexico.

PAUL BOSMAN

CHAPTER 7

Masked Bobwhite

No bird of the Southwest has stimulated as much debate as the Masked Bobwhite. The quail's late discovery and early disappearance, limited distribution, and susceptibility to livestock grazing have created a continuing aura of controversy. That our knowledge of the bird's existence in Arizona is almost entirely due to the efforts of one man is only one aspect of a remarkable history.

Although the pioneer ornithologist Elliott Coues reported bobwhites residing in southern Arizona and Sonora, Mexico, as early as 1864, he neither saw nor collected any. Coues's (1903) listing of this species in Arizona was based solely on reports of southern Arizona settlers, and it remained for the indefatigable Herbert Brown, Arizona's first resident naturalist, to obtain a specimen, describe this new form to the scientific world, and attempt to preserve the bird by reporting on its needs and its rare status. None of these endeavors proved easy, and the quail's discovery was steeped in acrimony.

Like many early Arizonans, Herbert Brown had a keen interest in mining ventures and spent significant amounts of time in the field, both in southern Arizona and Sonora. During the 1870s and early 1880s he traveled extensively in Mexico and on one of his trips heard and saw bobwhites in the grassy plains not far south of the international boundary. Probably at the urging of his friend and natural-history mentor, E. W. Nelson, Brown developed an active interest in this remote population of what was then an undescribed form of America's most familiar game bird. Always interested in contributing to scientific discovery and realizing that bobwhites extended into Arizona, Brown arranged for collectors to secure specimens.

In the spring of 1884 a man named Andrews collected a pair of bobwhites on the eastern slope of the Baboquivari Mountains and brought them to Brown in Tucson. Brown immediately published a short note about them in the *Weekly Citizen* and called the quail *Ortyx virginianus*, the scientific name at the time for bobwhite quail. This article was republished in *Forest and Stream*, the natural-history periodical of the day (Brown 1884).

R. R. Ridgway, of the U.S. National Museum, however, denied that bobwhite occurred in Arizona. Ridgway (1884) assumed that Brown had mistaken Mearns' Quail for bobwhite and published a note to that effect in *Forest and Stream*. Brown had unfortunately left his specimen in the care of a friend and the skins had spoiled. Stung by Ridgway's denial, he nonetheless sent the mummified body of the female and the salvaged head and other parts of the male to G. B. Grinnell, publisher of *Forest and Stream*. Grinnell forwarded these remains to Ridgway, who identified them as *Ortyx graysoni*, a bobwhite found in extreme southwestern Mexico (Grinnell 1884).

Brown meanwhile had obtained another pair from east of the Baboquivaris, which was examined in Tucson in late 1884 by such noted ornithologists as W. E. D. Scott, H. W. Henshaw, F. Stephens, and E. W. Nelson (Brown 1904). Stephens, another collector, managed to obtain a male bobwhite near Sasabe, Sonora. This bird, which was to become the type specimen, was sent to William Brewster at the American Museum of Natural History for identification. Brewster (1885), perhaps as an intended irony, named the bird *Colinus ridgwayi* after his colleague.

The next year Brown described the bird's habitat and distribution and pointed out that all of the quails collected to date were the same bird identified by Ridgway as *Ortyx graysoni*. Ridgway (1886), however, did not accept Brown's summary and, ignoring what would have been a sympatric occurrence of two species of bobwhite, considered both of the identifications as valid until proven otherwise! Brown collected more specimens and left the resolution of the quail's taxonomy to J. A. Allen (1886a, 1886b, 1886c, 1887).

The scientific name of the Masked Bobwhite remained *C. ridgwayi* until publication of the American Ornithological Union's checklist in 1944, when it was changed to *C. virginianus ridgwayi*, relegating the Masked Bobwhite

Fig. 7.1. Male Masked Bobwhite.

to subspecific status. Examination of sixty specimens from Arizona and Sonora later led Banks (1975) to agree that all populations in these two states were of a single subspecies, possessing variable plumage characteristics, and the trinomial designation to racial status remains in effect. There is no evidence that Masked Bobwhite had contact with other races in historic times, although its resemblance to *Colinus virginianus graysoni* suggests a recent link with the black-headed bobwhites of the Pacific coast of southwestern Mexico (e.g., Johnsgard 1973). Brown's initial description, derived almost a century earlier, had been correct.

Masked Bobwhite males are readily identified by their cinnamon-red breasts and black heads and throats. Their overall russet color is characteristic of the males of several bird species that overlap the Neotropic and Nearctic realms—the Cinnamon Teal and the Ruddy Duck, for example. The solid black head of the type specimen is atypical, and a varying amount of white is usually present above the eye and occasionally on the throat (Allen 1886b; Banks 1975; Fig. 7.1). Females closely resemble those of other races of bobwhite and are practically indistinguishable from the analogous bobwhite *C. v. texanus*, found in subtropical Texas and Tamaulipas, Mexico.

Masked Bobwhites are smaller than more northern races and the same size as bobwhites in southern Georgia and northern Florida at approximately the same latitude (Tomlinson 1975). They are also the smallest of Arizona's quails. Tomlinson's (1975) sample of twenty-six adult males, trapped in fall and winter in Sonora, Mexico, ranged between 5.3 and 6.4 ounces and averaged 6.0 ounces. Nineteen adult females ranged from 5.2 to 6.9 ounces and averaged 5.7 ounces. Young bobwhites reach adult size at about 126 days of age, when the eighth primary is molted. As with other quails, the juvenile primary wing coverts are barred and readily distinguishable through the first winter from the more uniformly colored coverts of the adults (Leopold 1939).

DISTRIBUTION

Historical accounts and collections show that Masked Bobwhites were restricted to level plains and river valleys in Sonora and extreme southcentral Arizona between 500 and 3,850 feet elevation (Brown 1885, 1904; Van Rossem 1945; Ligon 1952; Tomlinson 1972a). The bird's primary residence was the grassy *sabanas* and *llanos* within Shreve's (1951) "Plains of Sonora" and "Foothills of Sonora" subdivisions of the Sonoran Desert. In Arizona the birds were limited to the Altar and Santa Cruz valleys (Brown *in* Allen 1886a; Fig. 7.2). All areas of historical habitat are characterized by a mean annual rainfall from twelve to sixteen inches, 75 percent of which can be expected during July through September (D. Brown and Ellis 1977). Freezing temperatures are infrequent and rarely last longer than twenty-four hours. Reports of Masked Bobwhite outside these climatic parameters are unsubstantiated by specimens and other corroborating evidence.

The bird's eastern and southern distribution was, and is, limited by the transition of open savannas, with their summer-active grass and forb understories, into dense thornscrub. Bobwhites are replaced in the more structurally diverse thornscrub communities of Sonora by Elegant Quail, and Masked Bobwhites have not been documented south or east of the Río Yaqui.

To the west and northwest, decreasing summer precipitation excludes Masked Bobwhite from the Central Gulf Coast, Lower Colorado Valley, and Arizona Upland portions of the Sonoran Desert. In 1849 Audubon

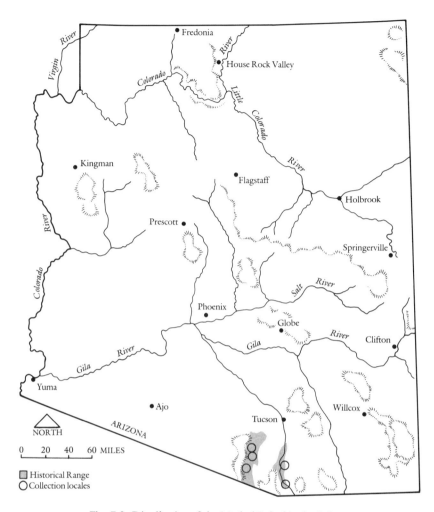

Fredonia

House Rock Valley

Virgin River

Colorado River

Little Colorado River

Kingman

Flagstaff

Holbrook

Prescott

Springerville

Salt River

Phoenix

Globe

River

Clifton

Gila River

Colorado River

Gila River

Yuma

Ajo

Willcox

Tucson

NORTH

ARIZONA

0   20   40   60 MILES

☐ Historical Range
◯ Collection locales

Fig. 7.2. Distribution of the Masked Bobwhite in Arizona.

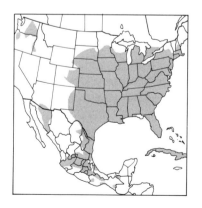

(1906), on leaving Altar, Sonora, for the Papago country, noted, "Plenty of the California partridge [Gambel's Quail] are here, but the black-breasted is [now] nowhere to be seen." Northward, and above 4,000 feet elevation, the subtropical scrub and grass understories of Sonoran savanna grassland give way to leaf succulents and sod-forming perennial grasses of warm temperate affinity. At the northern limits of Masked Bobwhite range in the Altar and Santa Cruz valleys of Arizona, semidesert grassland replaces Sonoran savanna grassland and the bobwhite is supplanted by the Scaled Quail.

Present Distribution

From 1967 through 1970, Tomlinson (1972b) conducted an extensive search to determine the distribution of the Masked Bobwhite in Sonora. Habitat type was an important consideration, and likely areas were searched with the aid of a dog during the fall and winter. Cactus Wren and Verdin nests, which are lined with the feathers of resident birds, were dismembered and examined for bobwhite feathers, and the bird's night roosts, marked by distinctive droppings, were sought. In the summer breeding season, taped female calls were played to elicit responses from calling males.

Masked Bobwhite were found in only two sites: the Benjamin Hill–Carbo area and a very limited region east of Mazatán (Tomlinson 1972b). Subsequent investigations showed Masked Bobwhites to occupy discontinuously an area of approximately five hundred square miles surrounding Rancho El Carrizo south of Benjamin Hill. The small population of bobwhites in the area east of Mazatán could not be located in 1974 and was thought to have been extirpated by heavy grazing (D. Brown and Ellis 1977).

Given the extensive areas uninvestigated, the bird's secretive habits, and the difficulty in locating low-density populations, it is possible that other Masked Bobwhite populations exist. Tomlinson's investigations were of necessity confined to accessible areas, and such promising regions as the Yaqui Indian lands west of the Sierra del Bacateté were not visited. Tomlinson (pers. comm.) thought the region between the Ríos Matápe and Tecoripa south of the Presa Alvaro to be particularly worthy of future investigations. Given the widespread deterioration and disappearance of savanna grasslands throughout Sonora, however, any population as yet undiscovered would almost certainly be limited. Even within the small range of the extant population, the birds are absent over wide areas.

HABITAT

Masked Bobwhites have always been associated with weedy bottom-lands, grassy and herb-strewn valleys, and forb-rich plains. Canyons and arroyos are avoided. Herbert Brown (1885) accurately observed that in southern Arizona Gambel's Quail "were found in rough canyon-like coun-try; scaled quail in wide grassy plains; and bobwhites on the mesas and in the plains but not in the canyons."

In the summer of 1884 Stephens (1885) noted several bobwhites near his camp in Altar Valley, which he described as possessing "the best grass we saw on the route" (Tucson to Puerto Lobos), and unsuccessfully attempted to collect a bobwhite in "this open prairie." Recalling conditions in Altar Valley between the time of his arrival in 1885 and the turn of the century, pioneer rancher Manuel King stated that

Sacaton and Johnson grass [the observation of this exotic grass at such an early date is in error] covered the entire Altar Valley from the slopes of the Baboquivaris to the Cerro Colorado and Sierrita Mountains. Only an occasional tree was growing and haystacks of native grasses, harvested by farmers and ranchers, were common everywhere in the fall and winter.

He described Masked Bobwhite as then "numerous" (Arrington 1942c).

Both Brown (*in* Allen 1886a) and Stephens (1885) reported that Masked Bobwhites used sacaton (*Sporobolus wrightii*), a coarse bunchgrass restricted to bottomlands, as escape cover. Some scrub cover is also important, how-ever, and Brown and Stephens both made mention of mesquites and other brushy cover, then restricted to drainageways and bottomlands.

J. T. Wright, who collected Masked Bobwhite in Sonora in 1931, told Tomlinson (1972a) "that the country at that time consisted of wide, grass-covered valleys with certain grasses reaching over the heads of the native white-tailed deer." Van Rossem (1945), another collector, stated that the Masked Bobwhite was a resident of "grass plains, river valleys and foothills in the lower Sonoran Zone." J. Stokely Ligon (1952) reported on his return from capturing Masked Bobwhites in Mexico that "this quail is definitely a dweller of deep-grass-weed habitat, a type of cover incompatible with heavy use by livestock."

These observations and others have been reinforced by studies of re-leased birds by Goodwin and Hungerford (1977), who found that from October through June, Masked Bobwhite preferred weedy areas with dense ground cover beneath tree-shrub overstories (Fig. 7.3).

Fig. 7.3. Area south of Benjamin Hill, Sonora, where J. J. Levy and S. Gallizioli found Masked Bobwhite in 1964. Arizona Game and Fish Department photo.

Masked Bobwhite habitat then, is an open savanna grassland within dry-tropic scrub. The scrub species may be characteristic of either thorn-scrub or Sonoran desertscrub, and at the extreme northern edge of the Masked Bobwhite's range are primarily velvet mesquites. The potential for abundant grass cover in this region is seasonal, as is the occurrence of a great variety of summer-active forbs and weeds. The original nature and composition of these grasslands is conjectural, but grass and forb species frequently encountered at relic sites are four root-perennial gramas, (*Bouteloa rothrockii, B. aristidoides, B. parryi, B. filiformis*), several subtropical three-awns, false grama, tanglehead grass, vine mesquite grass, ragweed, purslane, spurges, pigweed, and spiderlings. Cane beardgrass, Arizona cottontop, sideoats grama, and less often, black grama, are restricted to higher elevations, drainages, and rocky northern exposures. In the more representative areas, blue grama and such semidesert grassland shrubs as burroweed and snakeweed are localized or absent. Much of the bird's native range in Sonora, however, has now been cleared and is populated by the introduced bufflegrass, an exotic range grass that forms extensive monocultures.

Trees and scrub are always present but vary in composition and density from site to site. Many kinds of thorny shrubs and trees occur in the southern and eastern portions of Masked Bobwhite range. Frequently encountered species in bobwhite habitat near Benjamin Hill, Sonora, include mesquite, ironwood, paloverdes, retama, guycan, acacias, tomatillo, *Caesalpinia pumila, Croton sonorae,* desert hackberry, kidneywood, coursetia, tree ocotillo, limberbush, false mesquite, and partridge peas. Cholla and columnar cacti of several species, though not always prevalent, are conspicuous.

LIFE HISTORY

Masked Bobwhites remain in coveys until late June. As with other quails, the birds form pair bonds while still within the covey unit, and some are paired as early as March. Pairs gradually separate from the covey as the nesting season approaches, and loose coveys containing several pairs and single males are seen through late June and early July.

In the only study of native Masked Bobwhite in Sonora, Tomlinson (1972b) determined that this race does not normally start breeding until July, when summer rains begin. The onset of the breeding season is heralded by the well-known *bobwhite* call of the male, usually given from some conspicuous perch in or near heavy grass cover. Call-counts during 1968 through 1970 showed that males began calling between June 25 and July 15 and stopped between September 4 and 20. Calling frequency reached a peak between August 10 and 24, after which it declined rapidly. It thus appears that gonad recrudescence continues during a period of declining photoperiod. The peak of nesting coincides with the period of peak calling activity. The nest is on the ground and constructed and concealed in grass (Brown 1885), so that nesting may be postponed until sufficient grass or other herbaceous growth is available.

Nesting success appears to be related to the amount and distribution of summer precipitation and correlates with the intensity of male calling activity. Tomlinson (1972b) determined that the Masked Bobwhite hatch began in late July, reached a peak between September 5 to 20, and continued on even into early November. His earliest sightings of young were in late September, when most broods consisted of small chicks. The breeding, nesting, and hatching cycle is thus timed to coincide with the production of green feed, the growth of concealing cover, and the availability of invertebrate foods and seeds produced by the summer rains—a pattern characteristic of other southwestern quails in their respective habitats.

Newly hatched broods have five to fifteen young that, with the adults, form the nucleus of the fall–winter covey. Unproductive adults and young separated from other broods may join a covey, but covey size rarely exceeds twenty birds and in November averages about twelve (Tomlinson 1972b).

Bobwhites shift from the more open grasslands in late summer and early fall to savanna margins. The tall growth of grasses and weeds provides ideal screening cover as the birds feed on the new shoots, leaves, and flowers of legumes and other forbs. Insects, particularly grasshoppers, are plentiful and are essential for the chicks. Later in the fall, perhaps in response to large numbers of migrating raptors, the quail retreat into more brushy habitats. Here they forage between weed patches and tangled thickets searching out seeds of legumes (Cottam and Knappen 1939). Tomlinson (pers. comm.) found that Masked Bobwhite at Rancho El Carrizo made extensive movements in search of food and water during winter months. Such seasonal feeding and behavior patterns are not unlike those of bobwhites in Texas and elsewhere (see, e.g., Tharp 1971).

MANAGEMENT HISTORY

It was fortunate that Herbert Brown sought to report on Arizona's bobwhite when he did. By the mid-1880s the Masked Bobwhite was already disappearing from the state. Brown (1885) reported:

On the road from Bolle's Well west to the Coyote range, these quails were frequently to be met with, but teamsters and travelers have killed or frightened them off. One of the former assured me that he had killed as many as five at one shot. Ten miles south of Bolle's, in the Altar Valley, we came across a small covey—there were, perhaps, a dozen in all. The bright, deep chestnut breast plumage of the males looked red in the sun, and gave the birds a most magnificent appearance. We secured but one, a male, the rest secreting themselves in the tall sacaton grass, which at this point was between four and five feet high, and as we had no dog we did not follow them in. Our next place to find them was on the mesa southeast of the [Baboquivari] Peak, where we camped to hunt for them, but they were scarce, and we managed to secure but few.

Brown continued to try to obtain bobwhite, but the birds were becoming increasingly scarce. Cattle were on the range in ever-greater numbers, and the summers of 1885 and 1886 were dry. In a letter of February 9, 1886, Brown wrote J. A. Allen that the collectors whom he had sent out especially for these birds reported that in four days of searching in the Altar Valley they came upon only one flock. On December 15, 1886, Brown wrote in his journal: "Ira Carter whom I sent to the Baboquivari to look for bobwhite quail (*Colinus ridgwayi*) returned today after a fruitless search. He was away thirteen days and failed to even see or hear one of the quail sought."

Brown went on to report that he obtained one female from the Sycamore Ranch in the Baboquivaris that had been collected on December 14. According to E. A. Mearns's field notes, a Mrs. W. S. Sturges killed one out of a flock of three near her house at La Osa Ranch near Monument Boundary 140 just prior to Mearns's arrival on December 8, 1893. These were the last observations of bobwhites reported from Altar Valley, but three years later, on November 22, 1896, Brown recorded in his journal:

Was agreeably surprised tonight upon the receipt of four *Colinus ridgwayi*, 2 males and two females from Geo. Atkinson. He killed 6–4 females and 2 males in a field near Calabasas. . . . He thinks there were no less than 20 in the flock.

These birds from the Santa Cruz Valley were the last bobwhites collected in Arizona; all twenty-six birds were collected through Brown's efforts.

A prolonged drought began in the summer of 1899, and the bobwhite had probably vanished from Arizona by the turn of the century. In his incisive summary of the bobwhite's history in the state, Brown (1904) noted:

The causes leading to the extermination of the Arizona Masked Bob-white (*Colinus ridgwayi*) are due to overstocking of the country with cattle, supplemented by several rainless years. This combination practically stripped the country bare of vegetation. Of their range the *Colinus* occupied only certain restricted portions, and when their food and shelter had been trodden out of existence by thousands of hunger-dying stock, there was nothing left for poor little Bob-white to do but go out with them. . . . The Arizona Bobwhite would have thriven well in an agricultural country, in brushy fence corners, tangled thickets and weed-covered fields, but such things were not to be had in their habitat.

The circumstantial evidence that overgrazing and drought brought about the birds' demise is overwhelming. All observers agree that during the drought of 1891–93, the million or so cattle on Arizona ranges, mostly in the southern part of the state, devastated plant and animal life alike (Brown 1900; Hollon 1966; Wilson 1976).

The history of the Masked Bobwhite in Sonora is also one of diminishment. Birds were collected around agricultural fields near Cumpas and Bacoachi in 1886 and 1887 (Brewster 1887; Van Rossem 1945), but none has been reported from these areas since, and Bent (1932) feared that the

Masked Bobwhite was close to extinction. It was therefore encouraging when J. S. Ligon (1942) found Masked Bobwhite to be "still fairly numerous locally as late as 1937 in central and southern Sonora." Although the arrival of livestock in Sonora predated Arizona's cattle boom of the 1880s by more than a century, heavy grazing was not as pervasive. It was not until the Cárdenas administration in the late 1930s that the large landholdings of northern Mexico were apportioned into small ranches, necessitating the development of numerous stock waters and the proliferation of cattle into formerly ungrazed areas.

When L. L. Lawson (1951b) and Ligon (1952) returned to Sonora to obtain wild stock for propagation in 1949 and 1950, they found that the situation had changed dramatically since Ligon's previous visit: "ranchmen who had formerly known of the presence of the birds advised that they seemed to have vanished overnight" (Ligon 1952). After considerable effort, only twenty-five bobwhite were obtained in 1950.

No further observations of Masked Bobwhite were reported from Sonora until 1964, when Arizona Game and Fish biologist Steve Gallizioli and Tucson ornithologists Jim and Seymour Levy, located a population south of Benjamin Hill after finding the areas visited by Ligon near San Marcial denuded of grasses and destitute of quail (Fig. 7.4; Gallizioli et al. 1967). This general area contains the only extant native populations known today.

Fig. 7.4. The condition of most Masked Bobwhite habitat in Sonora after 1950. Heavy cattle grazing has denuded the level bottomlands where the birds formerly resided. Arizona Game and Fish Department photo.

Early Restoration Efforts

Using stock obtained in Sonora, Ligon (1942, 1952) released about two hundred bobwhites in ten areas of Arizona and southwest New Mexico (D. Brown and Ellis 1977). Most of these releases were well above the elevations of historic distribution and none of the releases resulted in the establishment of a population. Two other unsuccessful releases of propagated birds in northern Arizona in 1945 along the Lower Colorado River near Joseph City and Holbrook were probably an attempt to see if Masked Bobwhite might survive in country that superficially resembled Plains Bobwhite (*C. v. taylori*) habitat. Areas within the bobwhite's known range were not selected as release sites because Ligon and Arrington (1942c) could not find suitable range conditions anywhere in historic habitat. Ligon may also have concluded that the bird's historic range included plains and semidesert grasslands (Ligon 1942; Phillips et al. 1964). Whatever his reason, two additional releases of wild-trapped bobwhites to plains grassland in Arizona and New Mexico in 1950 also failed.

In 1963 and 1964 Jim and Seymour Levy and personnel at the Arizona-Sonora Desert Museum began separate studies of penned Masked Bobwhite using breeding stock obtained from Ligon (Walker 1964; Gallizioli et al. 1967). The Desert Museum's propagation project in Avra Valley was terminated in 1964 when two Tohono O'odham boys entered the breeding pens and released or ate the few remaining Masked Bobwhites. The Levys, with assistance from the Arizona Game and Fish Department, tried to persuade a Sonoran landowner to set aside a portion of his ranch as a preserve, but after some initial encouragements this attempt to manage native rangelands for Masked Bobwhite fell through. In 1966 the Levys donated their remaining four pairs of pen-reared Masked Bobwhites to the U.S. Fish and Wildlife Service. These birds, and fifty-seven wild bobwhite captured near Benjamin Hill, Sonora, in 1968 and 1970 became the propagation stock for the Patuxent Wildlife Research Center (Tomlinson 1972b).

In 1969 the U.S. Fish and Wildlife Service, in cooperation with the Arizona Game and Fish Department, began searches to locate suitable reintroduction sites in Arizona. Four areas in Altar Valley were eventually selected in 1970. The Arizona sites were higher in elevation (2,400–4,300 feet) than the bird's Sonoran habitats (950–2,700 feet), were generally rockier, and the subtropic vegetation depauperate by comparison. All were subject to livestock use, and the ground cover appeared less thrifty and diverse than in Sonoran habitats. The release areas were less than ideal but represented the best sites available (D. Brown 1970c, 1971a).

In 1972 the U.S. Fish and Wildlife Service leased 1,840 acres of the Las Delicias Ranch in Altar Valley from the State Land Department as a Masked Bobwhite release area. These pastures, along with a Bureau of Land Management section on Rancho Seco near the Las Guias and Cerro Colorado mountains, were to provide nesting habitat free from grazing. Postrelease investigations showed the desirability of obtaining bottomlands in either Altar Valley or Santa Cruz Valley (D. Brown and Ellis 1977), and 1,150 acres of habitat on Buenos Aires Ranch along Altar Wash were leased as a bobwhite habitat study area between 1978 and 1981. When it became apparent that released birds did indeed prefer bottomland habitats, the Las Delicias and Rancho Seco leases were abandoned.

The first pen-reared birds from the Patuxent Wildlife Research Center in Laurel, Maryland, were released into the wild in 1970. Many of the birds suffered deformities from excessive debeaking and confined rearing. After 1971 the quail were held in Tucson for three months prior to release, but until 1974 all the bobwhites were released with little conditioning to the wild; most disappeared within two months. Mortality from predation was abnormally high (Ellis and Serafin 1977).

In 1974 two reintroduction techniques were employed to produce more release-worthy stock (Ellis et al. 1978). One was a modification of the foster-parent–adoption methods described by Hart (1933), Stoddard (1931, 1946), and Stanford (1952). The most promising foster parents proved to be wild-caught Texas Bobwhite males sterilized by bilateral vasectomy (Ellis and Carpenter 1981). These birds readily adopted Masked Bobwhite chicks, after which they were released on the study sites. The second technique was a modification of the call-box conditioning program proposed by Hardy and McConnell (1967:29) in which released birds are called back to a predator-proof pen by a caged female each evening.

These techniques were perfected and tested with thousands of birds released between 1974 and 1979 (D. Brown and Ellis 1984). With both pre-release and postrelease training programs, captive-bred birds were better prepared for survival in the wild. Many of the birds released in 1976 survived into the winter, and by the onset of next year's summer rains an estimated thirty birds remained near release sites on the Buenos Aires Ranch. The following October a pair of Masked Bobwhite was sighted with at least three chicks. This observation was the first documented overwinter survival and demonstrated that progeny could be produced in the wild by propagated stock.

By 1979 a sizable wild population was present on the Buenos Aires Ranch, and the number of calling males had increased from twenty-one in 1977 to seventy-four in 1979 (Goodwin and Hungerford 1981). Thereafter, uncontrolled grazing on the study pastures, combined with summer drought, resulted in sharply reduced populations (Goodwin 1982, 1983). Releases were terminated, and only nine birds were detected in 1982 (Levy and Levy 1984; Ough and deVos 1984). Although the feasibility of reestablishing Masked Bobwhite had been demonstrated and valuable insight into the bird's habitat requirements obtained, the most valuable lesson was the reiteration of the quail's vulnerability to grazing pressure. A refuge managed exclusively for Masked Bobwhite was necessary.

To evaluate the suitability of ranges that had undergone brush removal, releases of almost three thousand pen-reared adult, immature, and chick bobwhites were made at three locations in Sonora, mostly from 1980 through 1982 (D. Brown and Ellis 1984). The success of these releases is doubtful (Mills and Reichenbacher 1982). Prospects were poor at all three sites because of intensive livestock grazing and the low quality of the birds released (none had received any conditioning).

In 1985, after nearly two years of controversy, the Buenos Aires Ranch was purchased by the U.S. Fish and Wildlife Service and established as a Masked Bobwhite refugium. Although reports of Masked Bobwhite in Altar Valley persisted, they could not be verified. It thus appeared that the introduced population had died out, despite moderate and above-average summer precipitation between 1981 and 1984. The hope was that the elimination of grazing from key habitats would now allow some new birds to survive periods of declining population levels. A reintroduction program using the Texas Bobwhite adoption technique was therefore reinitiated in 1985 in conjunction with the total exclusion of livestock grazing (Dobrott 1985). Although past successes give cause for optimism, only time will tell if a Masked Bobwhite population can be reestablished in historical habitat in Arizona. Meanwhile, the birds persist only in declining and widely fluctuating numbers south of Benjamin Hill in Sonora, Mexico.

POPULATION DYNAMICS

Call-counts can be used to measure yearly variations in quail numbers and breeding success (e.g., Bennitt 1951; Rosene 1957; Smith and Gallizioli 1965; D. Brown et al. 1978). Two call-count routes south of Benjamin Hill, Sonora, showed the number of calling males to steadily decrease following a series of dry summers (Tomlinson 1972b). Drought conditions were exacerbated by the presence of livestock on both areas, but bird numbers recovered on the less intensely grazed Rancho Grande route only with the return of more favorable moisture conditions after 1976 (Fig. 7.5).

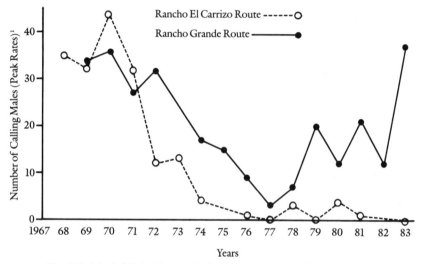

Fig. 7.5. Masked Bobwhite population trends on two call–count routes in Sonora, Mexico. Data from Tomlinson (1972b), Ellis and Serafin (1977), Goodwin (pers. comm., 1982), Mills and Reichenbacher (1982).

Masked Bobwhite thus appear to follow a population pattern similar to that of Mearns' Quail. The amount of summer precipitation determines the quantity of herbaceous vegetation produced and correlates with repro-ductive success. However, the percentage of young birds in the fall popula-tion does not vary as greatly as among Gambel's Quail, and total quail numbers are probably determined more by overwinter carryover than nest-ing success. This variation in survival is dependent on the amount of resi-dual ground cover, so that population size is related to grazing intensity and the amount of rain received the *previous* summer. Should summer precipitation be inadequate and an insufficient quantity of concealing grass and forbs be produced, or if grazing removes most of the annual production, fewer birds survive than are produced. Prolonged summer droughts, coupled with heavy grazing pressure, are the reasons for the bird's endangered status.

SEARCHING FOR BOB

I had expected an exotic landscape to accompany such a legendary bird, and I was not disappointed. Tree ocotillos, caterpillar cactus, and the bright, blue-flowered guycan were only a few of the spectacular plants that greeted me. Guided by Seymour Levy and accompanied by Ron Anderson, I was at last to see Rancho El Carrizo, the fabled habitat of the Masked Bobwhite. Many times I had heard how Seymour's brother, Jim, and Steve Gallizioli had rediscovered an indigenous population of Masked Bobwhite here twenty years after the bird had been reported as extinct.

The winter of 1970 had been preceded by a series of wet summers; nesting success and survival had been good, and we were confident of finding our quarry. Roy Tomlinson, then working on Masked Bobwhite in the area, had reported fair numbers of the quail and had recently trapped fifty-seven to send to Patuxent Research Station for brood stock.

At the entrance to the ranch was a *No Hunting* sign that went on to say that we were entering a game refuge. Ron and I were impressed by the abundant ground cover of last summer's grasses interspersed with an overstory of thorny shrubs and trees. Presently we came to the open valley of Arroyo Carrizo and the ranch headquarters. Somewhere on Rancho El Carrizo was a brush-cleared pasture said to be ideal for these grass-loving quail. The ranch *patrón* was Juan Pedro Camou.

Camou was a descendant of French immigrants who had come to Mexico during the Napoleonic Wars. The family had been "given" this ranch in the desert by the revolution-dedicated Cárdenas government as compensation for expropriating their once-extensive holdings in the great grasslands of northeast Sonora. Juan Pedro had a car dealership in Hermosillo, so ranching was an avocation, not a livelihood. Nonetheless, the ranch showed care and attention. The necessary labor was done by campesinos who lived in a tiny village separated from the main house in traditional hacienda fashion.

Today *El Patrón* was absent. A *vaquero* told us that there were plenty of
the *perdiz rojo* in a pasture to the northeast where an American was trapping
them. It did not take long to find the right pasture; there were only two
cleared areas, each about three hundred acres. One of them had recently
been cleared and burned, but the other was rank with weeds and dried
grass. A few Hereford bulls bellowed their discontent at our arrival, but as
elsewhere on the ranch, cattle were sparse. The brush had been left in piles,
and a number of paloverdes and large cacti had been left standing for shade
and variety. There was no question but that this was the pasture where we
should look for Masked Bobwhite.

Before we could start a serious search, the birds made an appearance on
their own. Driving the perimeter of the clearing, we drove right up to a
covey. Only when we stopped did we see the bait on the ground and Tomlinson's overturned traps. After setting a couple of the Stoddard traps, we
decided to take a hike. Even though it was now midday, the March weather
was cool and the native savanna beyond the pasture invited exploration. The
three of us fanned out in the underbrush where the covey had vanished.

Few of my many excursions have been as enjoyable and informative as
that hike in Sonora. The late winter sun cast a pleasant warmth and a fine
light. I headed through the dense ground cover of knee-high grasses toward a low range of hills to the west, where a fire was burning.

Within moments, I flushed a buck white-tailed deer. The animal got up
almost at my feet and gave me a great scare. Another one—a doe—got up,
and then another. Assembly calls of both the scattered bobwhite covey and
the more numerous Gambel's Quail that had been flushed along the way
accompanied my tramp. Later I found a shed antler and the tracks of *bura*
(mule deer). I was truly in a paradise of game.

In the hills thick thornscrub, some of it now alternatingly blazing and
smoldering, impeded my progress upslope. Had the source of the fire been
the distant lightning flashes I had seen earlier that morning? There was also
evidence of past fires—charred mesquite trunks and scarred cacti. Yet the
country looked wonderfully rich. The washes were well wooded and the
trees festooned with vines and creepers. The thornscrub was impenetrable
where not opened by fire, and the shrubbery was covered with trailing
plants surrounded by an abundance of forbs and grasses.

What was most impressive was the vista behind me. The straw-colored
grasses, intermixed with gray deciduous shrubs, provided a subdued backdrop to the scattered spinach of ironwoods and conjured up an image of

the African bush. I could readily visualize jaguars roaming this tropical landscape; one had recently been taken just south of here on Rancho Tabiquito. As if to enliven my musings, three javelina—two adults and one half-grown—trotted by, temporary refugees from the creeping ground fire that was now burning itself out on the thin soils of the mountain slopes.

Later that day we saw more bobwhites on Rancho Hereford, another of Camou's holdings. A cock obliged us by being caught in one of Tomlinson's traps and had to pose for photos while his colleagues scurried off into a tangle of thornscrub. Everywhere grasses flourished, for sixteen and a half inches of rain had fallen the previous summer. The birds' future seemed assured. No farms or subdivisions were moving into this country and the ranch was in good hands. The small clearings only added variety to the landscape and provided an "edge effect." Little did we realize then how quickly this distinctive southwestern landscape was to change.

Wheek—wheetehe—heeah: the female separation call spewed forth from the tape recorder accompanied by a background of mechanical churning. The imperfection of the accompanying whirr was of little consequence, and the ruse elicited the desired response: the distinctive *bob-white* of a bachelor male. His call summoned a reply from another a good bit farther off. Tomlinson grinned, and I could see that Paul Webb was visibly excited at hearing his first wild bobwhite. As for me, I was uneasy and disappointed. Not because only two bobwhites were heard where there should have been a dozen or more, but because of the changes in the countryside of Rancho El Carrizo.

We had come in late at night and bedded down as a violent summer thunderstorm, typical of Sonora's "monsoon" season, was passing through. The humid air and a chorus of amphibians promised another subtropic adventure to rival the one four years earlier, and I was not prepared for my subsequent disappointment. The clearings and "tamed" pastures had greatly proliferated. Worse still, the native grasses were gone, not just in the pastures but in the now-retreating wild country. It was true that last summer had been abnormally dry, but the grazing plan had changed, too. Numerous cow plops and the background of constant bellowing attested to that. We heard only five *bob-whites* on Tomlinson's call-count that August morning.

I have been back to Rancho El Carrizo several times since, but each time there were more changes. Most of the country is in bufflegrass pasture. The Camous, who had ranched there since the 1940s, have left. Ejidos have

moved into the once-expansive savannas; slab-sided Brahmas have replaced
the white-tailed and mule deer, and the vines and creepers have disappeared. Masked Bobwhite are still to be found south of Benjamin Hill, but
not on Rancho El Carrizo. The magic was gone.

Whenever I find myself in Sonora in an area of grass and brush, I wonder
if Masked Bobwhite might be present. If so, perhaps the aura of the old
Rancho El Carrizo might be recaptured. In some places and in some years
such places as the sloping plain south of Trincheras, the vicinity of the old
Waddell Ranch in Valle de Agua Caliente, and the *llanos* near San Marcial,
where Audubon, Wright, Ligon, and Tomlinson found bobwhites, still appear suitable for these reclusive birds. And what about areas that have escaped the visits of ornithologists? Somewhere in the hinterlands of Sonora,
in some remote area not yet subject to the onslaught of humanity that is
modern Mexico, could another remnant population be holding out?

But these are just musings. The only reports of Masked Bobwhite are
vague and unsubstantiated. My inquiries are met with faded recollections
or answers that are too encouraging. Rural Mexicans are eager to please. I
have torn apart hundreds of Cactus Wren nests and have yet to find a
Masked Bobwhite feather that could be identified with certainty. Sonora is
a big state though, and few Americans visit the back country anymore.

So the rumors persist. Masked Bobwhite were recently said to have been
seen in the bag of quail hunters camped at Presa Obregón. The Yaqui lands
adjacent to the Sierra del Bacateté are an intriguing possibility. Indians at
Potám claim to know the bird well, but the Yaquis are hesitant to permit
entry to their domain. And bob is a secretive bird and prone to reveal his
whereabouts only in the heat of midsummer. Perhaps a small population
still exists unnoticed to all but the local *vaqueros, peones,* and *indios,* who
know every plant and animal.

I will just keep searching.

Paul Bosman

CHAPTER 8

Scaled Quail

The handsome Scaled Quail (*Callipepla squamata*) is the second most commonly encountered quail in Arizona and the preeminent game bird in New Mexico, trans-Pecos Texas, and the central plateau of Mexico. Both sexes display white, conical crests—hence the common name of "cottontop." The scaled, or "scalie," appellation is appropriate, however, as the birds possess a distinctive scalloping on the breast, nape, and belly. Their dorsal plumage is an overall tan with a bluish gray tinge, giving them the local name of "blue quail" among Texans, New Mexicans, and early Arizona settlers.

Southern Arizona birds are the grayish "Arizona," or *pallida*, subspecies, though some individuals exhibit russet-orange horseshoes on their bellies characteristic of the *castanogastis* subspecies found in south Texas. The occasional Scaled Quail seen in northern Arizona along the Little Colorado, Puerco, and Zuni rivers are presumably of the nominate *hargravei* subspecies, which is even paler, grayer, and slightly larger than *pallida* (Rea 1973). The type race, *squamata*, is confined to the Central Plateau of Mexico.

Scaled Quail are larger than Gambel's Quail. Adult males average 7.3 ounces, females 6.7 ounces. Unlike other quails, the sexes appear similar in the field. The sex of adults and most fall juveniles can be ascertained by the throat feathers. When examined closely, the males are seen to have uniform buffy cream throats, whereas these feathers on the female are finely streaked (Wallmo 1956a). As with other quail, the outer two juvenile primaries and secondary wing coverts are retained through the winter, and first-year birds in the fall bag are easily identified. Scaled Quail wings can also be differentiated for management studies from those of Gambel's Quail by the Scaled Quail's rustier tinge and slight scalelike margins on the leading coverts; Gambel's Quail wing feathers have a more olive hue and the outer coverts have a distinctive midstripe.

Occasionally hybrid Scaled Quail × Gambel's Quail crosses are encountered (Fig. 8.1). These so-called "Scrambled" Quail are usually reported from marginal Scaled Quail areas and are probably the result of the mating of a first-year female Scaled Quail with one of the numerous excess male Gambel's Quail. Like Scaled Quail × Bobwhite crosses in Texas, these hybrids are thought to be sterile (Wallmo 1956b).

DISTRIBUTION

Scaled Quail are birds of the Chihuahuan Desert, adjacent semidesert grassland, and the southern, scrub-invaded portions of plains grassland. They are primarily found in west Texas, New Mexico, and southeast Arizona and descend southward through Chihuahua, Coahuila, Nuevo León, Durango, Zacatecas, and San Luís Potosí to Hildago and the Valley of Mexico. Northward, Scaled Quail reach into southeast Colorado, extreme southwest Kansas, and the Texas and Oklahoma panhandles. Northeast Sonora and south-central Arizona represent the bird's natural western limits (Aldrich and Duvall 1955). Introduced populations are reported to be established in irrigated valleys in northern Nevada and in Washington (see, e.g., Johnsgard 1973).

In Arizona, Scaled Quail are primarily found in the southeast quarter of the state, with widely spaced coveys also present along the Little Colorado River from Springerville northward to the Sanders-Chambers vicinity (Fig. 8.2). The best populations are in and adjacent to Sulphur Springs Valley, the sloping bajadas northeast of Oracle Junction, and the mesas and foothills of the mountains bordering Altar Valley. Some extralimital observations since 1960 include south of the Gila River between Guthrie and the river's confluence with the San Francisco River, several locations in Avra Valley, the Great Plain south of Pisinimo on the Tohono O'odham Indian Reservation, near Brandenburg Mountain north of Aravaipa Creek, and

Fig. 8.1. Male Gambel's Quail × Scaled Quail hybrid from near Barkerville in Pinal County. Such crosses are relatively rare and usually occur at the fringe of the Scaled Quail's range. The author has encountered only one such hybrid in more than twenty years of quail hunting. Arizona Game and Fish Department photo.

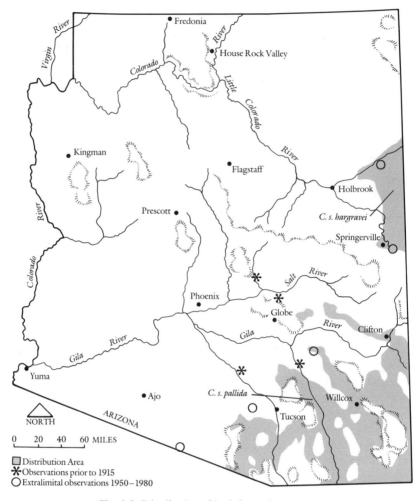

Fredonia

House Rock Valley

Virgin *River*

River

Colorado

Little

Colorado

Kingman

Flagstaff

River

Holbrook

River

Prescott

C. s. hargravei

Springerville

Colorado *River*

Salt *River*

Phoenix

Globe

Gila *River*

Clifton

Gila *River*

Yuma

Ajo

C. s. pallida

Willcox

NORTH

ARIZONA

Tucson

0   20   40   60 MILES

▢ Distribution Area
✳ Observations prior to 1915
◯ Extralimital observations 1950–1980

Fig. 8.2. Distribution of Scaled Quail in Arizona.

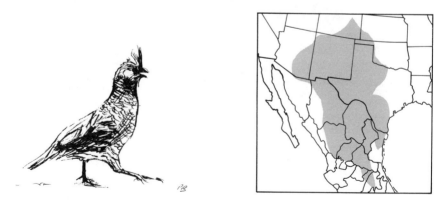

the vicinity of Barkerville in Pinal County. An isolated population also persists in the Brushy Tank area on the San Carlos Indian Reservation (Rea 1973).

Prior to 1925, Scaled Quail were present in Tonto Basin north of Roosevelt Lake, along the lower Salt River, five miles east of Globe at Cutter, and near Picacho Peak (Mearns 1884–86; Swarth 1914; Bent 1932; Phillips et al. 1964). Hargrave (*in* Rea 1973) found Scaled Quail bones in archaeological remains along the Little Colorado River Valley, in the San Francisco Mountain region, near Williams, and in Ventana Cave. Thus, the bird's range was formerly more extensive than at present.

HABITAT

As befits an essentially grassland species, Scaled Quail are not particularly fond of steep slopes and rugged country. Preferred habitats are open plains, rolling hills, low ridges, and mesas. The birds utilize scattered shrubs under three feet tall but avoid dense thickets, tall brush, and tree-lined washes.

Although I have seen large numbers of Scaled Quail in the heart of the creosote-dominated expanses of the Chihuahuan Desert in Coahuila, their habitat in Arizona is more typically semidesert grassland (Fig. 8.3). Here perennial bunchgrasses are interspersed with such low shrubs as burro-weed, snakeweed, and dogweed. Soapweed yucca is common, and mimosa, or wait-a-minute thorn, is an important cover plant, as are acacias and mesquites. Cacti, particularly chollas and prickly pears, are also usually present. Other important shrubs include desert hackberry, condalia, desert-spoon, beargrass, and little-leaf sumac. Scaled Quail are often found around old homesteads, and brushy grasslands near maize and other agricultural fields are especially attractive to them. Where the shrubs become too dense and the country loses its open character, this species gives way to Gambel's Quail.

Scaled Quail habitats are typically warm temperate, that is, the growing season can be expected to be from 125 to 150 days long. Cold temperate environments tend to lack the necessary diversity of low shrubs, and the subtropical Sonoran Desert has too little ground cover and is populated by short trees, tall scrub, and Gambel's Quail. Otherwise, the most important element of Scaled Quail habitat is summer precipitation. With the exception of some introduced populations in Great Basin farming areas, the

Fig. 8.3. Scaled Quail habitat in Sulphur Springs Valley, Cochise County. The short shrubs intermixed with perennial grasses are principally burroweed; the tall shrubs are soapweed yuccas.

birds are restricted to areas receiving at least six inches of summer rainfall (Campbell 1968; Campbell et al. 1973; D. Brown et al. 1978).

Scrub invasion is the Scaled Quail's most persistent enemy in Arizona and the reason why the species is now outnumbered ten to one by Gambel's Quail in many of its former strongholds. Overgrazing, summer drought, and fire suppression all favor the proliferation of woody plants over perennial grasses and the replacement of scalies by Gambel's Quail. An almost total conversion of perennial grasses to trees and shrubby plants is thought to account for the disappearance of Scaled Quail from the Tonto Basin and other western fringe areas. Some shrubs are necessary, however, and areas completely cleared of mesquites and all other brushy plants have locally reduced Scaled Quail populations (McCormick 1975).

Scaled Quail in southeast Arizona are most commonly encountered between 3,500 and 4,600 feet elevation, the extremes being 2,800 and 5,500 feet. The infrequent coveys found at the higher and colder locales in extreme east-central Arizona occur at elevations between 5,500 to 7,000 feet. Like their lower-elevation counterparts, these birds are in country of moderate relief: mesas, riverbottom breaks, and gentle slopes. The grasses, instead of warm-temperate species, are sand dropseed, blue grama, and other grasses of the plains and Intermountain West; the scrub components are junipers, yuccas, four-wing saltbush, greasewood, and other cold-tolerant plants (Fig. 8.4).

Scaled Quail may drink regularly when water is available, but it is not essential to their distribution, and some coveys exist miles from permanent water.

LIFE HISTORY

Like other quails of the Southwest, Scaled Quail attain sexual maturity their first spring. Some birds begin forming pair bonds as early as late February and early March. During courtship the male feeds the female tidbits and engages in ritual chasing. By late March most hens have selected a mate, and both pairs and excess males are well dispersed by mid-April. If

Fig. 8.4. Scaled Quail habitat between Spring-erville and St. Johns in Apache County.

the winter was wet and the weather warm, so that sufficient green foods are available, housekeeping begins in earnest. Some males will now be giving their announcement call—a single-note *squawk, shriek,* or *whock* that is analogous to the Gambel's Quail's *caw* call. This call corresponds to maximum testicular development, and is a good index to breeding condition.

The *squawk* call is usually given from an elevated perch such as a fence-post, mesquite tree, or yucca stalk. Although unmated males announce most persistently, calling elicits responses from other cocks in the vicinity, and all males are thought to call at some time or another. Calling serves to space rival males, and should two cocks come in too close contact, one will be repulsed by an antagonistic *squeel* call analogous to the Gambel's Quail's *meah*. Actual combats are rare, and there are no defined territories (Anderson 1974). Mated males call only when the hen is absent, and probably for this reason the height of calling activity coincides with the peak nesting period. This is usually in April or May, but the dates and intensity vary from year to year.

Unlike Gambel's Quail, Scaled Quail may initiate and maintain pair bonds through the summer, and a dry spring may find the peak of calling and nesting activity delayed until the onset of summer rains in late June, July, or even August. At this time the birds appear to favor open habitats, where the principal foods are green shoots, grass blades, green seed pods, and whatever grasshoppers and other insects are available. The greens provide a source of Vitamin A, and their abundance is directly related to the quails' reproductive activity and success.

Nests are on the ground, usually on a flat or an open ridge, and commonly placed at the base of a cholla, in a mat of prickly pear, or other protected situation (Bent 1932; Russell 1932; Wallmo 1956b). The nest is normally made of grass and often lined with feathers; a grass canopy may be provided in the most elaborate examples. From nine to sixteen (extremes are five and twenty-two) 1¼ by 1 inch eggs are laid in successive days, the total depending on the year and the intensity of breeding activity. The eggs are duller and tend to be less blotched than those of Gambel's Quail.

The male assists with nest building, remains in attendance, and may set on the eggs should something befall the hen. Incubation takes approximately twenty-one days, and the pair may renest if the nest is destroyed. Downy young may be seen as late as mid-September and even into October. This phenomenon gives rise to the widely held opinion that the quail "double clutch" in good years. Such is not the case; some birds delay nesting until conditions are suitable, and there is no evidence that two broods are ever raised in the same year (Campbell et al. 1973). The chicks are cinna-mon-buff with black and white markings and even in their juvenile plum-age show evidence of a future "cottontop." Like all quails the young are highly precocial and can make short flights within days of hatching. Should an intruder startle either parent, particularly the hen, the bird may flutter on the ground and feign being crippled in an effort to draw the danger away from the chicks.

The family remains together through the summer. As the chicks mature, parental bonds weaken, and aggregations of family coveys, thwarted pairs, and individual males may be seen in late September and early October. The youngsters complete their postjuvenile molt at twenty-two weeks of age, and by November most of them have attained the appearance and size of the adults. The youngsters' food selection increasingly changes from ants and other invertebrates to seeds, which eventually make up 70 percent or more of their diet (Wallmo 1956b).

Preferred foods in late summer and early autumn include carlowrightia fruits, leaves, and flowers, and the seeds of whitethorn acacia, caltrop (Mex-ican poppy), spurges, pigweed, Russian thistle, gumweed, and cultivated sorghum (Wallmo 1956b; Schemnitz 1961; Campbell et al. 1973). Cactus seeds and prickly-pear fruit are also readily fed on, and in early fall the quails' beaks and faces may be stained purple. Grasses and grass seeds are only infrequently taken. Insects are consumed in greater numbers by Scaled Quail than by any other quail, and water, though not essential, is taken with increasing frequency during dry periods if available. Scaled Quail are nonetheless efficient conservers of water, and Henderson (1971) thought this species better adapted to heat than Gambel's Quail.

Winter coveys of multiple families and assorted singles are the norm by November and commonly contain anywhere from fifteen to sixty individu-als, depending on population size and habitat quality. Extreme examples may range from as few as four or five to more than one hundred. The quail retire immediately after sunset to spend the night roosting on the ground in small groups of two to five birds scattered over several acres of low brush and grass. Although some predawn calling may occur, the birds are com-pletely diurnal and do not leave their valleys and ridgetop roosts before full daylight. Sometime after sunrise the covey is on the move, roosting groups reassembling through the use of gathering calls (Wallmo 1956b).

Daily activities often begin with foraging along a ridge toward a water source. Roost areas change nightly, and the time spent traveling to water varies. Not all coveys go to water each day, and even when they do, not all the quail drink. Most watering takes place between midmorning and noon but can occur at any time. In the middle of the day Scaled Quail usually seek shade, where they loaf and peck about before again feeding. Sandy areas are also sought for dusting.

Each covey has a regular winter range. A typical day's travel involves an ellipsoid movement encompassing twenty-five to one hundred acres (Wallmo 1956b). Collectively, these daily movements make up the covey's home range, which is irregular in shape and rarely more than a square mile in extent—considerably smaller than the 720 to 2,180 acres covered by summer-ranging birds (Wallmo 1956b; Campbell et al. 1973). The same area is commonly occupied by the same covey each winter, although mass dispersions take place in the fall of some years. Whether these movements are because of food failures or social pressures is unknown, but individual movements of more than sixty miles have been recorded in years of high population levels followed by low food supplies (Campbell and Harris 1965).

Scaled Quail seek protective thickets of mesquite, catclaw, mimosa, or prickly pear when pursued by predators or during winter storms. Where patches of brush are lacking, such man-made structures as old buildings and farm equipment may be used as cover. However, snowstorms or freezing temperatures are rarely severe enough in Arizona to cause significant mortality. The quail seem able to predict inclement weather, and they increase their feeding activity and retire to suitable cover beforehand. During these episodes, and also at other times, the covey may break up into small subgroups that remain separated for days at a time. Eventually, the covey reassembles, as the birds are remarkably attached to their home range. Despite scattering and temporary aggregations into collective coveys, there is only a minor and gradual exchange of individuals within coveys (Wallmo 1956b).

As winter progresses the birds move gradually uphill to the foothills. Here they forage on the seeds of a variety of shrubs and forbs: snakeweed, mimosa, mesquite, false mesquite, woolly tidestromia, crotons, crownbeards, bladder-pods, carpet-weeds, globe mallows, sunflowers, caltrops, and spurges. Grass seeds are relatively unimportant, although ants, snout beetles, and other insects are still taken when encountered (Campbell et al. 1973; Davis et al. 1975). With the warming days of early spring, greens again become available, and after a winter of quiescence, aggression between males increases. The covey disintegrates as another reproductive year begins, with only one pair now occupying the winter covey's former range (Wallmo 1956b).

MANAGEMENT HISTORY AND POPULATION DYNAMICS

Scalies generally account for only about 6 percent of the reported statewide quail harvest and have traditionally been hunted in conjunction with the more populous Gambel's Quail. Scaled Quail were not always provided for in the regulations, however, and periodically there have been recommendations to manage this species separately. During the mid-1940s Scaled Quail numbers were thought to be so low that one biologist recommended complete protection before the species became extinct (Eicher 1944a, 1945). The season was closed on all quail from 1946 through 1948, and when limited hunting was again allowed in 1949, most of the Scaled Quail range was excluded. The quail season was again closed in 1950, even though Scaled Quail populations were now thought to be improving (Lawson 1950). Cochise County was again closed during the 1951 season because of the poor reproductive performance of Gambel's Quail in southeast Arizona (Gallizioli 1951b). The 1971–72 quail season in the three southeasternmost game-management units opened on November 1, one month later than the rest of the state, in deference to the Scaled Quail's propensity to nest later than Gambel's Quail. Since 1979 the season on both Scaled and Gambel's quails has opened statewide on the second Friday in October and continued through mid-February with an aggregate daily bag limit of fifteen quail.

An overt attempt was made in the 1940s to improve both Scaled and Gambel's quail habitat by constructing 10-to-160-acre livestock-free enclosures upstream from water sources to ensure adequate nesting and protective cover (Griner 1940a, 1940b; Kimball 1941a, 1942c, 1945; Eicher 1943c, 1944b). These enclosures in Cochise County were eventually abandoned because of maintenance difficulties and the observation that quail populations fluctuated more in response to precipitation changes than to the presence or absence of grazing. The abandonment of the enclosures may have been premature, however, as most of the thirty-four test plots showed an increase in ground cover that might have demonstrated long-term population benefits for this species (Kimball 1945; Fig. 8.5). An increase in Scaled Quail food plants brought about by grazing, as reported by Davis et al. (1975), would be beneficial only if food shortages were the limiting factor to population increase.

Transplanting Scaled Quail to unoccupied grasslands has periodically been proposed (e.g., Kimball 1941c; Project Personnel 1968b). One transplant was made to the Springerville area in the early 1950s, but the relatively

Fig. 8.5. Quail Restoration Enclosure No. 21 on the Rucker Ranch in Co-chise County (Eicher 1944b). The improvement in ground cover in the enclo-sure (left) is readily discernible. These study plots were abandoned shortly after World War II. Arizona Game and Fish Department photo.

few scalies in northeast Arizona are thought to be descendants of native rather than introduced stock. A proposal to release Scaled Quail in the San Rafael Valley was dropped when small numbers of the birds were found to be already residing in these shrub-poor grasslands. An investigation of the Cordes Junction–Bloody Basin region showed that, although the habitat appeared superficially suitable, summer droughts—a key factor in Scaled Quail distribution—probably occurred too frequently to sustain a popula-tion over a protracted period of time. Because of their specific climatic requirements, there appears to be little potential to expand Scaled Quail distribution through trapping and transplanting.

The natural history and ecology of Scaled Quail was studied by Wallmo (1956b) in west Texas and by Schemnitz (1961) in the Oklahoma panhandle. Other investigations followed in Colorado (Snyder 1967) and New Mexico (Campbell 1968), but it was not until 1970 that Scaled Quail were studied in Arizona in Sulphur Springs Valley and on the Willow Springs Ranch near Oracle Junction (D. Brown et al. 1978). This research showed that call-counts could accurately predict Scaled Quail fall hunting success, that both winter and summer precipitation were important to nesting success, that Scaled Quail nesting success fluctuates less than Gambel's Quail's, and that the overwinter survival of adults and juveniles determined variations in population levels more than reproductive success. In this last finding, Scaled Quail were shown to be very unlike Gambel's Quail, in which more than 90 percent of the annual variation in hunting success depends on the vagaries of nesting success (Swank and Gallizioli 1954).

The effects of precipitation on reproductive success and hunt success were less clear. With the exception of one year (1973), reproductive success (percentage of young in the bag) was relatively constant (Table 8.1). Fall–winter precipitation was highly variable, however, and when seasonal combinations were compared with reproductive success, significant correlation was found with precipitation from October through March, October through date of recorded calling peak, and October through August. The relationship between April–August precipitation and reproductive success was not significant, in contrast to the findings of Campbell et al. (1973) in southeast New Mexico.

TABLE 8.1

Precipitation and Scaled Quail Call-Count Indices and
Hunt Information from Oracle Junction Area, Arizona, 1970–76

Year	Precipitation (inches)[a]			Call-count Index[b] and Date of Peak	Scaled Quail per Hunter Day (N)[c]	Immature Scaled Quail in Bag (%) (N)[c]
	Oct.–March	April–Aug.	Total			
1970	8.67	3.61	12.28			
1971	2.68	6.06	8.74	27–134 4 Aug.	0.32 (133/410)	52 (127)
1972	7.81	6.66	14.47	29–189 14 June	0.29 (192/649)	54.5 (176)
1973	15.53	5.23	20.76	40–290 7 May	0.44 (309/705)	79.8 (297)
1974	4.20	5.93	10.13	55–355 26 July	0.56 (214/381)	52 (196)
1975	7.39	5.99	13.38	27–186 21 May	0.33 (215/658)	49 (219)
1976	4.10	5.91	10.01	25–145 14 May	0.23 (174/755)	39 (178)

[a] Precipitation data from Willow Springs Ranch Climatological Station
[b] Average of highest count and succeeding count; first figure is number of birds calling, second figure is number of calls recorded
[c] Figures in parentheses are sample sizes of number of Scaled Quail/hunter days reported

The period of peak calling activity varied greatly between years, ranging from May 7 to August 4 (Table 8.1). The onset of calling was observed to be stimulated by climatic factors, that is, warm temperatures, precipitation, or high humidity. In those years when winter precipitation was low (1971,

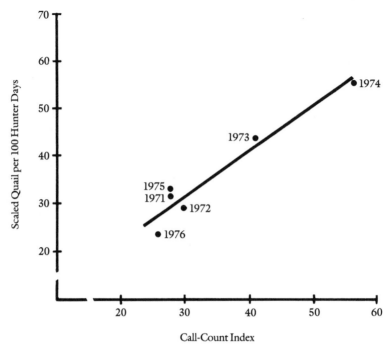

Fig. 8.6. *Relationship between call–count index and Scaled Quail hunting success.*

1974, 1976), calling activity was erratic throughout the spring and summer, and the calling peak was poorly defined; in 1971 and 1974 the calling peak did not occur until late summer with the commencement of that season's rains. Other investigators (Wallmo 1956b; Campbell et al. 1973) have found wide differences among hatching schedules for this species, with peaks from May through September.

Unlike Gambel's Quail, Scaled Quail show a relatively consistent breeding success. Since 1951 the percentage of young Scaled Quail recorded in the bag at Oracle Junction has ranged from 38 to 80 (Table 8.1). The percentage of young Gambel's Quail in the bag at Oracle Junction during the same period has ranged from 9 to 81. Schemnitz (1961) found Scaled Quail breeding success to be relatively uniform during his study in Oklahoma even though this period was generally one of drought. Campbell and others (1973) found the percentage of young in the bag in New Mexico to be between 44 and 84 for the years 1960 through 1968. It thus appears that Scaled Quail populations are not subject to the almost total failures of reproductive success that periodically occur among Gambel's Quail. In this respect they are intermediate between Gambel's Quail and Mearns' Quail, the latter species having between 57 and 79 percent juveniles in the bag during the period 1963–1975.

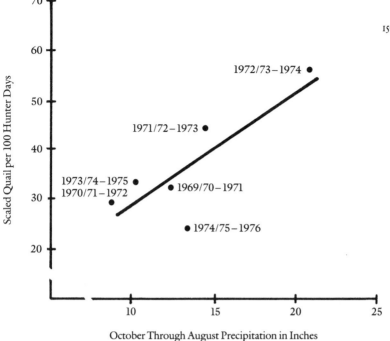

Fig. 8.7. Relationship between October–August precipitation and succeeding year's Scaled Quail hunting success. Data from Brown, Cochran, and Waddell (1978).

Seasonal precipitation did not affect the following season's hunt success, but there was a significant correlation between the *previous* year's October– August precipitation and hunting success (Fig. 8.7). This suggests that spring–summer moisture conditions contributed to population carryover and that survival was an important factor in determining call-count indices and, eventually, fall population levels as measured by hunt success.

Although the effects of moisture are of some importance to reproductive success, precipitation must be even more significant in terms of the production of food and cover. Several studies (e.g., Hoffman 1965; Campbell et al. 1973) have shown that the production of annual forbs is an important factor in food abundance and population carryover. Perennial grasses and dry-tropic scrub plants provide the principal cover for Scaled Quail. Residual grass cover in the Southwest depends on grazing pressure and the previous summer's precipitation (Cable 1975). This accounts for the general knowledge that Scaled Quail hunting is best on moderately grazed ranges during the years succeeding abundant rainfall.

This dependence on climatic factors does not mean that Scaled Quail populations cannot be improved. Good range practices that permit an adequate cover of residual grasses lower annual mortality and allow for increased local populations. Also, the removal of tall, dense, brushy vegetation on ridges can open up the habitat and improve nesting and roosting conditions for scalies. Both practices were satisfactorily tested in the Oracle Junction area, where the Page-Trowbridge exclosure formerly provided a pasture free from cattle grazing and two other sections were chained to remove a dense mesquite overstory. These areas supported more Scaled Quail in both favorable and unfavorable years than adjacent pastures. Conversely, pure grassland or completely cleared landscapes have been shown to be unsuitable for this species (Schemnitz 1961; McCormick 1975). Scaled Quail can exist in brush-deficient habitats only when artificial nesting and cover sites are supplied or if shrubby plants are allowed to reinvade. The birds' numbers depend on climatic vagaries *and* habitat condition; hunting pressure has been shown to have virtually no effect on population levels (Campbell et al. 1973; Brown et al. 1978).

HUNTING FOR SCALIES

Scaled Quail are not only more prone to run than Gambel's Quail, once shot over, they are more wary. Chances are that your first encounter with scalies will be to glimpse a covey moving out ahead of you. Listen carefully and you may hear their alarm calls, a high-pitched *chupah, chupah, chur* or *chink-chank-a*. You will not be able to walk them up, for they will outrun you. If you chase after them, you will still be hard pressed to catch up to the nucleus of the covey, smaller now as individual birds peel off to the left and right. If and when you do get them up, the flushing distance will be maximum range—forty yards or more. As often as not, you will not have an opportunity to bag even one bird. There has to be a better way.

There is. I like to hunt Scaled Quail the way I hunt Gambel's Quail but with some important differences. To find scalies, I spend the early morning on the long sloping ridges where they roost, for it is here that the birds will begin their foraging. I will be prepared for a long hike, as the density of Scaled Quail is usually less than that of Gambel's Quail and finding one covey an hour is reasonable success. I will watch for roosts, tracks, and dusting areas, and for Cactus Wren nests to dismember and check for the subdued, pale feathers that mean scalies are in the vicinity. I avoid washes and thickets unless I know that some birds have been already flushed by other hunters or a raw wind or the heat of the day has driven them to protective cover.

It is probably because of their open habitat that Scaled Quail are so prone to run. Indeed, the birds appear to prefer that mode of locomotion and almost all of their travel is on foot. A prudent course of action is to keep an eye to the ground well out in front. It is also advisable to listen for the soft *churr*s of communicating birds. More than once I have spotted scalies foraging toward me and, by standing quietly, have had them work their way into range before they discovered my presence.

Once the birds are alerted the only choice is to take after them. Where the ground cover is dense or if a stiff breeze is blowing or the weather is warm, the birds may hold until well within range. Otherwise, flush them at any distance, keep a careful eye on their direction of flight, and try to find them again. Scaled Quail usually do not offer much shooting on the covey rise. This is especially so in unfavorable years, when small coveys of mostly adult birds can be particularly evasive. What is needed is persistence and a good trailing dog, as scalies will, as often as not, again run on landing.

After one or two flushes, the birds will begin to hold. Scaled Quail singles in good cover "sit tight" to a dog and provide plenty of heart-thumping action. Once in the air, they fly stronger, farther, and higher than the other quails—more like Prairie Chickens, Sharp-tailed Grouse, or other grassland species.

After bagging only a bird or two, I often lose the covey. If it was a large one (twenty quail or more) or if other coveys are scarce, a waiting game may now be in order. After fifteen or twenty minutes the gathering calls will begin; their two-note *chu-ching*, or *ping*, call given by disturbed birds and the two-syllable *chuck-churr* separation call are immediately recognized by the serious quail hunter. Both calls are ventriloquial and make the bird difficult to locate. The caller is also likely to be moving, and reassembling birds are a challenge to pinpoint. Regrouping scalies also tend to flush at extreme range, and it is best to wait for the covey to reassemble before breaking them up again, a process that can require an hour or more. Even then the quail will flush more wildly than before, and the largest covey will rarely yield more than another bird or so.

A productive tactic for the day is to work the ridges for Scaled Quail for one or two hours and then hunt the hillsides, mimosa patches, and mesquite-lined washes for Gambel's Quail. This procedure increases the chances for a mixed bag and, in a mediocre quail year, provides for a reasonable amount of action. Because of the extreme distances that might be involved in shooting at Scaled Quail, I use an AA load of #7½s in a modified-choke 12 gauge.

Hunting scalies is a challenge. A bag of six or more of these most prestigious of quails makes for a memorable outing.

Paul Bosman

CHAPTER 9

Gambel's Quail

Arizona's most popular game bird, the Gambel's Quail—sometimes called Arizona Quail, Desert Quail, or Valley Quail—is familiar to hunters and suburban dwellers alike. Its jaunty, plumed topknot, carried by both sexes and not possessed by any other native quail, makes for ready identification. Ascertaining the bird's sex is usually no problem either; the bright russet cap, black face and bib outlined in white, and cream belly marked in the center with a black, often horseshoe-shaped splotch easily differentiates the male, or "cock." The female is more drab and lacks her mate's distinctive head markings. Like the male, she displays russet flanks conspicuously slashed with white. The backs of both sexes are a blue gray, and formerly the birds were sometimes called "blue quail," a name now more commonly applied to the Scaled Quail. The upper wing surfaces are an olive gray with a distinctive cream margin on the trailing edge of the secondaries; the buffy tail coverts are markedly streaked in rust.

As with all species of quail, the young of the year can be distinguished through their first winter by their spotted secondary wing coverts. The outer two primaries are also retained through the postjuvenile molt and are more pointed and worn than the adult's (Fig. 9.1). Otherwise, the young of the year in autumn closely resemble, and often outweigh the adults.

Except for the rare Masked Bobwhite, the Gambel's is the smallest of the southwestern quails. Adult males average only about 6 ounces, although an

Fig. 9.1. Wing of a seven-month-old Gambel's Quail. The spotted secondary coverts and more pointed outer two primaries identify a bird of the year.

occasional plump specimen will exceed 7. The females are slightly lighter, averaging between 5.7 and 5.9 ounces (Gorsuch 1934; Dunning 1984).

The quail is named after William Gambel, a naturalist from the Philadelphia Academy of Science who collected plants and animals along the Santa Fe Trail in 1841 and who encountered this species east of the "California Range." Of the several nominate races, two are recognized as occurring in Arizona. The Western Gambel's Quail (*Callipepla gambeli gambeli*) is found throughout central and western Arizona, and the slightly darker and more richly colored Eastern Gambel's Quail (*C. g. sana*) is reported to inhabit the higher elevations of eastern Arizona from the Chiricahua Mountains north to the vicinity of Whiteriver (Aldrich and Duvall 1955; see also, however, Phillips et al. 1964).

DISTRIBUTION

The Gambel's Quail is the only gallinaceous game bird endemic to the Sonoran Desert. Southwest Arizona and western Sonora are the metropolis of the quail's distribution, with the species extending into all contiguous states (Gullion 1960a). Eastward, through southern New Mexico and extreme northern Chihuahua, the bird's distribution becomes increasingly restricted to drainages, culminating in the Rio Grande Valley downstream to about Big Bend National Park in Texas (Wauer 1973). South of Arizona, Gambel's Quail occur throughout most of western Sonora and Sinaloa wherever there is reliable winter precipitation and the structure of the thornscrub is not so dense as to completely favor their Elegant Quail competitors.

Gambel's Quail in Baja California Norte are confined to the arid northeast corner, and the species is replaced south of San Felipe and in the remainder of the Baja Peninsula by its close relative, the California Quail. In Alta California, Gambel's Quail are restricted to the east side of the peninsular ranges, where the species comes into contact with both California and Mountain quails. In Nevada and extreme southwest Utah the quail is unevenly present in the valleys and foothills of the Mohave Desert. Intermittent and widely fluctuating populations also occur eastward in southern Utah along tributaries of the Colorado River, ascending up the San Juan and Grand river drainages into Colorado (Aldrich and Duvall 1955).

The limits of historic distribution of Gambel's Quail in Arizona (Fig. 9.2) are in some doubt. Because this desirable bird is easily trapped, numerous introductions into both occupied and unoccupied habitats were attempted by private and public parties between 1885 and 1930. At least some of these releases were near the Mormon settlements of Holbrook, Snowflake, and Vernon on the Little Colorado River drainage in northeast Arizona and at Pipe Springs on the Arizona Strip (McLean 1930; Bent 1932; Gullion 1960a; Monson and Phillips 1981). For this reason it is not known whether quail reported near Moenave (Griner et al. 1941) and other locales along the Little Colorado River represented native or introduced stock.

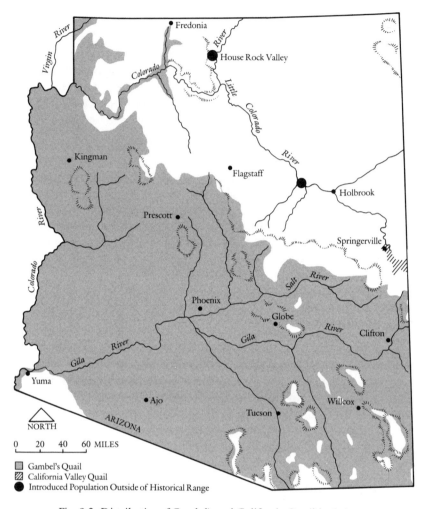

Fig. 9.2. Distribution of Gambel's and California Quail in Arizona.

Within the map:

Fredonia

Virgin River

Colorado River

River

House Rock Valley

Little

Colorado

Kingman

Flagstaff

River

Holbrook

River

Prescott

Springerville

Colorado

Phoenix

Salt River

Globe

Gila River

Clifton

Gila River

Gila

Yuma

Ajo

Tucson

Willcox

NORTH

ARIZONA

0   20   40   60 MILES

Gambel's Quail
California Valley Quail
Introduced Population Outside of Historical Range

Sometimes persisting for years, most of these populations eventually died out without additional releases. Of the several thousand Gambel's Quail trapped and released during federally funded restocking projects between 1939 and 1955, the only transplants thought to have been made outside the birds' native range in Arizona were in November 1950 along the Little Colorado River and its tributary, Canyon Diablo. Gambel's Quail persisted near Winslow until the severe winter of 1967–68, when the population all but disappeared. A supplemental release of quail from Robbin's Butte Wildlife Area in the early 1970s may have served to dilute what cold-tolerant stock remained. As of 1988, Gambel's Quail are not known to occur in the Little Colorado River drainage or on the Hopi and Navajo Indian reservations.

Otherwise, Gambel's Quail may be found in suitable habitats throughout sub-Mogollon and northwest Arizona below about 6,000 feet elevation, including tributary drainages into the Grand Canyon upriver to at least Cataract Creek. An isolated population persists at Kane Springs in House Rock Valley (Tom Britt, pers. comm.).

HABITAT

If one plant could be said to be associated with Gambel's Quail, it would be the mesquite (*Prospopis juliflora*), and the ranges of the two species largely overlap. The mesquite is not essential to the bird, but both find optimum conditions in the same habitats. This is especially so along drainages, and mesquite-lined rivers, creeks, and arroyos below 5,500 feet elevation are characteristic havens for Gambel's Quail in Arizona. Springs, seeps, and stock tanks, though not crucial for the bird's distribution, are favorite focal points.

Other well-populated Arizona habitats are wash-laced bajadas and outwash plains within the structurally and vegetatively diverse Arizona Upland subdivision of the Sonoran Desert, the denser scrub regions of the Mohave Desert, scrub-invaded semidesert grassland, and the lower, more open chaparral communities (Fig. 9.3). These habitats support the majority of both hunted and residential populations, and key quail indicators other than mesquite are desert hackberry, ironwood, catclaw acacia, saguaro, prickly pear, several chollas, jojoba or coffeeberry, any of several allthorns, and scrub oak. Dominant understory plants may be brittlebush, triangle-leaf bursage, shrubby buckwheat, burroweed, jimmyweed, turpentine bush, or snakeweed.

Fig. 9.3. Gambel's Quail habitat near Hillside in Yavapai County. Such open chaparral—grassland habitats consistently support Arizona's highest quail populations.

At lower elevations, below 2,500–3,500 feet, saltbushes (particularly quail-bush) are important as cover, and washes and riparian areas become an essential component of quail habitat. This is especially so along the lower Gila and Colorado rivers, where the birds are most often observed near dense thickets of saltcedar, arrow-weed, screw-bean, and other riparian vegetation (Fig. 9.4). Other superior quail habitats can be found at the edges of agricultural areas, particularly those adjacent to tamarisk-choked river channels or other brushy cover. Shrubby fence rows and waste areas are required components of cultivated quail habitat, however, and the increasing tendency toward clean farming has greatly reduced the amount and quality of what were formerly productive quail areas.

In southeast Arizona—in the Pinaleño and Chiricahua mountains, for example—Gambel's Quail extend upward into oak woodland or encinals, and in central Arizona, such as in the Bradshaw Mountains, quail may even be found up into the pines. The birds avoid dense chaparral, however, and most pinyon-juniper woodlands are too cold and have too little plant variety to support more than token numbers of quail. The few quail within Great Basin desertscrub are confined to drainage bottoms, and the birds are generally absent from the extensive creosote plains of the driest and hottest portions of the Mohave and Sonoran deserts.

All in all, productive habitats for Gambel's Quail in Arizona can be almost any brush locale having such thorny legumes as *Prosopis*, *Acacia*, and *Mimosa*, accompanied by cacti, leaf-succulents, and shrubbery. Some of the best quail areas now include shrub-invaded grasslands, which, in addition to being invaded by species of thornscrub, share the physiognomy and many of the plant genera of the coastalscrub, or "soft chaparral," habitat of California Quail.

LIFE HISTORY

The beginning of the reproductive year is announced by the cock's single-note *cow*, or *caw*, call. These calls are most often given from some elevated perch, and each bird has a distinctive tone to its cry. Only those males in breeding condition and advertising for a mate call, and depending

Fig. 9.4. Gambel's Quail habitat along the lower Gila River, Yuma County. Dense thickets of the introduced saltcedar are poor quail habitat but provide excellent cover when adjacent to other riparian vegetation or farmland. Photo by Harley Shaw.

on the year, they may account for anywhere from less than 25 to more than 75 percent of the population (Hungerford 1960a). Calling is most pronounced among unmated birds and those whose hens are absent. For this reason, peak calling activity coincides with the height of reproductive condition and nest initiation—usually between mid-April and the first week of May, the actual dates depending on temperatures and plant phenology.

The calling and nesting period is earlier and more concentrated in favorable years than in unfavorable ones, when nesting is prolonged and irregular. At these times many of the pairs dissolve their partnerships, and coveys of unpaired adults are seen as early as May. In the driest years this monogamous species may not form pair bonds at all. Hungerford (1964) showed that breeding behavior and development of the reproductive organs were dependent on the quantity of green feed produced by winter rains and correlated with the amount of Vitamin A stored in the quails' livers.

Gambel's Quail in spring primarily feed on greens and succulent vegetation, especially the leaves and flowers of the native Indian wheat (*Plantago sp.*) and the exotic filaree (Erodium). The leaves and flowers of mesquite, paloverde, and mimosa are taken along with the seeds of these and such other legumes as deer vetch, lupine, and locoweed. Saguaro pollen, and later the fruit and seeds, are important dietary items where the giant cactus is present. Ants and other insects are increasingly fed on as the nesting season progresses (Hungerford 1962).

The nest is usually a scrape bordered by small twigs and sparsely lined with grass stems and a few feathers. Like the calling males, the nests are not concentrated near water but are located rather randomly throughout the habitat, usually under a shrub or some other protected locale such as a prickly-pear patch. Tree nests are occasionally constructed where suitable platforms can be found from five to thirty feet above the ground (Neff 1941; Senteney 1957).

The usual clutch is ten to twelve eggs, although nests in dry years may contain five or fewer, and as many as twenty have been recorded (Bent 1932). Clutches of more than fifteen are usually the result of more than one hen, and "dump nests" are not uncommon. The dull white-to-buff eggs are smooth, slightly glossy, and irregularly splotched in brown. The normal arrangement is for the hen to do the incubating while the male stands guard. The male has a strong parental interest, and should something befall the hen, he will incubate the eggs and adopt the orphaned chicks.

Incubation requires twenty-one to twenty-three days; afterwards the nest site is immediately abandoned, and ants clean up any remaining eggs or dead chicks (Gorsuch 1934). The downy young, light buff striped in cinnamon, are precocial and follow the parents on their forays. For the first few days of life, the chick's food is entirely animal matter: beetles, small worms, moth caterpillars, and grasshoppers. The chicks are brooded and shaded by the hen for about ten days, after which they roost in low bushes with the adults (Gorsuch 1934). They are not fully independent, however, for about two and a half to three months, and summer and early fall coveys are made up of family groups, adopted young, and unsuccessful nesting adults from adjacent territories.

The peak of the hatch is in late April or May, with some clutches hatching as early as late March and others as late as August and even September (Hungerford 1960a). This wide range of dates and the annual variations in numbers of late-hatched chicks have given rise to the assumption that Gambel's Quail renest and that second hatches take place in some years.

Gorsuch (1934), Senteney (1957), and Hungerford (1960a) were convinced that second nestings did not occur. These investigators thought that, although some birds whose nests were destroyed might renest, the bird's decline in reproductive condition in June precluded a second brood.

Gullion (1956a, 1960a, 1960b) was of a different opinion. In 1952, after a wet, mild winter, nesting in southern Nevada uplands began in late February and peaked in mid-April. Most of the young he observed at water between June 28 and July 12 of that year were "weaned" and appeared independent of parental care. A number of broods were accompanied only by males, and Gullion (1956a) assumed that the hens were renesting. Although he had no proof that "double brooding" did occur, he cited two age classes of young and a 15:1 ratio of chicks to adults (88 percent young) as evidence that such a phenomenon occurred.

If second hatches do occur, such attempts are rare and of minor importance to Arizona quail populations. The nesting of Gambel's Quail during the hot, dry month of June is infrequent and has little effect on population levels. Summer brood surveys in mid-July rarely showed even 10 percent of the young quail to be less than one-quarter grown (e.g., Gallizioli and Day 1954). Although the occasional rains that fall in April and May can have a positive impact on Gambel's Quail reproduction (Hungerford 1960a; Raitt and Ohmart 1966), the effects of such late precipitation are minor. In one such year, 1967, only 6 percent of the quail in the bag at Oracle Junction were under ten weeks of age and hatched after the midsummer brood count. Even this small increase in late-hatched quail is thought to be the result of renesting attempts and a prolonged reproductive season that allowed early nonnesting adults to nest.

Summer finds the family settling into a routine. Upon awakening at first light, the adults leave their dense nighttime roosts—commonly a large hackberry—after a few *cuts* and some social twittering. The familiar *yhuk-ka-ka* assembly call is usually given by one or both parents to make sure all are present. The quail then begin foraging on foot, often along a wash toward water or a preferred feeding area such as waste grain found at a corral (Gorsuch 1934). Taking the lead, the male stands guard while the other birds water and feed. The usual tendency is to water early in the day, and observations of daily concentrations of watering quail have led to the conclusion that water is essential to the quail's welfare (e.g., Grinnell 1927; McLean 1930; Gullion 1960b).

Other investigators, however, have convincingly argued that water is not necessary for Gambel's Quail (Vorhies 1928; Leopold 1933; Gorsuch 1934; Lowe 1955). Nonetheless, it was taken for granted that quail survival and distribution could be increased by the provision of water, and the development of "gallinaceous guzzlers" became increasingly popular through the 1940s and 1950s (Glading 1943; Kimball 1946a, 1946b; Wright 1953, 1959; Gullion 1954, 1958, 1960b). In the 1960s Hungerford (1960b, 1962) showed that the availability of succulent green foods, not water, was the natural limiting factor for quail populations.

The practical aspects of water developments for quail were resolved by an Arizona Game and Fish Department study north of Phoenix (Gallizioli 1961a; Smith and Gallizioli 1963). Nine rainwater catchments were sealed off in January 1961 and 1962, effectively drying up two hundred thousand acres of quail habitat except for one intermittent stock tank. Despite the fact that 1961 was drier than average, quail call-counts and hunt success during both succeeding seasons were actually higher in the study area than in a comparable adjacent area where catchments continued to supply quail with water throughout the summer. It thus appears that, although water developments may concentrate quail within certain portions of a covey's range, these devices have little effect on quail numbers and distribution in Arizona.

Quail typically feed twice each day and spend the middle of the day loafing in a shady wash, dusting, sleeping, and taking sand for grit. If the birds are approached, they emit a nervous *whit-whit-whit*, and if pressed, they sound a *crear-crear* alarm call. The covey then scatters on foot or takes wing. The only time that undisturbed birds regularly take to the air is when going to roost or when crossing highways or other obstacles. More often than not they roost in the same shrubbery used the night before.

Even after the summer rains have started, quail continue to feed primarily on winter annuals—the seeds and leaves of deer vetch, filaree, and lupine. The leaves and seeds of mesquite and white-thorn acacia are also taken, along with seeds of saguaro, mimosa, carlowrightia, a mustard (*Sophia menziesii*), and climbing morning glory. Cholla and other cactus seeds and fruits show up in the diet with increasing frequency, and by September many quail may have faces and breasts stained purple from feeding on prickly-pear fruit. Ants are still a favorite summer food of both adults and chicks. Summer-emerging beetles, leafhoppers, and grasshoppers are eaten, but few summer annuals and almost no grasses are taken (Griner et al. 1941; Hungerford 1962).

Both seasonal and daily movements are small. Greenwalt (1955) and Gullion (1962) found that the maximum yearly movement of a covey was less than a mile, with 87 percent of the birds not moving more than 480 yards. The average range of a covey is only nineteen to ninety-five acres. Although there is some overlap with other coveys, most maintain a discrete territory that is possessed but not defended.

Fall, like the early summer, can be difficult for the quail, and in some years investigators have found a high loss of juveniles prior to the hunting season (Griner 1941; Gallizioli and Webb 1958). Seeds of winter annuals may now be in short supply, and it is at this time that dispersal first takes place. The search for food may take the covey into the range of other coveys, and by the winter months, aggregations of several coveys may be found in such food-rich areas as warm hillsides where early winter rains have produced a fresh flush of green annuals. The birds also appear drawn to salt blocks, perhaps because of an increased diet of mesquite beans.

Late winter and early spring sees the covey's greatest movements and the first evidence of pairing. Some individuals, primarily males and juveniles, now leave the parent covey (Gullion 1962), allowing genetic exchange between coveys. The males chase and nudge the hens and offer tidbits of select foods. As spring approaches, the coveys re-form with many of the same individuals present as in the previous fall. The covey then returns to the same general range occupied the year before to pair off, disperse, and begin the reproductive cycle anew.

MANAGEMENT HISTORY

The first quail season was established by the territorial legislature in an 1893 amendment to the game code. Quail were not to be shot, shipped, or sold from the first day of April through the first day of September. Trapping and netting were prohibited at all times, and for the first time the eggs of all birds were protected.

By the turn of the century quail hunting had become a popular pastime, and a generous season and lack of a bag limit gave Arizona a reputation for harboring "game hogs." According to the *Arizona Daily Star* and other periodicals, even the modest regulations of the day were ignored in the more "uncivilized" reaches of the state.

In 1909 the legislature limited quail hunting to an open season of October 16 through January 31, and this general season was retained in the state game code passed in 1912, along with a bag limit of twenty-five quail.

Little information is available on the vagaries of quail hunting between 1913 and passage of the new game code in 1929. Quail management consisted of trapping and transplanting quail to uninhabited or "depleted" areas, reducing the season length to close on December 31, and lowering the daily bag limit to twenty "Gambel or Valley Quail." In 1929 quail numbers must have been thought to be in need of improvement, as the season was shortened to November 1 through December 31 and the following year the newly appointed Arizona Game and Fish Commission reduced the bag limit to fifteen quail per day.

The most significant action taken in the 1930s was the publication of Gorsuch's (1934) life-history study and his conclusion that Gambel's Quail could best be increased by preserving and rehabilitating their habitat— primarily through the elimination of overgrazing. Gorsuch also recommended controlling the quail's natural enemies, better sportsmanship behavior by hunters, the enforcement of reasonable game laws, and continued study by qualified biologists. It was not until 1940 that this last recommendation was implemented. In the meantime, the only overt efforts to manage Arizona's premier game species were to make summer brood counts to appraise the commission of the year's quail hunt expectations, and to trap quail from farming areas where depredation complaints were received. Quail hunt regulations fluctuated with the vagaries of supposed population levels: the bag limit was reduced from fifteen to ten in 1934, increased to twelve in 1937, and dropped to ten again in 1939.

Arizona's first Federal Aid quail study focused on Cochise County, where the objective was to develop a satisfactory management plan and hunt regulations (Griner 1940a). Probably because of Gorsuch's influences, overgrazing and depredations by kangaroo rats and ants were considered the most deleterious influences in need of investigation (Griner 1940b). Small "inviolate" refuges near water sources were established, and it was recommended that the county be divided into four management units, one to be closed to hunting each year on a rotating basis. The reasoning behind this recommendation, which was never implemented, was to reduce hunt pressure on the same coveys year after year.

Other quail investigations in 1940 concentrated on visiting well-known quail locales, reporting on quail conditions, and making recommendations for refuges and water developments (Kimball 1940a–c; Griner 1940b–d; Lawson 1940c, d). Drought, overgrazing, and overhunting were considered the primary factors limiting quail numbers, although Griner (1940a) recognized the value of green growth to reproductive success—a phenomenon he attributed to the production of Vitamin B-1. Other quail related activities consisted mostly of responding to requests to trap and dispose of quail feeding on crops in the Safford, lower Gila River valley, and Yuma areas (Griner 1940e; Lawson 1940e).

The most substantial accomplishment in quail-management in the early 1940s was the purchase of tax-delinquent lands along the lower Gila River for quail habitat; similar plans for a management area near Tucson were thwarted when the land was acquired for Davis-Monthan Air Force Base. Another important achievement was the first mailing of a small-game hunt questionnaire to monitor the importance of quail to the state's license purchasers.

The winter of 1940–41 was abnormally wet, and much needed. Despite an excellent hatch, the hunt recommendation was conservative and only a fifteen-day season was authorized. Kimball (1941a–c) thought that drought and heavy grazing had taken too great a toll of the breeding stock during the previous years. The planned implementation of deferred grazing systems, then being promoted by range conservationists, was also thought to be potentially ruinous to quail, and a series of small enclosures was recommended as quail refugia.

The winter of 1941–42 was not so generous. Summer surveys showed a decline in young:adult ratios, even though the successful hatch of 1941 had boosted quail numbers to a new high. Because reproductive success was down, Kimball (1942a, b) unsuccessfully recommended shortening the month-long November season that had already been approved by the commission.

The following year's summer survey indicated a disastrous hatch and an extremely low population (Fig. 9.5), and it was reasoned that the high harvest enjoyed in 1942 had been a debilitating factor. That the percentages of young birds in the 1942 check station bags was considerably lower than those observed on July surveys was additional cause for concern. Much of the crop was thought to have been lost before the season began, and there was a fear that the hunt had reduced broodstock needed for the coming year. The 1943 season was halved to fifteen days.

Low quail numbers continued through the mid-1940s. Although the quail restoration plots in Cochise County showed some improvement in range conditions, little if any increase in quail numbers was noted (Kimball 1942c; Eicher 1943a; 1944a). Quail management focused on expanding and standardizing the summer brood counts, trapping and transplanting excess populations in agricultural areas (e.g., Arrington 1942b), and implementing conservative hunt regulations. Water development was given new impetus by Glading's (1943) work in California, and water catchments specifically to benefit quail were constructed in the Superstition Mountains and in Paradise Valley (Kimball 1946a).

The 1945 midsummer quail surveys showed another year of poor quail numbers, and some populations were deemed the lowest in recorded history (Kimball 1946b). Even the Yuma area, the perennial source of crop-depredation complaints and quail for restocking attempts, showed a marked decline. Hunting was thought to be additive to natural mortality, and Kimball (1946a) determined that a ratio of 2.1 young to one adult was needed to justify a hunt. This figure was based on Emlen and Glading's (1945) average annual monthly mortality rate for California Quail and past survey and check station data on Gambel's Quail in Arizona. The summers having ratios of young to adults above 2.1:1 (1940, 1941, 1944) were followed by fair to good quail seasons; those years when the young-to-adult ratio was less than 2.1:1 were succeeded by poor or decreased hunt success. The statewide young-to-adult ratio observed in 1945 was 0.4:1; there would be no quail season in 1946, 1947, and 1948 (Fig. 9.5).

A seven-year drought broke in January 1949. Summer quail counts that year showed a statewide young-to-adult ratio of 2.16:1, and a two-day season was authorized in two areas of southwest and east-central Arizona where ratios exceed the 2.1 minimum (Lawson 1949b). The bag and possession

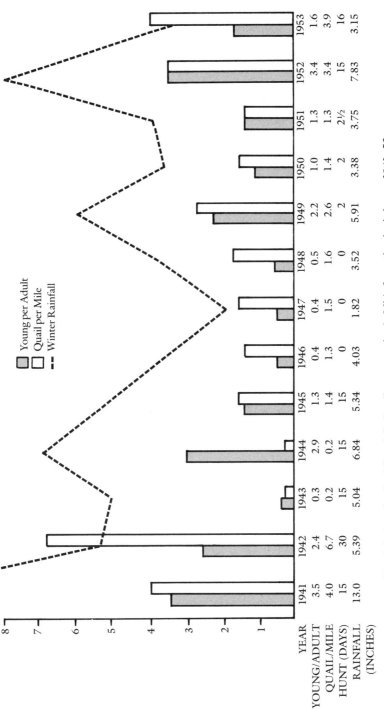

YEAR	1941	1942	1943	1944	1945	1946	1947	1948	1949	1950	1951	1952	1953
YOUNG/ADULT	3.5	2.4	0.3	2.9	1.3	0.4	0.4	0.5	2.2	1.0	1.3	3.4	1.6
QUAIL/MILE	4.0	6.7	0.2	0.2	1.4	1.3	1.5	1.6	2.6	1.4	1.3	3.4	3.9
HUNT (DAYS)	15	30	15	15	15	0	0	0	2	2	2½	15	16
RAINFALL (INCHES)	13.0	5.39	5.04	6.84	5.34	4.03	1.82	3.52	5.91	3.38	3.75	7.83	3.15

■ Young per Adult
□ Quail per Mile
--- Winter Rainfall

Fig. 9.5. Standardized Gambel's Quail survey and rainfall information in Arizona, 1941–53.

limit was five quail. The return to quail hunting was short-lived, however. Midsummer surveys in 1950 showed a Gambel's Quail young-to-adult ratio of only 1.04:1, and the numbers of quail seen per mile were at a new low.

Another miserable quail year followed in 1951, but Kimball's 2.1 young-to-adult criterion was now being scrutinized more closely. Gallizioli (1951a), on the basis of past survey and hunt data, questioned the rationale for closing the season in poor years. Most of the variation in quail hunt success appeared solely due to reproductive performance; population levels showed almost no relationship to previous hunt regulations and harvests. Sportsmen were also questioning the validity of the brood counts, contending that the surveys missed counting many young of the year. At their request, additional surveys were conducted and substantial increases in young quail were noted on many of the routes. Short, local hunts of two and a half days each were then authorized in several areas. Survey routes were expanded and survey procedures revised (Gallizioli 1951a), and a research study was instituted to determine the actual effects of hunting on quail populations (Gallizioli 1951b, 1952a; Webb 1953c).

Despite having a season in 1951, quail were abundant in 1952. Statewide young-to-adult ratios increased from 1.3:1 in 1951 to 3.4:1—within 0.1 of a youngster of the 1941 high. A December 1–14 season was approved with a bag limit of eight quail. The data generated from this and the 1951 hunt, coupled with preliminary research findings, showed how overly conservative past hunt recommendations had been. Swank and Gallizioli (1953, 1954) were now able to show that quail populations were almost entirely dependent on winter precipitation and the success of the hatch. Hunting had little if any effect. The two-week hunt in late fall with an eight-bird bag limit was continued (with local exceptions). Other longstanding management practices were eliminated or questioned. Trapping and transplanting practically ceased, refuges were abolished, and the value of water catchments was investigated.

Summer survey routes were modified in 1956, and a test run was made of a new call-count survey technique pioneered by Senteny (1957; Gallizioli 1957a). In 1957 a November–December season was recommended as banding studies had shown that no more than 25 percent of the population would be removed by hunting, that the percentage of quail removed was proportional to the density of birds present, and that hunting mortality was compensatory to natural mortality (Gallizioli 1957b, c).

Because earlier studies (e.g., Griner et al. 1941; Swank and Gallizioli 1953) had shown a high loss of young quail between the midsummer brood

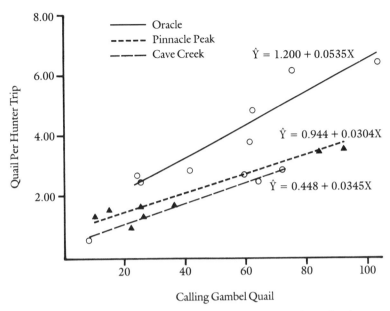

Fig. 9.6. Gambel's Quail call-count and hunt success information in three areas in Arizona. Data from Smith and Gallizioli (1965).

count and late fall hunting seasons, a split forty-day season from mid- to late October and from mid-December through early January was adopted in 1958 to harvest those juveniles "that were going to die anyway." The daily bag limit was increased to ten. Management efforts now concentrated on improving survey techniques, developing an annual statewide harvest estimate, and establishing a standardized season.

By 1965, hunt questionnaires were providing reliable hunt success estimates on a statewide basis and a split quail season during the month of October and from December 1 through the end of January was in effect. (The month of November was excluded in deference to cattle growers, who wanted this month to round up their stock without interference.) A fifteen-bird bag limit became the norm. Call-count surveys proved to be able to predict fall population levels with 97 percent accuracy and replaced the midsummer roadside counts as a survey technique in 1962 (Kufeld 1962a, 1964, 1965; Smith and Gallizioli 1965; Fig. 9.6).

November was included in the quail season in 1971 without objection from stock owners, and in 1979 the season was extended to mid-February to coincide with the closing of the Mearns' Quail season. A standard small-game season opening on the second Friday in October was also adopted that year, and this generous season of approximately 125 days has remained in effect to the present time.

POPULATION DYNAMICS

The success of the hatch accounts for 94 percent of the annual variation in Gambel's Quail hunt success (Smith and Gallizioli 1965). Changes in reproductive success are in turn strongly correlated with the preceding winter's precipitation (Fig. 9.5) and the production of Vitamin A in the spring feed (Gullion 1954; Hungerford 1960a, 1964). Population carryover, which averages about 60 percent but varies with the year and with population density, explains most of the remaining variation (Gallizioli and Webb 1959; Sowls 1960; Raitt and Ohmart 1968).

The correlation between winter precipitation and hatching success is not always linear, however. October–March precipitation amounts greater than about ten inches are superfluous and cannot improve reproductive success beyond the bird's maximum performance of about 80 percent juveniles in the fall population. Quail in riparian and irrigated farming areas do not experience the almost total reproductive failure caused by the absence of rain-induced green feed (Gullion 1958, Brown 1968a). Also, an exception to abundant winter rainfall resulting in high productivity appears to have occurred in 1981 after a period of three successive wet years when quail hatching success (and hunt success) declined. Gambel's Quail apparently are unable to sustain high levels of reproductive performance without intervals of drought as a rest period. This species is truly adapted to a boom-and-bust existence and is an evolutionary product of fluctuating climate.

Juvenile mortality is greater than adult mortality, and both juveniles and males are more vulnerable to trapping and shooting than adult females (Raitt and Ohmart 1968; Gallizioli 1967). Juvenile losses are greater in some years than others, and although Lawson (1950) and Swank and Gallizioli (1953) reported that large numbers of youngsters were lost between July and the end of September, other investigators showed young-to-adult ratios in fall hunt samples to exceed those observed on summer brood counts (Brown 1968a). Surprisingly, birds hatched in a "good year" retain a lower mortality rate throughout their lives than quail hatched in a dry year (Sowls 1960).

A large carryover of adults and juveniles following a successful hatch occasionally offsets a poor reproductive performance the following year. High survival of birds from the previous year allowed for better-than-average quail hunting in 1942 and 1953, when reproductive success was poor. Conversely, Gullion (1954) reported a mortality rate exceeding 90 percent during an exceptionally dry year in southern Nevada. Such a low number of survivors cannot regain a high population level in only one year of good reproductive success. Despite above-average rainfall and percentages of young in the harvest, hunting success in Arizona was below average in 1949, 1957, and 1972, each of which was preceded by several dry years and low population levels.

Hunting mortality is inversely dependent on the density of the quail population, ranging from as low as 4 percent of the population in poor years to as high as 31 percent in "bumper" years (Gullion 1954; Gallizioli and Webb 1958). Furthermore, hunting mortality is compensatory to natural mortality, and study areas subjected to high hunter pressure and the removal of quail by trapping had subsequent fall population levels equal to or greater than those of adjacent areas closed to hunting (Gallizioli 1957c; Gallizioli and Webb 1961).

The Effects of Grazing

Gorsuch (1934), Griner et al. (1941), Kimball (1946a), and others considered overgrazing to have a deleterious effect on Gambel's Quail. They reasoned that the resulting reduction in forage and ground cover contributed to an increased mortality of adults and chicks and was an important cause of low quail numbers. Although these early suppositions have been somewhat discredited by the knowledge that Gambel's Quail populations fluctuate as markedly on grazed ranges as on ungrazed allotments, the influence of livestock grazing on population carryover is of some consequence.

In an attempt to obtain some insights into the effects of grazing on Gambel's Quail populations, two areas were compared: Three-Bar Wildlife Area and Tonto Basin Study Area (Arizona Game and Fish Department, unpublished). The former had not been grazed since the 1940s, whereas the latter was heavily grazed. Both areas were good quail habitat, about the same size, and had precipitation stations. From 1977 through 1981, call-count and hunt data showed no significant differences in the percentage of young in the bag between the two areas, but the call-count index was higher on the ungrazed Three-Bar in all years but one, and hunt success was always greater there. Despite the same hatching success in both areas, hunters averaged almost a bird more per day on the Three-Bar than on Tonto Basin. Although it could be argued that quail hold better under conditions of more ground cover and may thus be more susceptible to hunters, the fact that the call-count index was higher on the ungrazed area four years out of five suggests that population carryover was also usually greater on the Three-Bar than on Tonto Basin.

Predation

As we now know, habitat quality and climatic factors determine fluctuations in quail populations, and it is difficult to realize now how much concern was once expressed about the effects of predation. In the 1930s predator control was thought to be as essential to small-game restoration as closed seasons. Much money and effort went into studies to identify the most serious predators and develop means to destroy them. Only when the results of these studies refuted popular opinion on the nature and extent of predator losses was it possible to investigate the real factors responsible for quail abundance and scarcity.

Quail, of course, are preyed upon. Some are taken by bobcats and by the efficient Cooper's and Harris' hawks. More significant, however, are losses to egg-robbing cotton rats, round-tailed ground squirrels, and such snakes as the coachwhip, gopher snake, and king snake. Gila monsters, too, are known to feed on quail eggs, but the number of eggs lost to these interesting reptiles is insignificant when compared to those lost to ants. According to Gorsuch (1934); not a single quail egg was found in thirty-seven Gila monsters captured in prime quail habitat. Gorsuch also refuted the alleged ravages of another opportunistic feeder, the Roadrunner. His collection of 128 Roadrunner stomachs contained neither eggs nor chicks, despite "common knowledge" that Roadrunners "clean out" whole broods and destroy the reproductive attempts of an entire season. Productivity, like mortality, is governed by climatic factors and habitat quality. Nest depredations in favorable years are offset by other nesting attempts. When conditions are unsuitable, no management measures to reduce natural predation will provide more quail. It should be noted, however, that Gambel's Quail thrive and reproduce in Sun City, Arizona, and other residential communities where cats and dogs are not allowed, while this bird is absent from comparable urban areas where pets are not restrained.

Diseases and Parasites

Quail are prone to a number of parasites, some of which can be life-threatening to the bird. Rarely, however, is an infestation sufficient to cause significant mortality (Gorsuch 1934; Gullion 1957). The only disease of consequence reported in Gambel's Quail is quail malaria, a malady present in populations in various degrees and not necessarily fatal (Hungerford 1955; Gullion 1957). Nonetheless, Gullion (1957) found malaria to occur in 95 percent of a declining population in one locality in Nevada, and this blood protozoan may be an important decimating factor in quail subjected to environmental stress.

The most common ectoparasites noticed by hunters are two species of bird lice, ticks (three species, of which the most prevalent is *Argas periscus*), and infestations of a small, red mite. Two species of large louse flies, vectors for bird malaria, are less frequently noted (Gorsuch 1934; Gullion 1957). Favus, a fungal infection, is occasionally seen at the site of old wounds, and some birds have swollen, arthritic toes and cankerous growths on the leg caused by staph infections (Gullion 1957).

Intestinal parasites are relatively common, especially roundworms in the caecum or lower gut. These may be in such numbers as to cause perotinitis, giving the intestines an even fouler odor than is typical of eviscerated quail. Another species of roundworm is sometimes found in the proventriculus, and tapeworms in the lower intestinal tract are not unusual (Gorsuch 1934; Gullion 1957).

All of these diseases and parasites are specific to birds and none is known to transmit human diseases.

WERE QUAIL MORE ABUNDANT IN THE PAST?

Quail numbers have always fluctuated dramatically over the years in response to the vagaries of winter precipitation and the success of the hatch. Nonetheless, the numbers of birds described by nineteenth-century travelers and residents of Arizona are difficult to envision and, if true, are greater than are now experienced even in the best of years. Such reports, said David Gorsuch (1934), "bear evidence that Gambel's quail populations of today are but remnants as compared with those of past years." Starker Leopold (1977), after researching the historical occurrence of the California

Quail, concluded that this species was also more prevalent in California in the period 1860–95 than later, and attributed changes in land use and the increasing replacement of annual forbs by exotic grasses after 1880 as the major reason for the decline. Were these biologists correct in these assumptions, or were the historical accounts exaggerations and memory more generous than reality?

The published diary of James M. Cutts (1965), a member of Lieutenant Emory's topographic expedition into Arizona in 1846, recorded "immense" numbers of quail in the bottoms of the upper Gila. Emory (1848) himself described "myriads" of the birds. John Durivage (1937) found quail along the Gila in 1849 to be "in the greatest abundance," and Benjamin Hayes (1850) commented on the "immense number" of quail near the junction of the Gila and Colorado rivers, describing the mesquites as "swarming" with them. S. W. Woodhouse, physician and naturalist with the 1851 Sitgreaves expedition across northern Arizona, termed the quail "excessively abundant" along the Lower Colorado River (Davis 1982).

Quail distribution also seems to have been more generous. Consider Mollhausen's (1858) descriptions of "partridge" numbers in 1854 along a tributary of Big Chino Wash in Yavapai County, where Gambel's Quail are now of sporadic occurrence at best: "We found them in such masses in Partridge Creek, that very few shots served to supply us all with an abundant dish." C. B. R. Kennerly (1856), passing through the same area in 1886, "found, in great numbers, Gambel's partridge. . . . While encamped here this beautiful bird afforded us fine sport with our shot-guns, and furnished us with many delicious meals." E. A. Mearns's field notes (1884–86) for 1884 also record large numbers of Gambel's Quail in the same general area, as well as on the Hualapai Indian Reservation, in Cataract Creek, and in the Grand Canyon—all locations where one is hard pressed to find a covey a century later.

A detailed description of quail numbers along the lower Gila during the presettlement period is provided by George O. Hand, a member of the California Volunteers. Hand kept a diary of his column's journey from Yuma to Tucson during the summer of 1862. The contingent augmented their meager rations by hunting, and Hand's entries often mention game. Near Gila Bend he (1862) wrote:

All along this day's march the quail were astonishing; big flocks of them two hundred yards long. I really think there were millions of them in each flock. If I were to tell my old friends in California that, they would say that I had lost my senses, and would not believe me.

Even allowing for some exaggeration and the fact that the winter of 1861–62 was abnormally wet according to California records, Hand's observations are remarkable by today's standards.

What about quail numbers in upland habitats? The birds must certainly have been abundant south of Tucson in 1885, before large-scale livestock ranching in the Altar Valley. Herbert Brown (1885) reported that Gambel's Quail "swarmed by the thousands" in the canyons where he searched for "hooded quail" (Masked Bobwhite). Also, in 1885, Mearns reported seeing "hundreds of large flocks of Gambel's Quail" along New River north of Phoenix—in May! That same year, Brown (1887) recorded that

[Arizona quail] have been very abundant. On the Salt and Gila rivers Indians and white men snared them by thousands. In September of that year [1885] I was in Phoenix and saw one man (a ranchman on the river bottom) drive in town with 600 live quail in one crate. They were purchased by a Mr. Whipley, a produce dealer, for 45 cents per dozen. The vendor was anxious to contract for 1500 more birds for the week following, but the offer was refused, as they were a drug in the market.

When Will C. Barnes (*in* Gorsuch 1934) arrived in the unsettled Tonto Basin in 1887, he found Gambel's Quail "not in thousands, but in actual millions, being present in countless numbers on all sides."

Brown (1900) explained why quail were not included in the list of birds having a closed season in the game code of 1887:

The Gambels are a hardy bird and under ordinary conditions multiply rapidly, and although not susceptible of domestication, increase enormously in the cultivated districts. In 1889 and in 1890 there was, so I was informed by the express agent, shipped out of the Salt River valley 3000 dozens. In 1887, I think, the first game law was introduced in the territorial legislature. The bill originated in the Tucson Gun Club, and its purpose was largely the protection of "Quail," but so great a pest were the birds regarded by the ranchmen of the Salt River valley that the legislators from Maricopa County threatened to kill the bill unless the clause protecting "Quail" was stricken out.

Brown described the effects of the drought of 1892–93 and the general ravages of overgrazing in Arizona during the last decade of the nineteenth century. As for the upland populations of Gambel's Quail, he noted that the desert country was now a void and that he "did not see a dozen Quail a day where formerly I had seen hundreds."

Brown (1900) also mentioned the great numbers of Gambel's Quail found in the lower Gila valleys:

The Mohawk valley, in Yuma county, is probably the most prolific breeding spot in the Territory. . . . In six weeks, in the fall of 1894, no less than 1300 dozens were shipped to San Francisco and other California markets. . . . I was told by one of the parties so engaged that he and his partner caught 77 dozens in one day. They used eight traps and baited with barley. Their largest catch in one trap, at one time, was eleven dozens.

Good quail hunting was also still to be had along the Gila, as indicated by an October 5, 1895, article in the *Arizona Daily Star*, which reported that "K. L. Hart and Jack Hallowell returned yesterday morning from a two days' hunt in the jungles near Gila Bend. They bagged 140 quail apiece." On October 24, the *Star* again reported on Hallowell's prowess—this time in the "jungles of Sacaton," where he bagged 110 quail. This is the last published account of a quail bag that would be difficult to obtain today.

Were quail really that abundant prior to 1900? And if so, why were they more numerous and widely distributed then than now? There are too many firsthand accounts to dismiss all these reports of incredible numbers as exaggerations.

It is perhaps informative that the period of greatest reported abundance of quail in Arizona coincides with that reported by Leopold (1977) for California Quail: 1860–95. Did the great drought and grazing abuses of the 1888–1904 period so damage the range in both states that quail populations could no longer recover their former abundance? Like a virgin forest once cut, were Arizona's native rangelands replaced by less vigorous habitats that would never again have the potential of their ungrazed predecessors? As Leopold (1977) postulated, was the culprit the replacement of native plants by a degrading succession from native forbs through exotic annual forbs to annual grasses?

If so, the synchrony of the period of abundance in the two states presents a problem. The introduction of livestock and the replacement of native grasses by Mediterranean annuals began much earlier in California than in Arizona. The shift to annual forbs did not begin in Arizona until after the turn of the twentieth century. If the replacement of perennial grasses by exotic forbs was a stimulant to greater quail production, as Leopold suggested, Arizona should have experienced its peak quail populations after 1885. Since such does not appear to be the case, other scenarios need to be investigated.

Most early reports of phenomenal quail numbers in Arizona are along perennial watercourses: the Salt River, Colorado River, Tonto Creek, and especially the lower reaches of the Gila (Fig. 9.7). The birds' numbers in the

Fig. 9.7. Undisturbed Gambel's Quail habitat along the lower Gila River north of Sentinel, May 1986. Water releases from Painted Rock Dam and the uncleared mesquite bottoms now support a large breeding population reminiscent of past conditions once found along the entire river.

uplands, though impressive by today's standards, were never so large, and no mention is made of "good" and "bad" years.

Could these large numbers of quail in the riverbottoms have been just concentrations of birds that came a great distance to drink? This is a reasonable hypothesis, but it does not conform to the biological facts. Studies have shown that water alone is not the key to quail abundance, and long treks to water have not been documented. Yet another hypothesis is needed.

We know that riverine habitats were richer then than now. Prior to the construction of dams, the rivers deposited their annual cargo of nutrients on the floodplains—nutrients that are now locked up in upstream reservoirs. The flush of greenery following spring floods allowed for a high breeding success among the quail each year; the dense riparian cover and low flows in winter provided a safe haven and a plethora of food seeds to support "myriads" of the birds. The fact that large concentrations of quail persisted adjacent to the lower Gila into the 1930s and 1940s and declined after the construction of dams and the complete capture of upstream flows

after 1941 lends credence to this theory. Since then, riparian habitat alteration and destruction, the cessation of wheat farming, and the invasion of
saltcedar have further diminished quail populations along the lower Gila
and other Arizona drainages.

Still, some nagging doubts remain. All four species of native quail now
have more restricted ranges than at the time of Mearns's and Brown's ram-
blings. Either the 1860–80 period was wetter in both winter and summer
than now, or the virgin uplands were also more productive than today's
habitats. If so, how do we know that the deterioration has ceased? Records
show that the number of quail checked at Oracle Junction in 1940, a dry
year following prolonged drought, averaged 6.6 quail per hunter day—a
success rate not attained now even in the best years. Were hunters better
then than now, or were there more quail? One has to wonder.

CALIFORNIA QUAIL

Along the Little Colorado River near Springerville, a quail call similar
to that of a Gambel's Quail is sometimes heard. Whether a male's spring
caw or a morning gathering call, there is something about the tone that
does not quite ring true. The *caw* call is not quite as shrill, and the *ku-ka-kow*
is a little deeper and a bit more melodious than the four-note *ku-KA-ka-ka*
heard farther south. Should the quail be pressed, it may give a sharp *whit—
whit*. These calls are those of the California Quail, *Callipepla (Lophortyx)
californicus*.

In addition to having similar calls, these exotics appear superficially like
our desert-dwelling natives, topknots and all (Fig. 9.8). Closer inspection,
however, reveals that the "helmet" of the California Quail cock is entirely
black, bordered in white, and that the crown lacks the Gambel's russet cap.
The yellowish cream chest and black belly patch of the slightly smaller
Gambel's Quail is replaced by a multihued scaled pattern, and the male
California Quail gives the impression of being a shade more slate blue.
Both sexes have a more speckled and flecked nape than their Gambel's Quail
counterparts, and the Gambel's distinctive, white-streaked russet flank
feathers are a more subtle ash brown.

This isolated Arizona population of California Quail resulted from introductions in 1960 by the Hooper Game Farm of stock obtained from
Oregon in 1960. The birds spread down the Little Colorado River to

Fig. 9.8. Pair of California Quail near Richville, Apache County, in April 1986.

Lyman Reservoir and up this drainage and its tributary, Nutrioso Creek, to the approximate boundary of the Apache-Sitgreaves National Forest and the limits of suitable habitat (see Fig. 9.2). These drainages remain intermittently occupied as of April 17, 1986, when I photographed a covey of twelve to fourteen birds near the old Hall place at Richville, twelve miles northwest of Springerville. Another covey, or at least an individual, was giving a gathering call upstream. At this time the quail were paired within the covey but had not yet begun *caw* calling.

On other occasions I have observed California Quail on brush-lined canal banks immediately adjacent to the shrubby floodplain of the Little Colorado River, in patches of raspberries and wild rose thickets (Fig. 9.9). Other important cover plants appeared to be coyote willow, four-wing saltbush, squawbush, and Rocky mountain juniper. Such habitats are analogous to those used by California Quail in northern California and Oregon, and their presence in the vicinity of Springerville is due to the suitable shrub cover, the ameliorating effects of the Little Colorado River and the absence of the native Gambel's Quail.

Fig. 9.9. California Quail habitat along the Little Colorado River near Richville. Small farms adjacent to brush patches and riparian scrubland next to the river provide food and cover in this cold temperate location.

Little is known about this population of quail, but their behavior, life history, and habitat requirements are most certainly similar to those of the California birds. For a comprehensive treatment of all aspects of this species the reader is referred to Leopold (1977).

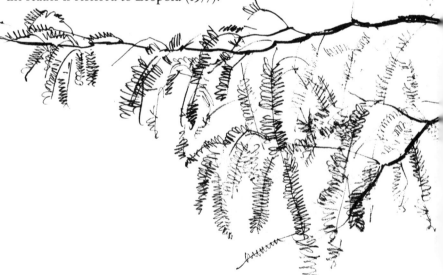

PART V

Cranes

The cranes are an ancient family with worldwide distribution. Two species occur in North America: the endangered Whooping Crane (*Grus americana*) and four migratory and three resident races of Sandhill Crane (*G. canadensis*). Although cranes bear a superficial resemblance to storks and herons, they have a distinctive evolutionary history and possess numerous morphological and behavioral differences. All are large birds with stout, daggerlike beaks, and fly with legs and necks extended. Cranes feed primarily on vegetable matter, and flocks of Sandhills are often seen foraging in Arizona's uplands.

The sexes have similar plumage and form lasting pair bonds after an extended and sometimes elaborate courtship. Clutches are small, usually only two eggs. Parental investment is high, however, and once fledged, the precocial chicks are long-lived. Young birds stay with the parents in family groups or join small flocks of other juveniles and do not attain sexual maturity for several years.

PAUL BOSMAN

CHAPTER 10
Sandhill Crane

No other Arizona bird projects the wilderness image as much as the Sandhill Crane. The birds communicate incessantly as they fly, and their unique, primitive-sounding creaks and grates are unmistakable. When seen, the callers are easily identified. No other large birds fly in ragged, extended formations with long, outstretched necks, spindly legs trailing behind a stubby tail, and propelled by steady beats of huge wings. Even on the ground their upright stance, overall light gray appearance, and flocking behavior readily differentiate them from herons, egrets, and other wading birds. No other such bird feeds in Arizona's fields or uplands.

The sexes have identical shades of slate gray plumage that may be rust stained with ferric oxide, a result of the birds' painting themselves with marsh debris. On closer inspection, the stout, bayonet-shaped beaks and unwebbed feet show these birds to be more adapted to a terrestrial existence than an aquatic one. The adults have a crown of bright red papilose skin on the forehead. This area on the young of the year is a rust brown, a character that can be used to distinguish juvenile birds through their first winter.

The Greater Sandhill Crane (*Grus canadensis tabida*), the more widely distributed race wintering in Arizona, weighs from 10.8 to 14.8 pounds and has a wingspan of up to seven feet. The smaller Lesser Sandhill Crane (*G. c. canadensis*) weighs between 5.4 and 8.2 pounds. The latter race also tends

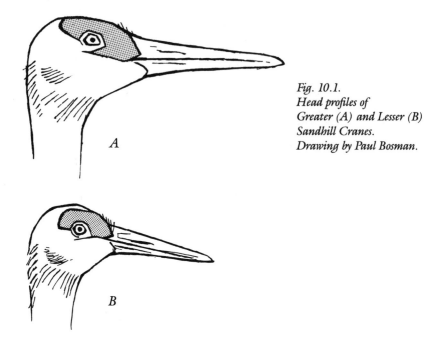

Fig. 10.1.
Head profiles of
Greater (A) and Lesser (B)
Sandhill Cranes.
Drawing by Paul Bosman.

to be darker in color, has a different tone to its call, and possesses a more abrupt head profile than the Greater Sandhill Crane (Fig. 10.1). But unless comparative birds are present, identification to race is difficult, and visual confirmation of subspecies can be difficult.

DISTRIBUTION

Two distinct populations of Sandhill Cranes winter in Arizona (Fig. 10.2). The largest population numbers between six thousand and twelve thousand birds, consists of approximately 40 to 50 percent Greaters and 50 to 60 percent Lessers, and takes up winter residency in Sulphur Springs Valley (Perkins and Brown 1981; Wrakestraw et al. 1983; Smith 1984). Although most of these birds roost on or near Willcox Playa, sizable flocks have also been observed roosting near Hooker Cienega on the Sierra Bonita Ranch and at Whitewater Draw two miles south of McNeal.

A second population of 1,750 to 2,000 Greaters also migrates annually from northeast Nevada to winter along the Lower Colorado River. Most

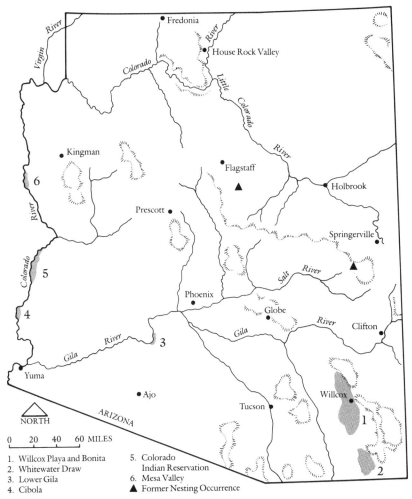

1. Willcox Playa and Bonita
2. Whitewater Draw
3. Lower Gila
4. Cibola
5. Colorado Indian Reservation
6. Mesa Valley
▲ Former Nesting Occurrence

Fig. 10.2. Winter distribution (shaded areas) *of Sandhill Cranes in Arizona.*

of these cranes roost and feed near Poston on the Colorado River Indian Reservation and on Cibola National Wildlife Refuge, with a few birds sometimes remaining to the north in Mesa Valley above Topock. Another small flock of 50 to 200 birds belonging to the Lower Colorado River Valley population winters on the lower Gila River between Gillespie Dam and Gila Bend near Cotton Center.

Crane observations away from these general areas are usually in late summer or early fall and are of migrating birds. Recent and historic observations away from known wintering locales include the Seligman area, Goodwin Mesa north of Bagdad, the Verde River near Camp Verde, near the junction of the Salt and Gila rivers, Picacho Reservoir, and along the Santa Cruz River south of Tucson. The occasional winter observations at San Simon Cienega and along the upper Gila River are thought to be of scattered flocks of populations that regularly winter in New Mexico.

HABITAT

Winter crane habitats can be divided into three categories: roost sites, loafing areas, and feeding fields (Lewis 1979b). Flocks of five to five hundred cranes typically leave a nighttime roost site around sunrise. The birds fly directly to cultivated croplands, where they will feed for two to six hours. From midmorning until noon, small flocks cease feeding and either return to the roost site or fly to a midday loafing area. After about three o'clock the cranes resume feeding, though some birds may not return to a feeding field until nearly sunset. Most cranes will again return to their roost site by half an hour after sunset, although some late feeders may not arrive until well after dark.

Shallow water, or at least damp ground, is the primary requisite of a roost site (Lewis 1976). Cranes rarely roost on dry ground and rarely stand in water more than 10 inches deep. Almost all roost sites observed in Arizona are wet ground or standing water less than 3.2 inches deep (Perkins and Brown 1981). Roosting areas in standing water are characterized by adjacent mud flats or other suitable landing platforms; cranes are apparently reluctant to land directly on water. Low dunes and sandy banks are further enhancements.

Another requirement for a roost site is unhindered visibility and freedom from human disturbance. Heavily vegetated areas and ponds with high banks are avoided. Cranes are especially wary when roosting and will

Fig. 10.3. Sandhill Crane roost site on the lower Gila River near Cotton Center. Shallow, quiet water, mud flats, and low, open dunes are characteristic of crane roost sites everywhere.

abandon a particular site if harassed. Typical roost sites are alkaline depressions such as Willcox Playa, marshy grasslands, and open, shallow ponds. Cranes using the Lower Colorado and Gila rivers roost on sandbars and the strands of barren river channels (Fig. 10.3).

If close to a feeding field, the roost site may also suffice for midday resting; otherwise a loafing area is selected. Favored sites are wet, grassy meadows of sedges, spike-rush, and other short-statured marsh plants. Lacking these, the cranes readily accept cultivated substitutes such as alfalfa and bermuda grass fields, giving the erroneous impression that they feed in pastures. Sacaton grass bottoms and fallow or abandoned fields are also used, and loafing-area requirements are not as specific as those for roosting sites or feeding fields. As with roosting sites, areas subject to human interference are avoided.

Almost all cranes in Arizona feed in cultivated grainfields. Native grasslands and other natural habitats are now infrequently visited, although the seed heads of wild grasses must have been a principal food source prior to large-scale agriculture (Baird 1859; Phillips et al. 1964). Corn is the most preferred food, followed in order by milo maize, newly planted winter wheat, oats, and lettuce (Perkins and Brown 1981). Cranes seen in cotton-fields and in truck crops are thought to be in the process of regrouping after being disturbed rather than feeding.

The desire for open landscapes is again manifested in fields chosen for feeding. Harvested, trampled, and disc-harrowed fields are preferred to standing crops. Distance is another important factor, as the cranes rarely fly more than ten miles from their nighttime roosts to feed. The distance is usually much less, and once a field is selected, the cranes use the same flight path each day. A particular field might be used for a day or two or for up to three and a half months. The first flock to locate or return to a feeding field often makes the selection for subsequent arrivals. Cranes are attracted to fields containing others of their kind and frequently pass over identical but unoccupied fields in favor of those where other cranes are feeding.

LIFE HISTORY

Cranes wintering in Sulphur Springs Valley are a mixture of the Lesser subspecies that nests in the arctic tundra of eastern Siberia, northern Alaska, and Canada, and the Rocky Mountain population of Greater Sand-hills that nests in the Intermountain West. The nesting range of the latter population includes northwest Colorado, northeast Utah, western Wyoming, east-central Idaho, and west-central Montana (Fig. 10.4). This population is the largest of four subpopulations of Greater Sandhills and shares a sympatric range with the Rocky Mountain population of Canada Goose (*Branta canadensis moffitti*). Few if any of the cranes wintering in Arizona belong to the poorly defined Canadian race (*G. c. rowani*) that nests in the muskeg marshlands of the Canadian taiga (Walkinshaw 1965a; Aldrich 1979).

Elko County in northeast Nevada is the principal source of the Greater Sandhill Cranes that winter along the Lower Colorado and Gila rivers (Drewien et al. 1976). Cranes nesting in northwest Utah and on the Duck Valley Indian Reservation, Nevada-Idaho, may also contribute to the Lower Colorado River Valley population (Fig. 10.5).

Sandhill Cranes do not normally form pair bonds until after their third year, and some birds do not pair until much later if at all (Johnsgard 1983). Courtship and initial mate selection begin on the wintering range and intensify during spring migration; most adults that are paired have selected

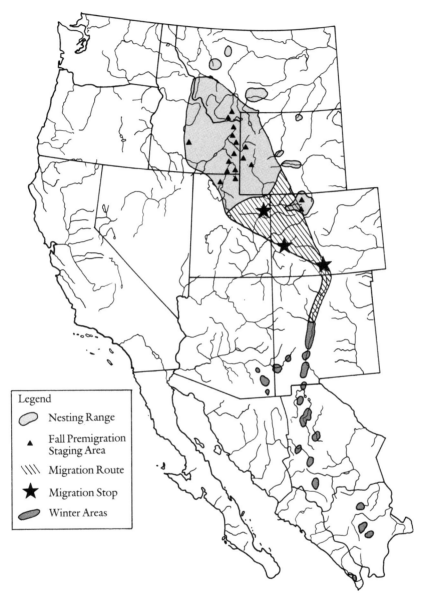

Fig. 10.4. Distribution of the Rocky Mountain population of Greater Sandhill Cranes (adapted from Drewien and Bizeau 1974; Wrakestraw et al. 1983).

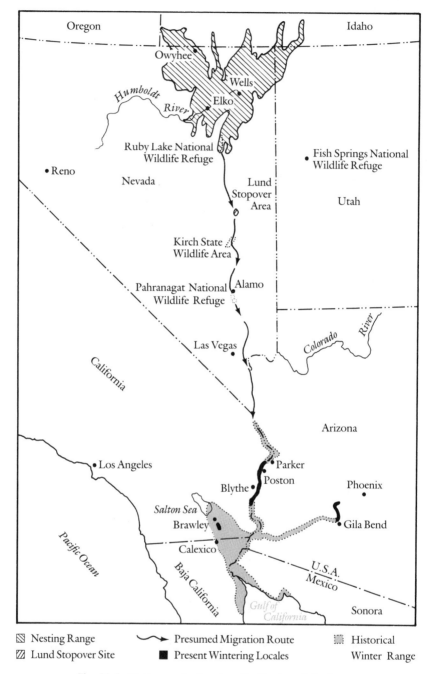

Oregon   Idaho

Owyhee

Wells

Elko

Humboldt River

Ruby Lake National
Wildlife Refuge

Fish Springs National
Wildlife Refuge

• Reno

Nevada

Lund
Stopover
Area

Utah

Kirch State
Wildlife Area

Pahranagat National
Wildlife Refuge

Alamo

Las Vegas

Colorado River

California

Arizona

• Los Angeles

Parker

Poston

Blythe •

Phoenix
•

Salton Sea

Brawley

Gila Bend

Calexico

U.S.A.
Mexico

Pacific Ocean

Baja California

Gulf of
California

Sonora

⬚ Nesting Range   ⟿ Presumed Migration Route   ⬚ Historical

⬚ Lund Stopover Site   ■ Present Wintering Locales   Winter Range

*Fig. 10.5. Nesting and wintering distribution of the Lower
Colorado River population of Greater Sandhill Cranes.*

mates by the time of their arrival on the nesting range. Courtship rituals include vertical head posturing and unison-call ceremonies accompanied by exaggerated strutting displays and ritual dancing (Fig. 10.6). Copulation takes place only after a nesting territory is located and successfully established, a process that may take several years. Once paired, the cranes are believed to remain mated until the death of one of the partners.

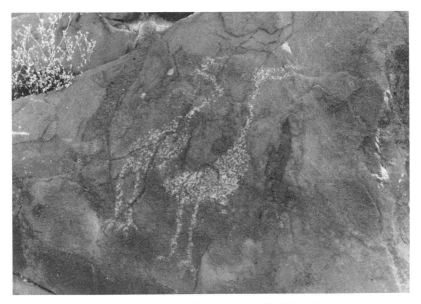

Fig. 10.6. Pictograph along the lower Gila River of two Sandhill Cranes apparently unison calling.

A pair's nesting territory may range in size from 3 to 160 acres, but is more commonly about 40 to 90 acres (Walkinshaw 1965b, 1973). The nest is usually a raised mound of vegetation within a marsh (Fig. 10.7), although some nests may be on dunes or dry ground. Two oval eggs, laid two to three days apart, are the normal clutch. The eggs are buff to olive colored, with brown, purplish spots, and measure 2.4 by 3.8 inches. The nights are chilly and coyotes and other predators are adept egg stealers, so both parents attend and incubate the eggs. Unlike doves and some other birds, in which the male incubates only during the day, either crane parent may sit on the nest at night (Walkinshaw 1965a). Incubation takes twenty-eight to thirty-two days (Lewis et al. 1977).

Fig. 10.7. Nest of Greater Sandhill Crane,
Gray's Lake, Idaho. Photo by Elwood Bizeau.

The "colts," as the young are called, usually hatch a day apart with one bigger (and stronger) than the other. After the precocial youngster eats an initial meal of its own eggshells broken apart by the parents, it follows the adults about. Both parents take the young on foraging trips, where they feed almost entirely on insects (Mullins and Bizeau 1978; Reinecke and Krapu 1979). Either or both parents defend the young, and except when feeding or incubating, the male is watchful of danger and "stands guard." Probably for this reason, once initiated, nesting success can be as high as 78 percent. Should the clutch be destroyed, renesting is not unusual (Drewien 1973).

After three months the colts are strong enough flyers to accompany their parents on forays to grainfields. By late August, aggregations of feeding flocks have gathered in valley staging areas in preparation for the trek south. Members of the Rocky Mountain population follow well-defined flyways into south-central Colorado, with large numbers of birds showing up in the San Luis Valley by mid-September. For the next month almost the entire population of these sixteen thousand or more Rocky Mountain Greaters concentrates in the area of Monte Vista National Wildlife Refuge before proceeding to winter in the Rio Grande, Animas, and Uvas valleys of New Mexico; Lake Babícora and other playa lakes in Chihuahua and Durango, Mexico; and Sulphur Springs Valley, Arizona.

The Lower Colorado River Valley population congregates in premigratory staging areas in Ruby and Lamoille valleys before passing through Lund (White Pine County), Nevada, and Pahranagat National Wildlife Refuge on their way to the Lower Colorado River (Drewien et al. 1976).

The first birds arrive in Arizona between the last weeks of September and the middle of October (Perkins and Brown 1981). Although all of the Lower Colorado River population has usually arrived by November 15, cranes in Sulphur Springs Valley continue to increase through the first week of January. Numbers then decline through early to mid-February before increasing again in late February or early March (Perkins and Brown 1981). Observations of color-marked cranes indicate that these changes in population numbers result from population shifts between Arizona and New Mexico and birds migrating to and from Mexico (Drewien and Bizeau 1974). Cranes along the lower Gila and Colorado rivers may move their wintering locales as food and roost conditions warrant. There has been a trend for birds to shift from the Colorado Indian Reservation to Cibola National Wildlife Refuge.

All cranes wintering in Arizona depart by mid-March. Most of the Rocky Mountain population again stops over at Monte Vista and Alamosa National Wildlife Refuges, or other areas in the San Luis Valley before returning to their respective nesting areas. March also sees almost the entire Lower Colorado River population arriving at their stopover in the wet meadows and irrigated playa south of Lund before traveling on to northeast Nevada in late March and early April. Cranes appear to have a strong fidelity to their nesting areas and return to the same site year after year even though suitable nesting territories may be in short supply. Sandhills are slow to pioneer new or former nesting ranges.

MANAGEMENT HISTORY

Sandhill Cranes are known to have formerly nested in Arizona at Mormon Lake and in the White Mountains on the Fort Apache Indian Reservation (Mearns 1890; Nelson 1885 cited in Bailey 1928). These nesting populations were eliminated during the settlement period. By 1900 the only cranes in Arizona away from the Lower Colorado and Gila rivers were incidental migrants and a few Greaters wintering along the San Pedro River (Slonaker 1912; Swarth 1914; Phillips et al. 1964). Even along the Lower Colorado River, where Coues (1874) found cranes numerous in the 1860s, few birds wintered in Arizona after the turn of the century. Most of the cranes were then continuing further south to the Colorado Delta region of Sonora (Battye 1909) and Baja California, Mexico (Price 1899; Stone 1905; Lumholtz 1912; Leopold 1949). Some of these birds may have then been members of the Rocky Mountain population, for Sheldon (1979) observed processions of cranes heading northeast over the Pinacate region on the Arizona-Sonora border in March 1915.

Although nominally protected by closed seasons in the United States since 1912, crane populations in North America continued to decline through the settlement years and the drought-stricken 1930s. By the early 1940s the Rocky Mountain population of Greaters was estimated to number fewer than two hundred birds (Walkinshaw 1949), and the Lower Colorado population was all but eliminated. Their low recruitment rate prevented the cranes from rapidly responding to improved conditions. Unlike the more prolific waterfowl, North American cranes did not increase in numbers until the 1950s (Drewien and Bizeau 1974).

By this time cranes were no longer using the Colorado Delta, the last reported sightings in Baja California Norte being in 1953 (Littlefield 1973; D. Brown et al. 1983). Presumably, the remnants of this population were the cranes that wintered farther north on the Colorado River Indian Reservation, where approximately 210 were censused in 1961 (Phillips et al. 1964). These birds and the small flock wintering between Arlington and Gila Bend were then the only cranes wintering in Arizona.

Growing numbers of cranes wintering in New Mexico valleys, combined with an expansion of irrigated small-grain crops, induced small numbers of wintering birds to pioneer the Willcox area in the mid-1960s. Willcox Playa provided ideal roosting conditions, short-stopping birds that formerly wintered in Chihuahua, Mexico. Cranes steadily increased, and by 1970 approximately 850 sandhills were wintering in Sulphur Springs Valley. The population wintering along the Lower Colorado River had meanwhile also grown to an estimated 850 birds (Lewis et al. 1977).

Both wintering populations increased dramatically through the 1970s (Tables 10.1, 10.2). Some depredation complaints from farmers were received, and the population in Sulphur Springs Valley had grown to a number that limited hunting appeared feasible. However, decreasing groundwater threatened to reduce irrigated croplands in the Sulphur

TABLE 10.1

Sandhill Crane Counts
in Sulphur Springs Valley, Arizona, 1970–86

Year	Number of Cranes
1970	850
1978	5,706
1979	5,746
1980	8,622
1981	4,327
1982	4,338
1983	5,635
1984	8,548
1985	8,347
1986	11,516

NOTE: The censused area includes Willcox Playa, Bonita, and Whitewater Draw

TABLE 10.2

Wintering and Migration Counts of the Lower Colorado River Population
of Sandhill Cranes, 1961–85

Year	Location	Number of Cranes
1961	Poston, Arizona	210
1968	Poston, Arizona	500
1970	Poston, lower Gila River, Arizona	850 (estimate)
1973	Lund, Nevada	1,003
1973	Poston, Arizona	1,100
1976	Poston, Cibola Nat. Wildlife Refuge, Arizona	1,850
1978–79	All known wintering areas	1,601
1979–80	All known wintering areas	1,681
1980–81	All known wintering areas	1,807
1982–83	All known wintering areas	1,510
1984–85	All known wintering areas	1,690

SOURCE: D. Brown et al. 1983; Smith 1984

TABLE 10.3
Sandhill Crane Hunt Information
in Arizona, 1981–85

Year	Permits	Hunters Afield		Hunter Days
		Total	Successful	
1981[a]	100	55	27	119
1982[b]	100	55	41	95
1983[b]	100	77	41	154
1984[c]	104	72	53	110
1985[d]	150		56	

NOTE: Sex could not be ascertained for all birds, as some were
eviscerated.
[a] Four-day season (two weekends)
[b] Three-consecutive-day season
[c] Two two-day seasons
[d] Two three-day seasons

Springs Valley and it was thought that modifications of the Lower Colorado River channel might limit the recent population gains there. A study on the status of the Sandhill Crane in Arizona was therefore initiated in 1978.

The investigation determined that the threats to cranes, though real, were not imminent (Perkins and Brown 1981). Depredations in the Willcox area were alleviated by a shift from winter wheat to corn and other late-harvested grains. The most important information gathered was the identification of crane needs in Arizona. This knowledge and the acquisition of Willcox Wildlife Area in 1977 enabled suitable roosting habitat to be provided in dry years by pumping water into Crane Lake and closing the area to entry. It was also determined that limited hunting of the cranes wintering in Sulphur Springs Valley would have little effect on the Rocky Mountain population as this population was now estimated to number more than 16,000. When the number of Lesser Sandhills was included, more than 300,000 cranes were present (Lewis et al. 1977).

An experimental hunt was authorized in 1981, with a limit of two hundred permits and a season of no more than four days. A November season was prescribed to minimize the number of later-arriving Greaters and any foster-reared Whooping Cranes (*Grus americana*) that might accompany them. At least one of these spectacular birds had visited Sulphur Springs

		Cranes Harvested					
Total Cranes	Cranes per Hunter	Adults	Juveniles	Juveniles (%)	Males	Females	Males (%)
42	0.76	39	3	7	13	16	45
73	1.33	63	9	12.5	21	33	39
55	0.71	48	7	13	19	25	43
69	0.96	63	6	9	43	20	65
92		83	8	9	37	34	52
66	0.94			10.2			49

Valley in January 1981 (Perkins and Brown 1981). The bag limit was set at two cranes per season, all hunters had to check in and out of the hunt area, and Willcox Playa (the most important roosting site) was closed to hunting. Although the first two hunts were protested by the Animal Defense Council, an annual crane season became standardized in 1985.

Results of the first five hunts are shown in Table 10.3. No Whooping Cranes were present during any of the seasons, and the numbers of cranes using Sulphur Springs Valley appeared to be little affected (Table 10.1). Arizona crane hunters took fewer than one hundred birds each year—less than 1 percent of the state's wintering population.

POPULATION DYNAMICS

Sandhill Crane populations need to be carefully monitored because of their low annual recruitment rate (between 7 and 16 percent) (Table 10.3). Winter populations with less than 10 percent juveniles are considered to be static or declining; winter populations having more are thought to be expanding (Buller 1976; Drewien and Bizeau 1974). The Lower Colorado River population is censused annually either on its wintering range in Arizona and California or at its spring stopover near Lund, Nevada. The Rocky

Mountain Greater population, along with other races, is censused each winter in Arizona and New Mexico; the number of cranes wintering in Chihuahua and Durango is periodically estimated from aerial counts. These surveys are supplemented by spring counts in San Luis Valley at Monte Vista and Alamosa National Wildlife Refuges.

Hunted populations wintering in southwest New Mexico and southeast Arizona are conservatively managed to protect the less-numerous Rocky Mountain population of Greaters that is mixed in with the more numerous Lessers. Estimates place the percentage of Greaters at Willcox between 20 and 40, with the remaining birds being Lessers and possibly a few Canadians (Perkins and Brown 1981).

Measurements of hunter-killed birds at Willcox indicate only two distinct size groups of cranes (Smith 1984). Weight data showed an 11–14 pound group that approximates the weights of Greaters and a smaller 6–9 pound cohort that spans the weights of Lessers (Fig. 10.8). These weights, in conjunction with measurement data, indicate that about 60 percent of the crane harvest in mid-November is Greaters, and that the Canadian race, if present, occurs either in insignificant numbers or is indistinguishable from Greaters (see also Tacha 1981). The overall sex ratio of birds taken to date is about 1:1 (Table 10.3).

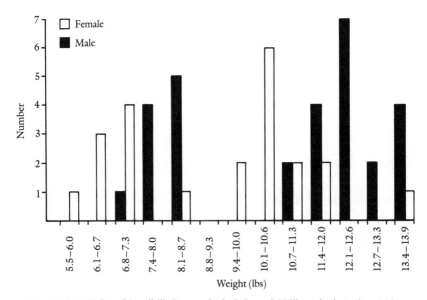

Fig. 10.8. Weights of Sandhill Cranes checked through Willcox check station, 1984.

Mortality from factors other than hunting are poorly known. Some wintering cranes have collided with powerlines, but such losses and those from predation are considered small (Walkinshaw 1956; Perkins and Brown 1981). In October 1980 an outbreak of Type C botulism (*Clostridium botulinum*) occurred, and 127 dead cranes were subsequently found on Willcox Playa—approximately 10 percent of the population then present. Harassment was successful in moving the main roost to unaffected ponds north of Willcox Playa and, whether because of this effort or colder temperatures, no sick birds were observed after November 15. The initial ingested toxin source was not determined. Such die-offs of cranes from botulism are unusual. The only other reports are one from Durango, Mexico (Nelson 1927), and one near Houston, Texas (Perkins and Brown 1981).

THE REWARDS OF CRANE WATCHING

Standing alone in the predawn blackness, I was overtaken by doubt and apprehension. Perhaps the cranes would not come. My early morning vigil would be for nothing. I stared toward Willcox Playa and where the big birds ought to be roosting.

Low, dark clouds obscured an earlier starlit sky. Lightning flashes periodically illuminated the Pinaleño Mountains to the north. Whatever thunder accompanied the approaching storm was too far off to hear. The incoming front had alleviated the bone-chilling cold so typical of the Sulphur Springs Valley floor in winter; would the change in weather affect the movement patterns of the cranes? Only time would tell. It was now five-thirty; the cranes would not be leaving their roosts until seven o'clock.

The scouting had been done, the feeding fields located. The cranes had used this same field only yesterday. Surely they would come.

The key to crane finding is knowing where they roost. Once a flock's nighttime refuge has been located, the birds can be intercepted on their early morning feeding foray. Without a suitable roost, the most attractive cornfield will remain empty. If cranes are feeding in an area, you can be assured that their roost is within a dozen miles.

To find these nighttime refugia, one must follow the cranes home after their evening meal. Locating the exact site may take more than a day: the big birds do not relinquish their secrets easily and may stage at a secondary site before continuing on to their main roost after dark.

The moon had set. At last a faint, burnt orange haze was visible in the east. A cold breeze stung my face, and my feet ached. I envied the cranes' shunt system, which allowed them to cut off the circulation to their legs and feet. How else could these survivors of Oligocene times be able to stand all night in two inches of near-freezing water?

Coyotes wailed, announcing the coming dawn. Flocks of ducks, resembling distant swarms of insects, were returning from the grainfields. Mallards and pintails predominated, their quacks and peeps mingling with the swishing whistle of wings as they passed overhead. Soon these winter visitors would alight on the shallow waters of the playa to spend the day secure from disturbance. It was six-thirty.

The gathering light activated the dawn chorus of the cranes, a gathering crescendo of throaty creaks, gurgles, and grating trumpets unique to the species. Then, as the din reached pandemonium proportions, whole flocks of the birds began taking to the air. Some of the aggregations were large—forty or fifty birds and more; others were family groups of three or four. Soon the squadrons were rising from the lake, calling incessantly as they wheeled and formed ragged chevrons that lined the horizon. There must be at least eight thousand in all. Many were coming my way.

The first formation was approaching. Their large size and light coloration suggested Greaters. More birds were lined out behind them, stacked up in waves like a great, raucous flight of prehistoric creatures winging off on some sinister mission. I lay down and hoped their sharp eyes would not spot me beneath my burlap blanket.

Seconds ticked by. If the cranes were still coming, they were now silent. I lay motionless in the cold and waited. Then I heard the *swish swish* of their huge wings overhead. I turned the burlap back and kneeled up. The giant birds were only thirty yards above me. I could see little balls of mud clinging to their feet and the red caps of the adults. A look of alarm was in their eyes as they flared and backstroked to gain altitude. There were twenty-seven cranes in that flock and more coming.

The flight was now at its height. Some of the cranes spied me, and the clamor of their alarm calls filled the air as the big birds fought their way to safer heights. Others methodically continued on their way, seemingly oblivious to my presence. The horizon, the sky overhead, the very atmosphere around me, was filled with cranes. The cold was forgotten in this avian celebration on the grandest of scales. I noted the time; it was 8:07 A.M.

PART VI
Pigeons and Doves

A widely dispersed family with primary residency in the tropics, pigeons and doves extend northward into the temperate regions of North America and Eurasia. As is to be expected in Arizona, a state with a large Neotropical region, the family is well represented. Included are three game birds—the Band-tailed Pigeon, White-winged Dove, and Mourning Dove—as well as the smaller Inca Dove (*Scardafella inca*) and Ground Dove (*Columbigallina passerina*). There is also at least one report of a Red-billed Pigeon (*Columba flavirostris*) (Tinkham 1942), and the White-tipped Dove (*Leptotila verreauxi*) can someday be expected to stray into Arizona from Sonora.

Columbids characteristically present subdued sexual dimorphism and maintain pair bonds through the nesting season. Both sexes assist in nest building and incubation, each partner having clearly specified duty shifts on the nest. Brooding and feeding of the altricial squabs is also shared, and the bond between the pair appears stronger than that between the female and young. Parental investment is high; clutch size is small and multiple broods may be produced each season. Arizona's pigeons and doves are for the most part migratory, with strong affinities to nesting areas and well-.defined wintering regions.

A gradual expansion of nesting populations into areas having only seasonally available food sources appears to have been the evolutionary force favoring migration strategies for most columbids. In contrast to northern migrants such as ducks and geese, the nesting and wintering range of columbids is commonly continuous with wintering populations sympatric with resident populations. Although the winter range of northern populations of columbids may be shared with local birds, banding data show little if any genetic interchange between the two populations, which are discrete and recognizable as races (e.g., Saunders 1968).

PAUL BOSMAN

CHAPTER 11

Band-tailed Pigeon

The usual introduction to bandtails is the clapping of wings as one bird after another flushes from a pine snag to shatter the autumn stillness. The birds make no cry of alarm, and except for their uniform plumage, remote location, and general wariness, they could be mistaken for domestic pigeons. The flock may contain a half dozen to a hundred or more birds. Yet many Arizonans are not even aware that Band-tailed Pigeons inhabit the state.

Arizona bandtails are of the Interior race *Columba fasciata fasciata*, which is paler and smaller than the *C.f. monilis* of the Pacific Coast states. Interior adults average just under 12 ounces with the males about 0.8 ounces heavier than the females (Dunning 1984). Both sexes have an overall blue-gray appearance, giving them the colloquial name of "blue rocks." It is only on close inspection that one notices the male's rosier breast and more pronounced iridescence on the nape; otherwise the sexes are similar. Adults in autumn can be differentiated from young of the year by their chrome yellow bills and feet, a white crescent at the nape of the neck, and a dark gray band across the top of the tail that gives the bird its name. First-autumn birds are also a more overall gray color, and the neck collar is faint or absent; the yellow colors of the feet are more subdued, and there is little or no iridescence.

Although plumage characters are distinct enough to allow experienced workers to classify the sex of adults, birds of the year must usually be sexed by cloacal examination (Braun et al. 1975). Juveniles possess light-tipped wing coverts and primary replacement patterns similar to those of Mourning and White-winged doves, and juvenile birds in the hand are easily identified (Silovsky et al. 1968; Fitzhugh 1974).

DISTRIBUTION

The Interior race of Band-tailed Pigeons has its ecological origin in the Sierra Madre Occidental of Mexico. The pigeons nest in all of the wooded mountains of Sonora and Chihuahua, northward through Arizona, New Mexico, west Texas, Colorado, Utah, and into central Wyoming (Fig. 11.1). Their occurrence in southern and central Nevada is scattered and irregular.

The northern boundary of the wintering range is inconsistent and apparently related to the availability of food. Pigeons remain through some winters in extreme southeast Arizona, extreme southwest New Mexico, southwest Texas, and in Chihuahua and Sonora (Phillips et al. 1964; Wauer 1973; Braun et al. 1975). Band recoveries show that most of the Interior population spends the late winter and early spring months in the high barrancas along the Durango-Sinaloa border.

Bandtails are birds of the mountains. Only between late spring and late summer do they leave their wooded fastness of pines and oaks to feed in grainfields or on the buds and fruits of early-ripening deciduous trees. Their regular distribution in Arizona is from 4,500 to 9,100 feet elevation, with most birds occurring between 5,500 and 7,500 feet. Only in exceptional years of scrub-oak acorn abundance do autumn-foraging bandtails descend to the lower limits of chaparral between 3,500 and 4,500 feet.

Pines and oaks are the mainstay of bandtails in both summer and winter. Accordingly, the bird's primary distribution in Arizona is in the central and southeastern portions of the state (Fig. 11.2). Some pigeons can almost always be found nesting in the Chiricahua, Pinaleño, Huachuca, Santa Rita, Catalina, Galiuro, Big Lue, Pinal, Sierra Ancha, Mazatzal, and Bradshaw mountains, on Mingus Mountain, and in the Blue country. Westward and northward, with the disappearance of Mexican pines and evergreen oaks, the distribution of bandtails becomes increasingly irregular. Populations are unpredictable in the White Mountains, on the Mogollon Rim, and on the North Kaibab Plateau where Gambel oak is a boom-or-bust

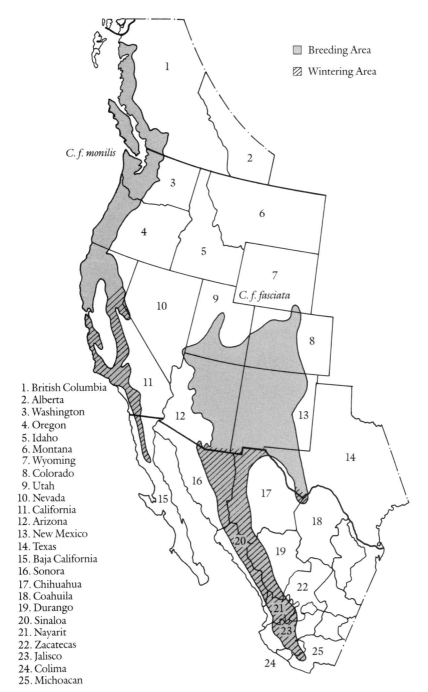

Breeding Area

Wintering Area

C. f. monilis

C. f. fasciata

1. British Columbia
2. Alberta
3. Washington
4. Oregon
5. Idaho
6. Montana
7. Wyoming
8. Colorado
9. Utah
10. Nevada
11. California
12. Arizona
13. New Mexico
14. Texas
15. Baja California
16. Sonora
17. Chihuahua
18. Coahuila
19. Durango
20. Sinaloa
21. Nayarit
22. Zacatecas
23. Jalisco
24. Colima
25. Michoacan

Fig. 11.1. Breeding and wintering distribution of the Coastal and Interior races of Band-tailed Pigeons (from Braun et al. 1975).

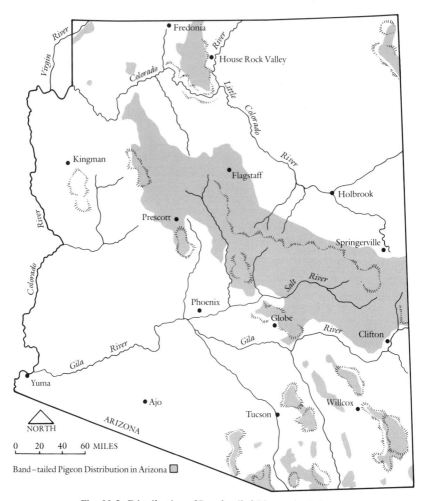

Fig. 11.2. Distribution of Band-tailed Pigeons in Arizona.

supplier of mast. Even in "good" years the distribution of bandtails is erratic and unpredictable, and an area that hosted hundreds of birds one year may be devoid of pigeons the next.

Only an occasional bandtail is seen in the Baboquivari Mountains, where Mexican Piñons (*Pinus cembroides*) are the only pines, and in the Hualapai Mountains, where evergreen oaks are practically absent. Bandtails are also irregular or scarce in the Lukachukai and Chuska mountains, in the Virgin Mountains on the Arizona Strip, and in the Cerbat Mountains.

HABITAT

Most Arizona bandtails nest within montane conifer forest communities of Douglas fir, white fir, and ponderosa pine, or in Mexican pine-oak communities within Madrean evergreen woodland (Fig. 11.3). Gambel oak and Rocky Mountain pinyon are important feed trees within the montane forest, and the principal components of the more southern pine-oak communities are Chihuahua pine, Apache pine, Mexican piñon, silverleaf oak, net-leaf oak, Arizona white oak, Emory oak, madroño, and alligator-bark juniper. The lower and more open encinal and lower-statured chaparral communities provide only marginal nesting habitat but may be frequented during periods of mast availability.

Fig. 11.3. Summer habitat of Arizona bandtails on the San Carlos Indian Reservation. The trees are ponderosa pine, Emory oak, alligator-bark juniper, and Arizona oak.

In northern areas, above 34° north latitude, bandtails nest in low numbers in subalpine forests of Engelmann spruce and subalpine fir up to 11,000 feet elevation. These birds feed on elderberries and other berry-producing shrubs in addition to conifer seeds. Depending on food availability, the birds will forage downslope in orchards or pinyon-juniper woodlands to as low as 5,000 feet elevation. Cottonwoods and other riparian deciduous trees are often used as perching sites particularly when adjacent to barley fields or other cultivated foods. Occasionally, bandtails are observed feeding on the fruits of Mexican elderberries, mulberries, and other plants within semidesert grassland and even Sonoran desertscrub (Neff 1947; Fitzhugh 1970).

LIFE HISTORY

Interior bandtails begin to leave their Mexican wintering locales sometime in March. The trip north is apparently direct, as some pigeons usually arrive in Utah, Colorado, Arizona, and New Mexico by the end of the month. Bandtails continue to arrive through April, coincident with the budding and flowering of deciduous trees and shrubs, and almost all the birds that are going to, show up by mid-May. The birds have a strong fidelity to their hatching and former nesting sites but may wander considerably as they seek out food sources prior to nesting (Braun et al. 1975).

If food supplies are adequate, courtship activities now commence. Some birds may even be paired at the time of their arrival. The males establish conspicuous perch sites and commence their soft, two-noted cooing that vaguely sounds like the hoots of a Great-horned Owl. Cooing, accompanied by ritual display flights that signify the onset of the breeding season, usually begin in April and can continue into September. As with doves and other columbids, the courtship flights are most often seen in the morning and early evening and consist of short arcing flaps and glides accompanied by soft chirping calls.

On the basis of call-counts and crop-gland activity, Fitzhugh (1974) determined that the bandtail breeding season in the Catalina Mountains north of Tucson peaked in mid- to late May and continued through mid-September. Two initial peaks of calling activity were noted, one in late May and another in mid-June, followed by secondary peaks thirty-nine to fifty-one days later. Fitzhugh surmised that the first initial peak was the major breeding period for second-year and older adults and that the second was a measurement of the breeding activity of the previous year's juveniles. Subsequent peaks were thought to precede second nesting attempts.

Band-tailed Pigeon nests are flimsy platforms of twigs constructed in the branches of any tree having suitable foliage. Nests have been found in Douglas fir, white fir, and in several species of oak and pine, and are usually eighteen to thirty-five feet above the ground. Both sexes participate in nest construction, which may take up to six days. Nests may be concentrated in the more productive habitats, but pigeons usually exhibit some territorial aggression, and colonial nest sites are unusual (Neff 1947).

The normal clutch is one glossy white egg, or occasionally two, measuring about 1.1 by 1.5 inches. Although nesting has been reported as early as April 2 and as late as October 25, most nesting in Arizona takes place between the end of May and the middle of September (Neff 1947; Fitzhugh 1974). The initiation and continuation of nesting attempts depend on food availability (Gutiérrez 1973). In most years many pairs nest twice, and in some years even a third time. However, other pairs nest only once, and some may not nest at all in some years.

After an incubation period of eighteen to twenty-two days (Neff 1947), a chick, or squab, is hatched. At this time both parent birds have developed "milk glands," subcutaneous glands lining the crop that secrete a thick, highly nutritious curd substance. This "pigeon milk," regurgitated with the parents' crop contents, suffices as the diet of the youngster for the twenty-four to twenty-six days required for brooding and fledging (Zeigler 1971; Gutiérrez 1973; Fitzhugh 1974).

Fitzhugh (1974) found a high degree of correlation between peaks of calling activity and subsequent crop-gland development. Males retained active crop glands longer than their mates, and Fitzhugh reasoned that the males were still feeding fledged young while the female was physiologically preparing for the next nesting. About fifty days are required to complete a nesting cycle from courtship through fledging (Zeigler 1971; Fitzhugh 1974).

Throughout the summer, pigeons feed on mulberries, elderberries, currants, other fruits and berries, pine seed, Emory oak and other acorns, and where available, cultivated grains. Like male doves, male bandtails leave their roost trees near the nest at first light when the female is still on the nest. After gorging on whatever food is in season, the birds visit water and/or a salt lick or other mineral site before returning to relieve the incubating female or to feed the squab(s). The female now feeds and waters, having incubated the egg(s) or brooded the young through the night and early morning hours. Midmorning finds most females and fledged juveniles actively feeding or visiting water tanks and mineral sites. The strong tendency for this species to supplement its diet with salt and to drink at mineral springs is unique among Arizona birds.

The middle of the day is often spent in small flocks, the pigeons often perched in a dead tree or other sites where vision is unobstructed and rapid escape is unhindered. Bandtails are great flyers and in their daily activities may travel up to twenty miles, with changes in elevation of more than two thousand feet. Flight is swift, and the pigeons pass through mountain saddles and dive down slopes with a great rushing noise. Even nesting birds display a flocking tendency, and the birds often travel and feed in groups of a half dozen to twenty or so. After a second feeding foray in the late afternoon, both parents return to the nesting area to roost. The female returns to the nest before dark; her monogamous mate perches in a nearby tree.

By September the feeding flights become somewhat nomadic as the bandtails search out mast crops and build up food reserves prior to migration. Gambel oak acorns, Rocky Mountain pinyon nuts, mountain elderberries, and cultivated grains and fruit are the preferred food items in the fall. Most pigeons depart by the end of September if foods are in short supply, as they almost always do in such high, northern locales as the North Kaibab and White Mountains. Few birds remain past mid-October even in central and southeastern Arizona, where adequate food supplies may still be present and the weather is mild. Housekeeping chores over, the birds head for Mexico.

Postnesting migrants are augmented by Colorado and New Mexico birds passing through west-central New Mexico and east-central Arizona, as they proceed southward through southeast Arizona into Mexico along both sides of the Sonora-Chihuahua border. Unlike the rapid northerly movement in spring, the fall migration is less hurried, and large flocks may linger for several days in food-rich areas. A few birds may spend the winter in the Huachucas or other southern Arizona mountains.

Once in Mexico, bandtails follow the Sierra Madre Occidental and its outliers southward, with most Arizona band recoveries occurring on the west, or Sonora, side (Fig. 11.4). Movement of Interior pigeons westward to Pacific coast states, while documented, are unusual.

By December Arizona's bandtails are concentrated in the high barrancas along the Durango-Sinaloa border. If oak and other high-elevation mast crops are depleted, the birds will forage at lower elevations on tropical fruits within adjacent Sinaloan deciduous forest and thornscrub before heading north again in spring (Braun 1973). Some bandtails, however, may occasionally stay on the wintering range, as band recoveries have shown that in some years birds that formerly summered in Arizona were taken in summer in Mexico. Whether these birds remained in Mexico because of an abundance of food supplies there or returned south after finding conditions unsuitable on the nesting range is unknown. It is known that bandtails are scarce or absent in Arizona in those years that foods are in short supply.

Fig. 11.4. Band-tailed Pigeon habitat of pines and oaks in western Durango. Such habitats are the wintering locales for Arizona's bandtails and also have their own nesting populations.

MANAGEMENT HISTORY

Band-tailed Pigeons are not mentioned in Arizona's territorial game codes or in the first state game code. The species was first recognized as a game bird in the Migratory Bird Law of 1913, and its totally protected status was retained in the more substantial Migratory Bird Treaty Act of 1918. Despite the bandtail's sporting qualities and attractiveness as a game bird, the season remained closed in Arizona, except that after 1930, permits could be obtained to take depredating pigeons between May 15 and July 31. Complaints that pigeons damaged fruit orchards and other crops continued, and in 1932 a fifteen-day season with a ten-bird bag limit was authorized for Arizona and New Mexico, despite the admonishment of New Mexico's foremost biologist, J. Stokely Ligon (1927), that "they do not appear to increase but remain in about the same numbers, an indication that they could not stand an open season in this state [New Mexico]."

Depredation complaints continued to be filed, and permits were issued to the extent that there was almost no closed season on the species (Fitzhugh 1970). After 1940 the season opened on September 16; prior to that time the opening of the regular season had been delayed until sometime in October, November, or even December, after the pigeons had left. Pigeons reportedly continued to increase in numbers (Neff 1947), and in 1944 twelve southwestern counties in Colorado were added to the area opened to hunting. Then, in the late 1940s, reports of depredations and pigeon numbers declined, and the season on the interior population was closed in 1951.

Although interest in the Band-tailed Pigeon as a game bird waned, it did not die. In 1966 the Arizona Game and Fish Department initiated a Band-tailed Pigeon study to determine if the birds were a huntable resource, if the spraying of pesticides in the national forests might be affecting their reproductive potential, and to learn more about their range, life history, and population dynamics. To facilitate band recoveries, an experimental season was opened in 1968. This study generated investigations in the other Four Corners states, and biologists from the region joined to coordinate their efforts. Regional banding goals were established, and the initial season in 1968 in Arizona and New Mexico was followed by seasons in Colorado and Utah in 1970. Crops were examined and classified as active, stimulated, or inactive (Zeigler 1971). All pigeons showing crop-gland development were considered to be potentially raising young.

In the first Arizona Band-tailed Pigeon season since 1950, 1,316 permits were issued, 851 hunters participated, and 2,085 bandtails were harvested. The harvest rate of banded birds in the hunt area was only 2.1 percent, and the population of pigeons was estimated at about one hundred thousand (D. Brown 1969). On the negative side, 81 percent of the adult pigeons exhibited some crop-gland activity, and it was recommended that the following year's season be set two weeks later, to October 11 through 19. Data on Band-tailed Pigeons were meanwhile accumulating. Arizona's pigeon range had been outlined and mapped, sizable banded samples had been obtained by trapping at salt stations, and only a trace quantity of pesticides had been found in ninety-seven pigeons examined.

In 1969 three additional game-management units were added to the area open to hunting. Almost one thousand hunters reported harvesting 2,820 pigeons (Table 11.1), and the estimated percentage of the banded population taken, or harvest level, was 2.4. The population in the expanded hunt area was estimated at about one hundred fifty thousand (D. Brown 1970d).

TABLE 11.1
Band-tailed Pigeon Hunt Information in Arizona 1968–85

Year	Hunters	Days Hunted	Avg. No. of Days Hunted	Harvest	Pigeons Bagged per Hunter Day	Pigeons Bagged per Hunter per Season
1968	851	1,498	1.8	2,085	1.4	2.5
1969	968	1,719	1.8	2,820	1.6	2.9
1970	1,069	1,815	1.7	3,545	1.9	3.3
1971	622	1,076	1.7	782	0.7	1.3
1972	576	968	1.7	453	0.5	0.8
1973	815	1,688	2.1	2,419	1.4	3.0
1974	858	2,039	2.6	3,063	1.5	3.6
1975	860	1,968	2.3	3,469	1.8	4.0
1976	817	1,902	2.3	2,800	1.5	3.4
1977	704	1,666	2.4	1,473	0.9	2.1
1978	594	1,323	2.2	1,439	1.1	2.4
1979	472	1,107	2.3	1,102	1.0	2.3
1980	788	1,794	2.3	2,408	1.3	3.1
1981	911	2,269	2.5	2,082	0.9	2.3
1982	865	2,291	2.6	2,378	1.0	2.8
1983	645	1,781	2.8	1,931	1.1	3.0
1984	736	2,128	2.9	1,139	0.5	1.5
1985	735	2,027	2.8	1,534	0.8	2.1

SOURCE: Mailed questionnaires (not adjusted for reporting bias)

Because only 48 percent of the adults' croplands were inactive, a later season was again recommended. The 1970 season was the most successful yet. Improved trapping techniques allowed for even greater samples of pigeons to be banded (Evans 1972), and the season was opened statewide. Despite the late season dates of October 17–25, a record harvest of 3,545 bandtails was reported.

By 1973 sufficient data were available to justify the continuation of a limited season, provided that the opening date was not before mid-October. Recoveries of pigeons banded in Arizona continued to show an overall first-year recovery rate (harvest level) of only 2.2 percent and an average annual harvest of about two thousand bandtails, considerably more than in any of the other Four Corners states (Braun et al. 1975). The most consistently productive areas were in the east-central portion of the state. With 30 percent of the harvest of the Four Corners states' banded bandtails estimated to be in Mexico, approximately sixty-five hundred birds a year were being removed from the U.S. population (D. Brown 1972d; Braun et al. 1975).

Subsequent seasons have had their ups and downs, but such is the nature of the bird—common one year and scarce the next. Hunters have to accept the fact that the birds' early departure soon after nesting means that the season in some years will not be open until after most of the birds have migrated; opening it earlier would risk shooting parent birds with dependent young. The prudent management strategy is therefore to maximize nesting success by delaying the season until most of the young are fledged.

POPULATION DYNAMICS

There has long been concern that bandtails are prone to overharvest because of their apparent low recruitment rate. The percentage of immatures in the harvest in Arizona and the other Four Corners states between 1968 and 1972 averaged only 23 percent, although this figure varied considerably by location and year. This variation, which is at least partially owing to differential migration of juveniles, confounded any accurate measurement of annual production.

Both daily and seasonal variations in crop-milk cycles have been described (Zeigler 1971), and the significance of the observed stages of glandular development in harvested birds is also difficult to assess. Pigeons have been observed feeding free-flying young, and Zeigler (1971) found that regression of some crop glands was not complete until ten days after the young were fledged. The age of independence of young bandtails is un-known, but under aviary conditions young pigeons were self-sufficient (feeding) at time of fledging (Braun et al. 1975). When all birds with glandu-lar development are considered active nesters, the extent of nesting activity is probably overestimated. The tendency for pigeons that have completed nesting to migrate early also results in some crop-gland activity being re-ported no matter how late the hunting season. It is not surprising, then, that no significant correlation was found between the percentage of imma-tures in the harvest and hunt success, harvest, or the percentage of adults having active crop glands.

The bandtail's relatively low reproductive rate is compensated by low mortality. The mean annual survival rate for pigeons in the Interior popula-tion is 64 percent for adults and 41 percent for juveniles: approximately one-half of the Band-tailed Pigeon population survives from one year to the next.

Band recoveries indicated a first-year harvest rate of less than 3 percent for Arizona and other Interior state bandtails. The mean annual first-year harvest rate of 1.5 percent for adults and 2.2 percent for juveniles is therefore well within the recuperative rate of this nonprolific species. In Arizona the harvest rate for adult females was slightly lower than for adult males (0.95:1.0), and banded juveniles were half again as vulnerable (1.5:1.0) as adults (Braun et al. 1975; D. Brown 1978b).

MOUNTAIN CLAPPERS

The familiarity of the noise registered instantly. The *whap whap whap* made by the flapping wings of a flushing Band-tailed Pigeon is a sound like no other in the forest. Distracted from my search for squirrel sign, I looked up to watch the departing bandtails. True to their habits, they wheeled about in a wide swath to alight on a dead pine snag. From there they cautiously eyed me and awaited my next move. If I were to approach to within a hundred yards, they would again drop from their barren perches and take flight with strong wing strokes slapping the air to gain momentum and speed. I had stumbled into their midday loafing area, and if not har-assed, they would be back tomorrow.

The next morning I selected a vantage point to await the return of the pigeons. The bandtail season would be open in a couple of weeks, and knowing their daily routine would mean birds in the bag. Although it was too late in the day to locate their feeding area, I could, by triangulation and a little luck, find where they had been going to water. Stock tanks and springs near salting grounds are an irresistible draw for bandtail concentrations.

Sure enough. After backtracking several flocks, I noted a focal point beyond a clump of large junipers. There I found a small spring development surrounded by salt blocks. Scattered ponderosas provided cover and roost sites. One old pine with a dead crown was loaded with pigeons waiting to drink. A return visit was definitely in order.

About two weeks later I was back. The sun had been up twenty minutes but the morning chill had not yet been dispelled from the shade of the pines. I had been waiting and shivering for an hour, knowing that only now could any birds be expected. Would they come? The season had opened the previous weekend and someone might have found my spot. Or the pigeons might have left the mountain. I doubted the former. There were no empty shotshells or feathers scattered about. The birds might well have migrated south, however, if their food stores had run out. Pigeons are mast feeders, and at this time of year their diet depends on a relatively few seed-bearing plants.

The first pigeons rocketed in over my shoulder with a great *whoosh*. They surprised me by coming from the downslope side of the mountain; I had expected them to come from above—from a secluded grove of Gambel oaks, their usual October food source. The five birds wheeled and alighted on the pine snag that was now miraculously sprouting bandtails. Where were these pigeons coming from, and what were they feeding on? No matter, I would be ready for the next arrival.

It was a single. The bird was coming from the same direction as the others, but was high up—maybe one hundred fifty yards or more. However, its attitude was such that it would pass directly over me on its descent to the pine snag. The bird was approaching at tremendous speed, and I blocked it out with my barrel when it was fifty yards overhead. I touched off a charge of high-base #6s and kept swinging. Stone dead, the bird's speed and momentum kept it going. It fell out of sight many yards downslope in a thicket of pines. No matter—my dog, Rosie, had seen everything and was on the way. By the time she returned with a mouth full of bandtail, two more birds were coming in.

The speed of these fellows was considerably less. Perhaps for this reason, I misjudged my lead and missed the first shot, getting the bird with my second barrel after it had passed by. The survivor made a place for itself on the snag while its former companion was still tumbling through the pine boughs. The dog was watching the wrong pigeon and I had to throw a rock in the direction the dead one had fallen. It took her almost five minutes to find it, following a trail of copiously shed feathers.

By seven o'clock a limit of five bandtails lay carefully arranged on the litter of pine needles. Marked green iridescence on the head and napes, and wine-colored breasts, showed four of the birds to be adult males. The light buff scallops on the trailing edge of the wing coverts indicated that the fifth pigeon was a bird of the year. It lacked any iridescence and was probably a female, an observation borne out when the bird was cleaned. All of the birds' crops were packed with pinyon nuts.

The hunt over, I sat back to watch the pigeons. Many more birds were now en route and coming through the low saddle behind me. Their great speed as they whistled past was impressive, and I decided that if I were to hunt here again, I would station myself in the saddle . A traveling bandtail moves along at more than sixty miles per hour—a challenging target for any gunner.

No other hunters were in the immediate area, and only the raucous cries of Scrub Jays and the rustlings of an Abert Squirrel interrupted the silence. The snag was tumbling with pigeons waiting to get down to the water. It was time to go.

Rosie caught sight of a large flock of pigeons circling overhead. She looked eager and bewildered. Why were these birds allowed to pass unmolested? And what of all those birds collecting on the dying pine?

Unable to communicate the intricacies of game management and bag limits to Rosie, I got up to leave. This gesture was understood. We were through hunting. Shaking off pine needles and sneezing on the offensive feathers, she happily plod along after me.

CHAPTER 12

White-winged Dove

No bird exemplifies Latin America as much as the White-winged Dove. Its coarse *who cooks for you* call, whether heard in Phoenix, Tucson, or Alamos, Sonora, always conjures up an aura of the Neotropics and a promise of exotic happenings.

The whitewing's hefty size and rounded-off tail give the bird an appearance between that of a dove and a pigeon. Its overall gray plumage, white epaulets on the wings, and white-tipped tail serve to differentiate this species from the more widely distributed Mourning Doves. Unless pressed by gunners, the whitewing's flight also appears slower, less purposeful, and more pigeonlike. On close examination, other distinguishing characters may be noted: a longer beak, an unfeathered, bright blue eye patch, and eyes that range from yellow-orange to orange-red. These accents of color, coupled with the bright red feet of the adults, ornament an otherwise first impression of grays, whites, and browns.

Adult males are especially handsome. Their brownish heads are crowned in reddish purple, as is the nape of the neck. The sides of the neck are iridescent, with flecks of gold, green, and purple. The female is similar but displays less purple and less iridescence. The black ear spot over her jowls is smaller and not as conspicuous, and the blacks, browns, and grays are not as intense. Nonetheless, the sex of some individuals cannot always be ascertained on the basis of plumage alone.

Juveniles, besides being more gray and lacking the adults' iridescence, have brown to hazel eyes and have browner more than red feet. Like the smaller Mourning Dove, juvenile whitewings retain light-tipped primary coverts through the juvenile molt and can be readily separated from adults up to about eighteen to nineteen weeks of age (Fig. 12.1). A rough approximation of hatching dates of juveniles can be determined by back-dating the number of replaced juvenile primaries (Saunders 1944 *in* Cottam and Trefethen 1968). The sex of juveniles cannot be ascertained by external criteria.

Fig. 12.1. Juvenile (top) and adult wings of White-winged Doves. Note the buff-tipped wing coverts on the juvenile wing.

Of the twelve subspecies of White-winged Doves described by Saunders (1968), two are thought to occur in Arizona (Fig. 12.2). The race encountered by most Arizonans is *Zenaidia asiatica mearnsi*—the Western White-winged Dove, a slightly larger and lighter colored race than the Eastern White-winged Dove (*Z. a. asiatica*) found in Texas and northeastern Mexico. Adult *mearnsi* range from 4.5 to more than 8 ounces if the bird has a full crop. The average weight is about 5.5 ounces, the males being only slightly larger than the females (Cottam and Trefethen 1968; Dunning 1984). Although definitive data are lacking, scattered populations of White-

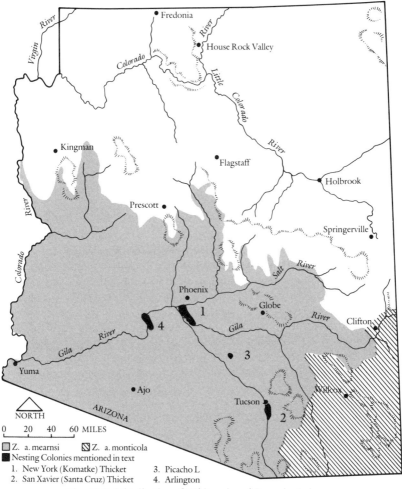

Fig. 12.2. Distribution of White-winged Doves in Arizona.

winged Doves within the Chihuahuan Desert and adjacent semidesert grassland in southeast Arizona appear to be the Mexican Highland subspecies, *Z. a. monticola*. This more sedentary race is described as having a longer wing and tail than *mearnsi*, and a smaller beak (Saunders 1968).

DISTRIBUTION AND HABITAT

The Western White-winged Dove's range in Arizona overlaps the boundaries of the subtropical Sonoran Desert and closely approximates the distribution of the saguaro. Low-density populations also extend into the

Mohave Desert and other warm temperate locations where cultivated grains and other man-supplied foods compensate for the absence of native foods. The occurrence of populations in the Verde Valley and other northern locales is thought to be evidence that White-winged Doves have expanded their range since the advent of human settlement (Gullion et al. 1959; Phillips et al. 1964). Otherwise, the bird's distribution is largely within flying distance of saguaros or other Sonoran Desert plants, with the highest densities in riparian thickets along the Lower Colorado, Gila, and Santa Cruz river drainages (Tinkham 1942; Pulich 1948).

Nesting pairs occur as low as 300 feet elevation along the Lower Colorado River to 4,500 feet or higher in southern Arizona's mountains and canyons. The higher-elevation birds, even when nesting in evergreen oaks or riparian deciduous trees, are usually within flying distance of saguaros or other subtropical food-producing plants. Tinkham (1942) noted that squabs in Florida Canyon in the Santa Rita Mountains were fed saguaro fruit pulp. The occasional pairs of *Z. a. monticola* encountered in southeast Arizona nest in ornamental cypresses and other trees around old homesteads, in residential areas, and along riverbottoms. These low-density populations seem to be nomadic and, unlike their subtropical relatives, do not regularly congregate in grainfields.

Fig. 12.3. White-winged Dove nest.

Fig. 12.4. Colonial nesting habitat of White-winged Doves. Sixty to 266 dove nests per acre have been recorded in these "saltcedar jungles" (Shaw and Jett 1960; Carr 1960).

Nests are usually located in densely branched, well-foliated trees twenty to forty feet high (Fig. 12.3). Paloverdes, ironwoods, mesquites, citrus trees, and introduced saltcedar or tamarisk are, in ascending order, preferred sites. Nesting has also been reported in Goodding willows, hackberries, and saguaros (Neff 1940a; Wigal 1973). Unlike Mourning Doves, white-wings rarely nest in shrubs under seven feet tall and almost never nest on the ground.

Groups of trees with interconnecting branches are especially favored, and dense thickets of mesquite and, more recently, saltcedar may support clumps, or colonies, of nesting whitewings (Fig. 12.4). Whitewings are more prone to nest in the interior of trees and thickets than are Mourning Doves, which commonly nest in the outer branches. Maximum nesting densities are in riverbottom thickets, where mature saltcedars are the choicest nesting locale, followed by mesquite bosques, citrus groves, and Arizona Upland communities within the Sonoran Desert (Neff 1940a; Lawson

Fig. 12.5. Arizona Upland nesting habitat of the White-winged Dove near "Owlheads," north of the Tortolita Mountains, Pinal County. This habitat is capable of supporting up to 0.5 White-winged Dove nests per acre (Carr 1960).

1949c; Shaw and Jett 1960; Carr 1960; Wigal 1973; and Butler 1977). Desert-nesting whitewings are not clumped, nor is nesting concentrated near water (Arnold 1943), nesting pairs being rather uniformly scattered throughout the desert landscape (Fig. 12.5). An increase in water sources reduces the concentration of watering birds but does not increase their overall density.

LIFE HISTORY

The first Arizona whitewings arrive in mid-April. The majority of the birds show up between April 22 and May 8; by mid-May most, if not all, of the migrants have returned, flying high via watercourses (Eicher 1944c). The spring migration, completed in about three weeks, is timed to coincide with the leafing out of the mesquite and the flowering of the saguaro. This synchronization is not accidental. Mesquite, hackberry, and other winter-deciduous trees, now clothed in foliage, are the birds' nest sites, and pollen from saguaro flowers provides a high-energy food for parents and squabs alike (Alcorn et al. 1961). Indeed, the whitewing's life cycle is closely attuned to the leafing, flowering, and fruiting of several Sonoran Desert plants, now including the leafing out of the introduced saltcedar.

Both sexes arrive at about the same time and some pairs may be already mated. Nesting territories are established and advertised almost immediately on arrival, and the same territories are often selected by the same birds year after year. Displaying males flap upward over their domain and then soar on fixed wings in curving, graceful arcs. From fifteen minutes before sunrise to about nine in the morning, and intermittently throughout the day, the males crow their *cook-cook, cook-coo* calls from select perches. These calls—or minor variations, including a shorter, nest-selection call given by the female—are coarse and distinct, and are the single most audible impression of the Sonoran Desert and its residential areas in late May and early June. Unmated and unaccompanied males call at almost twice the rate of mated birds, and the peak of calling activity coincides with the height of the incubation period (Viers 1970). In mesquite and saltcedar thickets the clamor of multiple coos may drown out all other sounds of birdlife.

By May 20 or thereabouts the calling approaches a crescendo, and nest building begins. Although both sexes pick up fragments of dead twigs from mesquite or other desert trees, the crude platform—only slightly more substantial than that of the Mourning Dove—is constructed mostly by the female. The nests are most commonly located in the crotch formed by two major branches in a tree or large shrub nine to twelve feet above the ground (Neff 1940a; Tinkham 1942). Even within the colonies, Arizona birds display some territoriality, and it is usual for a tree to contain more than one nest.

One to three, but most often two, creamy white eggs are laid on alternate days. The eggs are duller and average slightly larger (1.2 by 0.9 inches) than the glossier Mourning Dove eggs. Both sexes share in incubation; the female sits on the nest from midafternoon through midmorning of the following day. The male is on the nest during the heat of the day from approximately seven to ten in the morning through about three-thirty to five in the evening (Tinkham 1942; Eicher 1944d). Fidelity to the nest is stronger in the female than in the male, but both sexes are apt to flush more readily than Mourning Doves, and repeated disturbance can lead to nest desertion.

Incubation requires thirteen to nineteen days, depending on elevation and temperatures, and the first young are hatched around the end of June (Stair 1970). Nestlings usually hatch a day apart, with the result that one is noticeably larger than the other. The chicks, or squabs, are thinly covered with down and are blind and helpless. Fed "pigeon milk," a cheesy secretion formed in the crop glands of both parents, the squabs develop rapidly. Partially digested food and, later, seeds and other whole foods are added to the diet from thirteen to sixteen days after hatching, when the nestlings are ready to fledge. The squabs must be shielded from the heat of the direct sun during the day and brooded at night. Should an intruder arrive, either parent may feign injury and attempt to distract attention from the eggs or squab.

During incubation and squab rearing the parents maintain separate feeding patterns. The male feeds first, leaving its nighttime roost between five-thirty and six in the morning to forage on saguaro pollen and, in early June, on the developing pulp and seeds. Before midmorning he relieves his mate, who then leaves the nest to partake of the same diet. From mid-June through mid-July the birds feed on saguaro seeds and fruit (Tinkham 1942). Other desert foods include ocotillo nectar and seeds, elephant-tree fruit, jojoba nuts, and the seeds of prickle poppy and dove weed; where present, the fruits of the lotebush, or jujube, and organ-pipe cactus are taken (Tinkham 1942; Neff 1942). Most preferred food items are larger than those taken by the earlier-rising Mourning Doves. Cultivated grains are also sought, and visits to wheat, barley, and safflower fields become increasingly common as the summer progresses.

The birds water at least once, and often twice, a day, the males immediately after their morning feeding and in the late afternoon and the females at midday (Eicher 1944c; Stair 1961b). Flights of ten miles or more to water are not uncommon, and only in the most arid regions is water a critical factor in the bird's nesting distribution (Neff 1942). By four-thirty most females are back on the nest, and by seven-thirty to eight the males have returned to a nearby roost to spend the night (Eicher 1944d).

Most young of the first hatch fledge in late June or July; the earlier the hatch, the more successful the year (Lawson 1949c; Stair 1970). Should high-energy foods be abundant, as in cultivated areas, the colonial nesting birds will again increase their calling activity and renest (Viers 1970). There is plenty of opportunity, for the time from initiation of nest construction to fledging requires just a little over a month; birds in cultivated areas have better nesting success than those in the desert. Even in the densest riparian habitats, however, only between 40 and 50 percent of the nestings may be successful and the number of young fledged is only about 0.71 squab per nesting attempt (Tinkham 1942; Carr 1960).

The nestlings have a precarious existence. If the nest is disturbed, the startled parent may knock the squab out. Squirming youngsters also fall out or leave the nest too soon. Cats, rattlesnakes, and Gila monsters take their toll of downed birds, and the remains of wings and feathers litter the ground under the nesting thickets. Even when fledged, young whitewings are weak flyers and prone to easy capture by Cooper's Hawks and other raptors. Losses to such predators are compensated for by renesting, however, and fears that snakes, ground squirrels, and white-throated wood rats take a heavy toll of eggs and young have been overstated (Neff 1940a; Tinkham 1942; Arnold 1943; Eicher 1944c).

The cessation of nesting tends to be abrupt and is induced more by chronology than by temperature, weather, or (after mid-August) food shortages (Stair 1970). Most of the desert birds migrate almost immediately after only one nesting. Throughout July small flights of whitewings are increasingly seen passing southward high over southern Arizona valleys, and most birds have left the desert and towns by August 15. It is not known whether these flocks consist of parents migrating together or aggregations of individual whitewings.

The colony nesters and some desert birds within range of cultivated grains persist in nesting through the summer. As the second nesting draws to a close in late July and August, both juveniles and postnesting adults may shift to roost sites adjacent to feeding areas. As throughout the summer, whitewings rarely feed with other birds but follow their kind to feed in gregarious flocks. Favorite foods are maize, safflower, and barley. Unlike Mourning Doves, whitewings usually select standing crops in preference to harvested fields. These feeding flights can include hundreds and even thousands of birds, and farmers often complain about crop depredations. Actual losses are usually exaggerated, however (see, e.g., Kufeld 1966).

The stimuli for mass migration from cultivated valleys are not completely understood. Summer storms, a drop in nighttime temperatures, food shortages, and harassment have all been suggested as contributing factors. Nonetheless, there have been times when all or any of these events have had little or no influence on the onset of migration (Neff 1940b). Migration has also commenced in the absence of any of these phenomena once the young are off the nest (Lawson 1949c). In any case, with the approach of September, the whitewings become increasingly restless. Adults, especially when subjected to shooting, tend to migrate earlier than juveniles, and the later the season, the greater the percentage of young birds in hunters' bags (Gallizioli 1953b, 1955c). Once migration is underway, departure is rapid, and only a few late nesters with young on the nest and juveniles not yet physiologically able to migrate remain in Arizona after the first week in September.

The flight south is rapid and direct, and few birds are recovered as migrants either in southern Arizona or Sonora (Stair 1970). Sizable numbers of wintering whitewings are not recovered until the birds arrive on their wintering range, which extends from southern Sinaloa southward along the Mexican coast to northern Oaxaca (Fig. 12.6). Here the birds reside from November through March, feeding on cultivated grains and what natural foods are available, and roosting in riparian evergreen trees and mangrove swamps within tropical deciduous forest (D. Brown 1981). All Arizona whitewings, regardless of their nesting area, winter within this region without showing a particular fidelity for any specific area. Wintering Arizona whitewings overlap, but do not interbreed, with resident whitewings of the *palustris* race.

Fig. 12.6. Wintering locales of White-winged Doves banded in Arizona.

MANAGEMENT HISTORY

Some ornithologists have suggested that the range and numbers of White-winged Doves have greatly expanded with settlement (e.g., Phillips et al. 1964). Although the bird's range may have increased, whitewings were always abundant along the riverbottoms of the Sonoran Desert. The lack of comment from many early settlers is at least partially owing to the fact that most of them traveled in winter after the whitewings had migrated south. Consider Durivage's (1937:221 *in* Davis 1982) description of the Gila riverbottom near Gila Bend in early June 1849: "Quail and a species of dove were in the greatest abundance."

That both species of doves were plentiful along the lower Gila is also attested to by Dr. George H. Moran (1878), who wrote about the numbers of White-winged Doves he encountered between Fort Yuma and Maricopa:

The common dove, and a beautiful species (*Melopelia leucoptera*)—commonly called Sonora pigeon—abound in countless numbers. I marched to Yuma with troops in July, and returned in August, and cannot tell you how I wished for a shotgun.

E. A. Mearns's field notes also report good numbers of White-winged Doves in southern Arizona in the summer of 1886, prior to large-scale agriculture. Scott (1886) corroborated the abundance of whitewings in Pima County and along the San Pedro and Gila rivers in the 1880s, where he sometimes found "birds by the hundreds."

White-winged Doves did not immediately adapt to feeding on cultivated foods, as indicated by Henshaw (1875), Stephens (1885), and Bendire (1892), who did not report the birds to be especially numerous around Tucson between 1872 and 1882. In 1886 Herbert Brown wrote Bendire (1892) that "there are but few of these doves found in the immediate area of Tucson, but they are numerous all over the country generally." Perhaps, as indicated by some of Brown's other writings, incessant year-round hunting around the limited amount of agriculture near Tucson were responsible for the birds' scarcity.

Brown (1900) thought both whitewing and Mourning Dove populations increased in the cultivated districts during the 1890s because of a general drought and the lack of natural foods in the desert. He noted that the birds were destroyed by gunners in and out of season but received some protection when the amended game law of 1897 provided a closed season during March, April, and May.

Whatever the reason, White-winged Doves appear to have increased greatly in the Tucson area by the turn of the century, as noted by the *Arizona Daily Star* on May 28, 1904: "Hunters report that there are now thousands of Sonora pigeons in the valley." Swarth (1905) visited the then-great San Xavier mesquite forest along the Santa Cruz River south of Tucson in May 1902 and again in June 1903. He stated that the White-winged Dove was "by far the most abundant bird in the mesquite forest, and also the most conspicuous and noisy." He noted that Mourning Doves were "quite abundant, but so overshadowed by the [White-winged Dove] as hardly to be noticed." He also described the condition of the mesquite forest and feared for its future:

The river, running underground for most of its course, rises to the surface at this point, and the bottom lands on either side are covered, miles in extent, with a thick growth of giant mesquite trees, literally giants, for a person accustomed to the scrubby bush that grows everywhere in the desert regions of the southwest, can hardly believe that these fine trees *many of them sixty feet high* and over, really belong to the same species. This magnificent grove is included in the Papago Indian reservation, which is the only reason for the trees surviving as long as they have, since elsewhere every mesquite large enough to be used as firewood has been ruthlessly cut down, to grow up again as a straggly bush.

The closed season enacted in 1897 did not last long. Increased dove populations and the bird's penchant for wheat and cereal grains caused doves to be considered more pests than game. Gilman (1911) described the status of the whitewings in the San Xavier thicket in 1909–10:

They come in such great numbers that the wheat fields suffer and the loss is considerable. . . . At present there is no closed season and the beautiful birds may be shot whenever present. There was an attempt recently made to have them protected, but such a howl went up from the ranchers that nothing was done.

Whether this abundance was due to the refuge status of the reservation or to an increase in grain farming is not clear. It can be assumed, however, that the quality of the colony's remaining nesting habitat, coupled with grain cultivation, allowed the whitewings to recoup whatever losses they sustained from hunting.

In 1912 the first state legislature passed a dove season that opened on June 1 and continued through February 1. The bag limit on both species was thirty-five per day. This season soon became controversial, as some wanted further protection of the whitewings during the breeding season, whereas others considered summer hunting necessary because of the bird's migratory behavior and its damage to grain crops. This dispute continued for years, and the complex problem of the impact of nesting habitat, grain farming, and hunting pressure on whitewing abundance has never been fully resolved to the satisfaction of all parties (e.g., O'Connor 1939; Neff 1941; D. Brown 1978c).

Although the season after 1916 was not supposed to open until July 15, special dispensation for agricultural areas allowed June hunting to continue. Some thought that a decline in whitewing populations during and after World War I was due to the raising of cotton instead of grain (O'Connor 1939). Wetmore (1920), who studied whitewings in June 1919 in the Arlington Valley, where large tracts of mesquite bottomlands bordered a patchwork of new grain farms, was of a different opinion:

It has been common practice for many years for sportsmen to hunt white-winged doves during the months of June and July when the birds were ranging over the cultivated fields. Though this has been done under the guise of protecting crops it has been carried on in the main simply for sport, as the majority of the doves killed are shot in stubble fields from which the grain has been removed, or when in flight to or from the colonies in localities where they may be doing no damage. Occasionally men and boys even invaded the nesting colonies and slipped about among the low mesquites potting the male birds or shooting the females as they sat on their nests containing eggs and young. Others, waiting until the squabs were nearly grown, knocked the young doves from their nests with poles and gathered them in sacks for table use. Such harrying during the season when the birds are breeding can not be considered legitimate and can lead only to the decimation of the species. The mortality among young from the killing of their parents is tremendous.

Wetmore (1920) went on to predict that the large whitewing colonies along the lower Gila would soon disappear because of the rapid expansion of irrigation projects and the steady cutting and clearing of the mesquite forests.

Neff (1940b) reported that the large colonies of whitewings at Arlington, Sacaton, and other Gila and Santa Cruz river localities disappeared in the 1920s and that it was "the nearly unanimous opinion of Arizona's deputy game wardens that the whitewings have been decreasing every year." In 1937 the opening of the season was postponed to August 5 and a bag limit of fifteen birds was imposed. The only big flights were out of New York (Komatke) Thicket on the Gila Indian Reservation and along the Gila River between Arlington and Yuma (Neff 1940b).

Neff considered the harvests of 1937, 1938, and 1939 excessive, and the birds were judged to be even more sparse than before. In such then-remote Gila River areas as Agua Caliente and Texas Hill it was estimated that 75 percent of the twenty thousand birds present in 1937 were killed. Neff

(1940b) described the drought year of 1939 as "another disaster" for the whitewing. Meanwhile, mesquite cutting was taking a heavy toll on the dove's habitat. Tinkham (1941), and Arnold (1943) described the San Xavier thicket south of Tucson as only "a one-time great nesting colony for whitewings" no longer capable of supporting the large colony of "thirty years ago."

In 1940 the opening of the season was postponed to August 16, and in 1941 it was set back to September 1. Whether because of protection during the nesting season, the increase in saltcedar nesting habitat (Pulich 1948; Lawson 1949c; Shaw 1961a), an increase in cultivated grains during World War II, or a combination of all three factors is uncertain, but whitewings again began to increase. A statewide survey after the war showed good numbers of birds to be present along the lower Colorado, Gila, and Santa Cruz rivers (Pulich 1948). By 1948 nesting and hunting success were again considered "good." New York Thicket was still in generally good condition, and plans were made to preserve a hundred-acre remnant of the San Xavier mesquite forest that still contained seventy-foot mesquites (Pulich 1948).

Recognizing the importance of the White-winged Dove as a game species, the Arizona Game and Fish Department began systematically collecting hunt data in 1951, and an annual banding program was initiated in 1953 (Gallizioli 1953b, 1954b). Although a large percentage of the birds migrated prior to the season in some years (Gallizioli 1954b), hunt success during the first week of September was generally good and whitewings were still thought to be increasing in numbers. The 1954 season was the best in years, and Gallizioli (1955b) described one flight on the opening day of the season as containing "a minimum of 10,000 whitewings"; "flock followed flock in what appeared to be an endless stream. Limit bags were taken in from 15 to 30 minutes even by mediocre shooters." In some years the whitewings persisted for one to three weeks after the opening of the season.

A statewide call-count survey was begun on an annual basis in 1957, and check stations, band recovery, and hunt questionnaires were used to monitor the status of Arizona's whitewings. In 1957 the twenty-five-bird limit was reinstated. Ten years later a greatly increased cadre of hunters reported harvesting three-quarters of a million whitewings—an all-time record.

By the 1960s, however, the whitewings' prime nesting habitat along the Colorado, Gila, and Santa Cruz rivers and their tributaries was threatened by a number of projects planned by the U.S. Bureau of Reclamation, Army

Corps of Engineers, U.S. Geological Survey, and Maricopa Flood Control District. Despite numerous whitewing nesting studies (Stair 1958b; Shaw and Jett 1959; Carr 1960; Wigal 1973), that showed the value of riverbottom thickets, many prime nesting areas were altered or destroyed. Groundwater pumping, clearing, channelization, and fire all took a serious toll of the colonial nesting sites. By the mid-1960s the great mesquite forests at San Xavier, Komatke, and along the lower Colorado and Gila rivers were all but gone (Fig. 12.7). To make matters worse for the doves, cotton was rapidly replacing milo maize as Arizona's primary summer agricultural crop.

By the early 1970s it was becoming increasingly obvious that Arizona's whitewing hunting was on the decline. Hunt success and harvest data showed a downward trend, as did the statewide call-count index (Figs. 12.8 and 12.9). Moreover, band-recovery data showed that increasing percentages of the remaining colonies were being harvested (D. Brown 1970e). Hunters sought out those whitewing flights still in existence, and the birds needed protection from overharvesting to population levels below what the remaining habitat would support.

Instituting protective measures was not easy. The whitewing was not endangered as a species. What was threatened was the bird's status as an important game species, a status that many hunters thought would be jeopardized if the season and/or bag limit were reduced. Proposals to restrict the harvest of whitewings and shift hunting pressure to the more abundant Mourning Dove were met by strong and often acrimonious protests. Many hunters believed early migration or overharvesting in Mexico, not habitat loss and high hunt pressure, were behind the shortage of whitewings. However, Mexican harvests had not increased. Less than 30 percent of the band recoveries from heavily hunted areas were from Mexico—approximately the same percentage reported by Kufeld in 1963 (D. Brown 1970e). More birds were not leaving prior to September 1, there was just fewer late-nesting whitewings than before.

First-year harvest levels in some key areas were approaching 25 percent. Nesting densities in some of the best saltcedar thickets were lower than in the late 1950s and 1960s even though these habitats had increased in nesting quality in the interim (Wigal 1973). The twenty-five-bird bag limit had become not only unrealistic, but deleterious to the breeding stock.

Despite opposition from some hunting groups and the press, the department's recommendation for more protective regulations was adopted by the Arizona Game and Fish Commission in 1979. The bag limit was reduced to ten, and hunting in southern Arizona was restricted to the afternoon

Fig. 12.7. New York (Komatke) Thicket as it appeared in July 1941 (above) and July 1972. Groundwater pumping and upstream flow diversion resulted in the death of most of the large mesquites; woodcutting, once thought to be the greatest threat to these bosques, only scavenged the carcasses. 1941 photo by Lee Arnold.

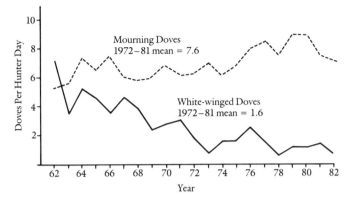

Fig. 12.8. Dove hunting success trends at
Arlington check station, 1962–82.

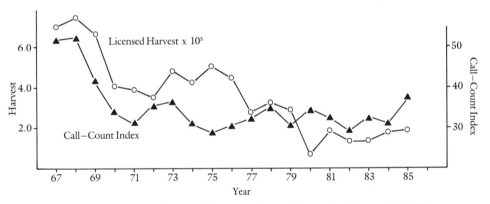

Fig. 12.9. White-winged Dove call-count index and harvest in Arizona, 1967–85.

hours. Afternoon-only shooting proved unpopular, however, and in 1980 the bag limit on whitewings was reduced to six with hunting allowed only during the morning. These stringent measures allowed whitewing populations to increase, and in 1981 the six-bird limit was retained and the half-day season rescinded. These bag limits and a fifteen-day September season have proven effective, and harvests and hunt success have increased along with some recovery in the call-count index (Fig. 12.9). Although it is not expected that the White-winged Dove will regain its former numbers, the regulations now allowed the existing habitats to sustain the maximum number of birds possible.

POPULATION DYNAMICS

White-winged Doves are potentially long-lived birds but are subject to high population turnover. Almost 6 percent of the band recoveries are from birds four years old or older (Kufeld 1963; D. Brown 1970e), and some exceptional individuals have survived in the wild for more than a dozen years.

Call-count surveys have been shown to index breeding and fall population levels accurately (Viers 1970; D. Brown and Smith 1976). Annual changes in nesting success are more difficult to measure. September age ratios, which have varied from 54 to 79 percent juveniles in the bag, are related more to migration chronology than reproductive performance.

Extended first-year recoveries show annual harvest levels ranging from less than 1 percent in desert areas to more than 20 percent in heavily hunted locales (Kufeld 1963; D. Brown 1970e). In contrast to Mourning Doves, banded adult female White-winged Doves are not recovered at a significantly lower rate than males, and the most recent data show the vulnerability of adults of both sexes to be about equal (D. Brown 1978b). Juvenile whitewings, also unlike Mourning Doves, are more heavily harvested than adults (Kufeld 1963; D. Brown 1970e).

Mean annual mortality rates of adults in heavily hunted areas have ranged from 43.8 to 72.2 percent; first-year mortality rates for juvenile whitewings in these same areas have been between 60 and 80 percent (D. Brown 1970e, 1978b). Statewide the mean annual mortality rate is 23.1 percent for both age classes.

Whitewings are not particularly prolific. Carr (1960) found the average number of squabs per nest to be about 1.7 regardless of habitat type, and Webb (1967b) reported that only an average of 1.09 of these youngsters survived to fledge, a figure intermediate between the 53 to 58 percent nesting success found by Tinkham (1942) and the 75 percent nesting success reported by Arnold (1941) and Pulich (1948). Any of these estimates is sufficient to maintain a population in the desert areas with only one nesting attempt, given the bird's overall annual survival rate in these locales of 77 percent for both adults and juveniles.

Because colonial nesting birds in the more productive (and heavily hunted) habitats nest twice each summer, their productivity per pair is around 2.2 young per year. Such a productivity rate would result in a fall population of about 54 percent young. This level of productivity would be barely sufficient, however, to sustain the population at Arlington in the 1960s, then subject to a mean annual survival rate of 56 percent for adults and only 40 percent for juveniles (D. Brown 1970e), and it was inadequate to sustain the same population in the early 1970s when the mean survival rate dropped to 27.8 percent for adults and 24.1 percent for juveniles (D. Brown 1978b).

It is thus apparent that local populations of White-winged Doves are vulnerable to overshooting. Nor do harvest levels have to be especially great. Comparison of five years of banding and hunt data from Arlington and Picacho Lake show declining populations at Arlington, where the annual harvest rate averaged just over 10 percent of the population. White-winged Dove harvests and hunt success showed neither a noticeable increase or decrease during the same period at Picacho Lake, where the mean annual harvest rate was less than 8 percent (D. Brown 1978b).

Other Mortality Factors

White-winged Doves are apparently more resistant to various strains of trichomoniasis caused by *Trichomonas gallinae* than Mourning Doves. Consequently, significant episodes of whitewing mortality from this protozoan parasite are unknown. The only "die-off" reported for this species in Arizona was the mysterious deaths of several hundred, mostly adult, whitewings near Maricopa in late July 1958. Laboratory examination showed the presence of *Salmonella* and two blood parasites, *Plasmodium* and *Haemoproteus* (Stair 1959), but the cause of the deaths could not be positively ascertained. Otherwise, the only incidences of mass mortality of White-winged Doves have been associated with the misuse of chlorinated hydrocarbons when spraying cotton.

THE WAY IT WAS

It would all begin in the intense heat of midsummer. With the coming of the summer "monsoons," it was time to visit the nesting colonies, those humid green thickets of doves clamoring, cooing, coming and going. The purpose of these visits was not so much to check on the strength of the population, which was assured, but to determine the direction and pattern of the developing feeding flights.

In the mid-1960s whitewings were an important cash crop, a commodity joyfully harvested by resident gunners, California celebrities, and foreign dignitaries. Hotels were booked months in advance. The hamlets of Buckeye, Coolidge, Florence, and Maricopa would, for a few days in September, achieve a significance out of all proportion to their size and commerce.

In those days I was, in turn, the Arizona Game and Fish Department's wildlife manager in Gila Bend, Casa Grande, and Tucson. A principal duty of a wildlife manager in such districts was to monitor the whitewing colonies and inform on their activities. The question most often asked as harvest day approached was, "Where are the whitewings?" It was my job to know.

Serious scouting did not begin until mid-August and the determination of the final feeding flight patterns. It was these August mornings I recall most fondly. Often accompanied by C. J. (Jack) Mantle, the commissioner from Tucson, I would proceed to the great colonies at Picacho Lake, Komatke, and Santa Rosa. There, in the predawn darkness, we awaited the ritual. Mourning Doves would be the first to leave, followed by the rising sun, and then the first whitewings—adult males leaving their nighttime roosts to feed. After another fifteen minutes, the skies were filled with layers of birds, all headed for the grainfields.

We would follow the main mass of whitewings as well as lateral rural roads allowed, oftentimes having to relocate the now-distant swarm with binoculars or by following up stragglers. Determining the location of the main flight was not always easy, as some of the birds would breakoff and go to satellite feeding areas. It was a prestigious badge to be in on the best field and the largest concentration of doves.

Once the feeding field was located—most often ripe maize—a strategy had to be developed to ensure a good field position relative to the oncoming flight. The birds' approach pattern was therefore carefully noted. The objective was to find an open area, bordered by some shady cover, had to be found on the incoming side of the field. Dropped birds must not fall in the maize, cotton, or any other place where they could not be promptly and easily retrieved. No time must be wasted looking for downed doves when the flight was on. The ripeness of the grain would be evaluated and its condition on September 1 predicted. If the grain was cut, most of the whitewings would go elsewhere—hence a need to monitor the flights right up to opening day. Rarely was a field posted against hunting.

Some of those feeding flights were truly wonderful. By the middle of August the young of the year would be added to the hordes and the population doubled. Throughout the day, doves flew in and out of the feeding fields. Flushed whitewings would get up in thunderclaps of flapping wings, only to scuttle to the other end of the field to resume their gorging on ripe grain. The air would be full of birds.

One particular moment stands out in my memory as epitomizing those halcyon days. Cascades of still-nesting females, youngsters, and nonbreeding birds were coming in to a field north of Picacho Lake, while throngs of earlier arrivals were perched on the maize heads. When a harvester began flushing birds out of the standing grain, the exiting birds were so densely packed that they obliterated our view of the field and obstructed our passage. Forced to await the whitewings' departure, we stood in awe as the umbrella of milling birds literally shadowed us from the midmorning sun. We were enveloped in White-winged Doves. I have no idea how many there were; there must have been tens of thousands.

It was bad form to shoot whitewings as they left their roosts, and shooting the birds over water meant waiting until the heat of the day. No, the killing must take place at a feeding field. Several suitable fields had to be examined before the right one was found. Sometimes the birds' approach was wrong, or there was no proper shade or place to hide. Some otherwise attractive fields were just too far from a roost site or were off the flight path. A flowing canal or other water source nearby was an important draw for hunters with dogs. No retriever could function long in 115° heat without copious quantities of water. The main ingredients of a good field, however, were the ripeness of the grain and the size of the flight. There were too few such fields and too many hunters to accommodate, so the best field was a closely shared secret.

Scouting for flights was not the only preseason activity. "Dove Nights" were annual features at sportsmen's clubs and sporting-goods stores. The one I remember most was Ward's Dove Night in Tucson. The audience numbered in the hundreds. Drawings, raffles, and above all, free information made for a gala occasion. Shooting and dove-hunting experts offered advice, and Game and Fish Department personnel supplied information on promising locations. Everybody left with something, and not a few hunting vests, shotshells, and shotguns were sold in the process.

The week preceding the opening of the season saw other rituals. The most discussed gossip, aside from where the best field was, was who was selling the lowest-priced shotgun shells. It was a great loss of face to have purchased a case at $2.10 a box and then find out that the same shells could be had for $1.99 a day later somewhere else. To hedge their bets, many hunters waited until the final frenzy of competition before making their purchase. On August 31, sporting-goods stores stayed open until 9:00 P.M. when shotshells sold at the lowest prices. No one bought shells *after* the opening of bird season.

Dove hunting was a shoot, and a stationary one at that. Anyone could, and did, participate, and the whole family went along. The only hardships were the early hours and the heat, and shotguns were more likely to be forgotten than ice chests loaded with cold drinks. One environmental hazard that could not be fortified against was the crowd of novice and careless shooters; few openings passed without a serious accident or death. Getting "stung" by hunters shooting at low-flying birds was an all-too-common occurrence.

Opening day was a ritual of singular purpose and complex emotion. September 1 will always bring images to my mind of dove hunters' breakfasts, last-minute checks of shotshells and licenses, stops at ice vendors, and the predawn drive to the shooting field. Not the least of the rites was the stop for coffee and the urgent chatter about last-minute preparations. Cluttered and smoky, the coffee shops filled with dove hunters, standing, sitting, and waiting in clusters for their foray to the field.

I was never late to my self-assigned stand and could not imagine who was in those headlit cars, throwing up roostertails of silt as they hastened to a parking rendezvous while the east was already advanced in light. Soon a veil of dust hung over the field, an opaque haze that screened the coming dawn. Gradually, the pale topaz light in the east changed to yellow-orange, then to orange-red. One year a violet-pink dawn became a blood-red backdrop for huge cumulus clouds edged in silver and gold.

At first light Mourning Doves began to flit in and out of each hunter's personal horizon. The first shots were heard, but the doves were scattered and flying haphazardly. *The* birds were still to come for those who were truly stalking the standing grain of a whitewing field. Only when the sun was in view would the whitewings come, first in trickles of ones and twos. Then the flood would be on!

The whitewings arrived in great waves, in an undulating slow-flowing motion, stacked into levels moving at different speeds. They were determined and deliberate until the opening barrage, when the birds would wheel and whirl about as mass confusion broke out. Whole sections of the flight dropped to earth on reaching the firing line. Like World War I infantry advancing from trenches, the hunters moved forward in synchrony to retrieve their prey, thereby adding to the general pandemonium.

The whitewings circled wide, regrouped, and again and again tried to enter the field. The toll was terrible. It was not unusual for 90 percent of the flight to be downed; scores of birds were lost in the maize or soared off, too inconvenient to retrieve. Those birds remaining pulled back disconcertedly to sit in the fence-row margins of mesquite and wait for things to quiet down. By ten o'clock they too were dead or back in the field feeding on the heads of safflower or maize stalks. Although their ranks were considerably reduced, even these midday feeders still outnumbered most of today's flights. By three o'clock other hunters had come and the shoot began anew, but at a less intense rate. After three days the whitewings were gone.

After 1970 the magic, too, was gone. Killing large numbers of whitewings was no longer right. Never mind the biological logic that the demise of the big flights was merely a function of the habitat's inability to support their former legions; we were participating in a heritage that was dying, and it was unseemly. There was no longer joy to be had in the killing fields.

I am told that great flights can still be found in Mexico, in southern Sonora, Sinaloa, and even farther south. The grain and the brush are there in proper combination. As close to Arizona as Caborca, in northern Sonora, both whitewings and Mourning Doves can still be had in incredible numbers. But it's not the same. There is no wildlife manager in Morocito, Sinaloa, and Ward's does not have a Dove Night in Caborca.

PAUL BOSMAN

CHAPTER 13

Mourning Dove

The Mourning Dove is the most common and widely occurring bird in Arizona. Throughout the state this columbid regularly ranks number one in the number of individuals seen—almost invariably it will be in the top five.

Nor is this abundance a southwestern phenomenon. The Mourning Dove is the nation's most popular game bird and is found in all forty-eight contiguous states as well as in Mexico, the Greater Antilles, and southern Canada. The annual harvest in the United States alone approximates fifty million (Keeler et al. 1977). Each year fifty to eighty-five thousand Arizona hunters bag one to two million doves, making this species also the state's number-one game bird.

The Mourning Dove is readily recognized by even the most casual observer of birds. Its trim, streamlined body, accentuated by a tiny head and sharply tapered tail, is familiar to all. A rattling whistle given by primary feathers during takeoff and with certain wing beats is unique and, once heard, makes for ready identification. Mourning Doves are differentiated from the only generally similar White-winged Dove by a shorter beak, a more uniform tan coloration (whitewings present an overall grayish appearance), and a lack of white everywhere except the outer tail feathers. Both species show a smudge of black below the cheek, but only the Mourning Dove displays black spots on the upper wing surfaces.

In flight, the Mourning Dove's faster wing strokes, greater speed, and more evasive flight pattern can often be used to differentiate the two species. Mourning Doves have been clocked at forty-three to forty-five miles per hour with occasional bursts up to fifty-five (Brooks 1943; Bastin 1952). Dove hunters must take care, however, as the bag limit on the two species is usually separate, and hunters are required to know the species *before* they shoot.

All Mourning Doves in Arizona are the Western subspecies, *Zenaida macroura marginella*, a slightly smaller and paler race than its Eastern counterpart, *Z. m. carolinensis* (Aldrich and Duvall 1958). The average weight of adults is about 4.0 ounces for females and 4.3 ounces for males (Dunning 1984). Maximum weights are 5.5 ounces for females and 6.0 ounces for males (Nelson and Martin 1953). The more richly colored adult males can be distinguished at all times of the year from the browner females by pinkish rose breasts, flecks of metallic green and other iridescence on the nape, and slate blue crowns.

Birds of the year can be identified until four to five months after fledging by the light tipping on the margins of the wing coverts, and their approximate hatching date can be ascertained by the number of replaced primaries (Fig. 13.1). All of the juveniles' primary feathers are replaced in about one hundred fifty days; in September those doves hatched in April can be differentiated from adults only by the lack of wear on the outer two primaries and the presence of a bursa of Fabricus (Swank 1955a).

DISTRIBUTION AND HABITAT

Nesting Mourning Doves occur from the lowest elevations along the Colorado River through montane conifer forests of ponderosa pine (Fig. 13.2). Almost any landscape having suitable nest trees has some doves, and the bird may even be found nesting on the ground in open prairies. Only in the limited alpine and subalpine regions above 8,500–9,000 feet elevation is the dove's melancholy call not a conspicuous sound of spring.

Mourning Doves are not, however, uniformly distributed. Call-count data collected by the Arizona Game and Fish Department show that the highest numbers of breeding doves are within Arizona Upland communities of Sonoran desertscrub. Progressively fewer birds are heard through semidesert grassland, chaparral, ponderosa pine forest, pinyon-juniper woodland, Mohave desertscrub, and Great Basin desertscrub. The

*Fig. 13.1. Mourning Dove wings. The juvenile's coverts (top) are
light-tipped; the adult's are more uniformly colored.*

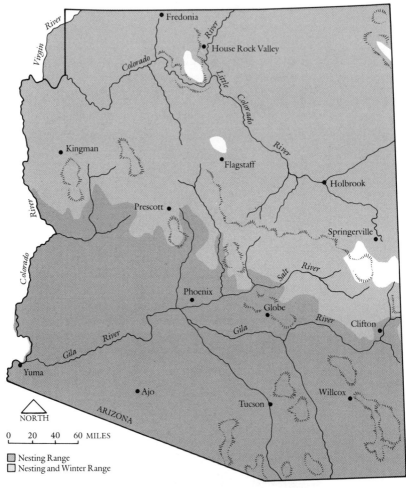

Fig. 13.2. Distribution of Mourning Doves in Arizona.

Nesting Range
Nesting and Winter Range

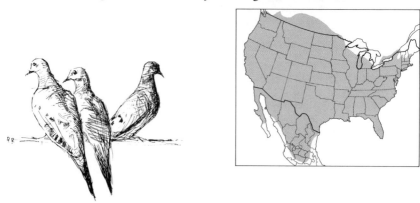

greatest nesting densities, however, are in wooded areas: mesquite bosques, cottonwood- and willow-lined watercourses, saltcedar thickets, and mature citrus orchards near cultivated grainfields. Above average nesting densities have also been recorded in cemeteries and residential areas.

Although ground nests are not uncommon in grasslands in good condition, most Mourning Dove nests in Arizona are in densely branched trees, tall shrubs, and cholla cacti. Trees twenty to thirty feet high, with dense foliage and horizontal limbs, are especially favored. Unlike White-winged Doves, Mourning Doves in riverbottom habitats show a slight preference for mesquite trees over saltcedar (Carr 1960; Shaw and Jett 1960). Call-count surveys conducted in downtown Phoenix and Tucson in 1973 showed calling activity here to be approximately the same as within the Sonoran Desert vegetation that these cities replaced. A factor conducive to nesting is an abundance of seed-producing forbs. Perhaps for this reason, there appears to be a relationship between winter precipitation and the number of calling doves in desert areas. Conversely, more doves may be heard in montane habitats in dry years.

Agricultural areas play an increasing role in the dove's feeding habits as the summer progresses. This species feeds more on small seeds than its whitewinged cousin, and weed-strewn waste places are an important component of Mourning Dove habitat. Harvested fields may be heavily frequented as these ground-foraging birds seek out waste seeds of sunflowers, safflower, barley, wheat, oats, maize, and corn.

With the cessation of nesting in late summer and early fall, the birds abandon most of the high country above 4,500 feet elevation. Grainfields and wild annuals become increasingly important before and during migration. After September 15, doves are often conspicuously absent from some productive food areas while other localities may host large numbers of migrants. Although transient doves get along by resting on fences and telephone lines, suitable roost sites are necessary to hold wintering birds for any length of time. The same tree-lined washes and city parks are just as important to the birds in January as they were in June.

LIFE HISTORY

Although Mourning Doves have been observed nesting in the warmer valleys during every month of the year, courtship activity, even in southern Arizona, does not usually begin until mid-February. By March the male's soft, tender courtship call of *coo-who-who-who* becomes increasingly common and by the end of April can be heard throughout the state. The peak of calling activity varies by location and year (Irby 1964) but is usually in April or early May in southern Arizona and in mid-May in the northern parts of the state. Juveniles hatched late the previous year may not begin calling and nesting until June (Irby and Blankenship 1966; R. Brown 1967). Unmated males call and advertise more than mated ones, but paired males do call, especially when the female begins incubating.

When not calling from a prominent perch, sexually advertising males may engage in soaring display flights, forming graceful arcs and curves. Both calling and territorial displays continue intermittently through the summer as successive nestings are initiated. Although there may be some temporary infidelity and a new nest site is sometimes chosen for subsequent nestings, the doves remain bonded to their chosen mates (Irby 1964; Mackey 1965). There is some evidence that the number of males in the population exceeds the number of females (Hanson and Kossack 1963). Perhaps for this reason, flights of twos and threes are common, the trios consisting of a mated pair and an unmated male (Goforth 1971). Whether some mated pairs migrate and winter together is unknown, and it is only assumed that all birds renew pair bonds each year.

Banding data show that nesting adults of both sexes, but especially males, have a strong affinity to their hatching and earlier nesting locales. Almost 95 percent of all banded Mourning Doves recovered in Arizona are recovered within one degree of their banding locale (Kufeld 1963).

The nest is a platform haphazardly constructed by both sexes, the male usually supplying the female with dropped twigs while she builds the nest. Rarely, and then only in a rudimentary fashion, is the nest lined with grass and down. The usual location is ten to forty feet above the ground on a horizontal fork of a short, densely branched tree (Fig. 13.3). Mourning Doves will accept a variety of sites, however, and nests have been found in fields, in cholla cactus, on man-made structures, and in many kinds of multibranched shrubs. A favorite site in urban and residential locales is the shelf formed at the junction of the fronds and the trunk of a Washington fan palm.

The usual clutch size is two, and eggs are laid on consecutive days. Occasionally, nests have been found with three eggs. The eggs are pure white, somewhat glossier than those of the White-winged Dove, and measure 1.1 inches in length and 0.82 inches in diameter (Bent 1932). Incubation takes only fourteen to fifteen days and is shared by both parents. Mourning

Fig. 13.3. Mourning Dove nest in a mesquite tree. Photo by Todd Pringle.

Doves tend to "sit tighter" than White-winged Doves and are more reluctant to flush when disturbed. The normal routine is for the female to set on the eggs from about three in the afternoon until around eight o'clock the following morning, the male being on the nest during the midday heat. The same sequence occurs when the squabs are fed, and doves seen in the middle of the day in summer are usually females feeding and watering prior to resuming their shift.

The squabs hatch without feathers and must be brooded and protected from the heat. Both parents feed the young regurgitated "pigeon milk." Growth and development are rapid, and the squabs are usually able to leave the nest twelve to fourteen days after hatching—less than a month after the initiation of nest building.

If the season is not too advanced, another nesting cycle will commence, and a new nest is sometimes built before the young of the previous effort have fledged. Up to seven nestings per pair have been recorded in a single season; the average number of nesting attempts in the lower Gila riverbottom near Arlington was 4.4. Nesting success can be highly variable from year to year and among individual pairs. Of the average 1.8 squabs per Mourning Dove nest recorded by Carr (1960) in the Gila riverbottom, only 0.7 squabs per nest were successfully fledged, the others succumbing to predators, disease, or heat.

Mourning Doves have no special physiological mechanisms to conserve water, so desert-dwelling birds must drink almost daily to maintain their body weight in hot weather (Bartholomew and MacMillen 1960). The species's success in inhabiting arid environments while subsisting almost entirely on dry foods is based on their ability to fly long distances to water. MacMillen (1961) found that doves drink approximately 7 percent of their body weight each day, twice as much as their minimum requirements. The usual pattern is for most Mourning Doves to water from about seven to eleven in the morning, with peak numbers drinking between eight and nine-thirty (Eicher 1944d). Another flight to water occurs just before dark (Gallizioli 1952b).

Mourning Doves selectively feed on small seeds throughout the year. A few greens and invertebrates are taken, but more than 99 percent of the diet at all times is cultivated grains and the seeds of annual forbs and roadside weeds and grasses (Browning 1962). Availability varies with the season, but in the spring and summer months favorite foods are the seeds of such species as horse-purslane, buckhorn plantain, doveweed, nutgrasses, and flatsedges. Other important seed sources at various times in the Southwest are red-maids, California poppy, careless-weed or pigweed, spurges, chickweeds, mustards, buckwheats, tepary beans, milk thistles, annual sunflower, Johnsongrass, cupgrass, barnyard grass, and Mediterranean canary grass (Davis and Anderson 1973). Favorite cereal grains include barley, wheat, maize, and even corn. In the higher elevations, pine seed, turkey mullein, and wild sunflower are the most common food items. Unlike White-winged Doves, Mourning Doves rarely feed on standing crops and almost always feed on the ground. After feeding the doves may frequent roadbeds and other gravelly surfaces to obtain sufficient grit to digest their coarse meal.

Even in southern Arizona, nesting is essentially over by August 15; 97.8 percent of the juvenile Mourning Doves shot in September hatch before that date (Gallizioli 1953b), and active crop glands in the adults are rare after September 1. Many of the early-hatched juveniles have migrated by late July, a full month before the major concentrations of premigratory birds begin forming in mid- to late August (Truett 1966; Blankenship and Tomlinson 1967; Miles 1976). Mourning Doves do not require large fat reserves prior to migrating. With the possible exception of a drop in minimum temperatures, weather and food availability appear to have little influence on migration chronology. Migration of Arizona's nesting population is usually underway by the first week of September, with 40 to 50 percent of the population leaving each week thereafter (Hanson and Kossak 1963; Miles 1976).

Once the last young are fledged, the sexes feed and flock together prior to migration. Although most doves banded in Arizona are recovered the first week of September within a few miles of their banding location, some birds will already be in Mexico by this time. Doves from northern Arizona and the inter-mountain states begin arriving in southern Arizona as early as August 15, and peak numbers of birds are present usually during the last weeks of August and the first few days of September. By September 15 there is a general movement out of the state, and most, but not all, doves seen after that date are migrants from farther north. A few doves appear to be residents, for in some years summer-banded doves are recovered in Arizona the following winter. As with waterfowl, Band-tailed Pigeons, and other migratory birds, most of Arizona's wintering Mourning Doves are from the intermountain region of Utah, Nevada, Idaho, eastern California, eastern Oregon, and eastern Washington (Kufeld 1963). Some Arizona and other intermountain-state doves also spend the winter in, or at least pass through, California's Imperial Valley as well as southern Arizona. Flocks may contain up to dozens of doves, but most flights are of singles, twos, and threes.

Arizona doves usually follow valleys and arroyos into Sonora. Most Western Mourning Doves, Arizona populations included, then drift down the west coastal states of mainland Mexico to winter in the Bajío, a large, subtropical agricultural basin in the transvolcanic region of Jalisco, Michoacán, and Guanajuato (Fig. 13.4; Blankenship and Reeves 1970). Most Mexican band recoveries are in October and early November, with progressively fewer doves taken through April, when Mexican recoveries cease.

MANAGEMENT HISTORY

Mourning Doves, or as they were once called, Carolina doves, have traditionally been hunted in Arizona along with White-winged Doves. During the territorial period both birds were hunted throughout the spring and summer in the expanding grainfields of southern Arizona:

It is doubtful if there has been better dove shooting in the vicinity of Tucson than at present. Quail are scarce, but the doves are flying in all directions. Hunters are bringing in hundreds of these delectable birds and the dove pot-pie is getting to be an every day luxury.

Arizona Daily Star, May 28, 1904

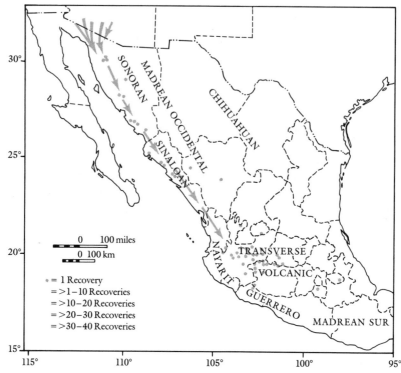

Fig. 13.4. Mexican migration route and recovery locations of Mourning Doves banded in Arizona.

Such sport was curtailed in 1913 when the state game code established a daily bag limit of thirty-five doves in the aggregate between June 1 and February 1. With ratification of the Migratory Bird Treaty Act in 1918, management responsibilities for doves and other migratory birds passed to the federal government. Subsequent regulations promulgated by the U.S. Biological Survey were more restrictive, and hunting Mourning Doves and most other migratory game birds was prohibited before September 1 (Anon. 1923).

By 1927, federal and state regulations had curtailed the Mourning Dove season in Arizona to September 1 through December 15, with a bag limit of twenty-five doves of both species. The next year the limit was reduced to twenty, and by 1942 it was down to ten. This limit, in conjunction with a forty-day continuous season beginning on September 1, remained in effect until 1956, when regulations were liberalized to allow a fifteen-bird bag limit and a fifty-day split season. Although the bag limit was again reduced to ten the following year, the split season has generally remained in effect, allowing the hunting of local doves in September and migrant birds in November and December.

Despite the Mourning Dove's ranking as the number-one game bird in Arizona, little was done to survey this populous species until the 1950s, and even then most of the emphasis was on the more prestigious and vulnerable whitewing. Mourning Doves were now receiving national attention, however, and under federal direction Arizona became a leading state in dove management. A banding program was started in 1951, and call-count surveys were begun the next year. In 1953 hunt information was collected through the use of check stations and wing boxes. These data showed that dove hunt success in Arizona was twice that of any other state and that more hunters shot more doves than any other game (Gallizioli 1953b). Such findings, coupled with threats to the bird's best riverbottom nesting habitats, fueled additional study.

Coo-counts, though unable to measure productivity, sufficed as a reasonable index to dove population trends. Because doves were such an important wildlife resource in Arizona, sufficient call-count routes were established to provide a statistically valid breeding dove index on a statewide rather than Western Management Unit basis. Results allowed for the detection of population changes greater than 35 percent and were found to correlate with hunt success the following autumn (Kufeld 1963; D. Brown and Smith 1976).

Band recoveries consistently indicated Mourning Dove harvest levels of less than 10 percent even in the most heavily hunted areas. High productivity, the early migration of immatures, and an abundance of small grains kept dove numbers from being overexploited through the 1960s. In 1968 Arizona breeding dove index was at a record level, and the estimated licensed harvest during the September season was an impressive 1,709,368 Mourning Doves.

There was trouble on the horizon, however. Changing farm practices, expanding residential areas, and the destruction of riparian thickets were taking their toll of Mourning Doves as well as whitewings. Populations began declining in the 1980s (Fig. 13.5). Half-day openings and zoned seasons, designed to reduce hunt pressure on White-winged Dove populations in 1979 and 1980, had mixed effects on the Mourning Dove harvest. In an effort to steer hunters away from White-winged Doves, the bag limit on Mourning Doves was raised to twelve and in 1981 the season was extended to seventy days.

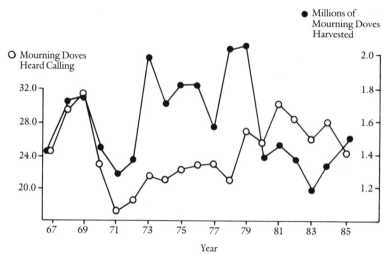

Fig. 13.5. Mourning Dove call-count index and
September harvests in Arizona, 1967–85.

The larger bag limit and longer season did not result in an increase in either dove hunters or doves taken. Twenty-five thousand fewer dove hunters took to the field in 1983 than in 1976. Nor has a longer late season had an appreciable effect; the number of birds taken during November and December has remained relatively constant (Fig. 13.6), comprising between 15 and 20 percent of the total harvest.

The disappearance of nesting and hunting areas in the Salt River Valley and other Arizona locales precludes a return to the huge Mourning Dove harvests of the 1960s. Declines in the breeding dove index in the intermountain states in the 1980s suggest that there will be little improvement in the numbers of migrant doves in the near future. Nonetheless, the Mourning Dove, with a reported bag of 1,606,000 birds in 1986, was still the number-one game bird in Arizona. The 73,315 licensed dove hunters were outnumbered only by the state's 77,754 quail hunters.

POPULATION DYNAMICS

Because of variations in migration chronology and the propensity for early-hatched juveniles to migrate before their parents, spring and fall

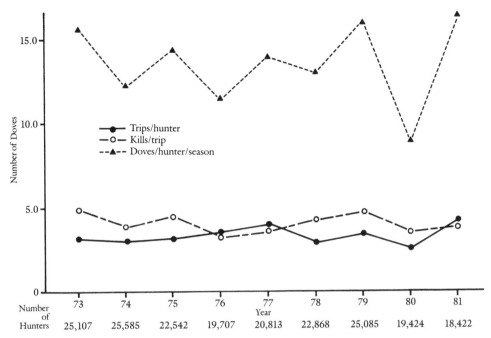

Fig. 13.6. Hunt success of late-season Mourning Dove hunters in Arizona, 1973–81.

population indices in Arizona show little relationship to measured changes in reproductive success (Irby 1964; D. Brown 1968b). September check-station data show no correlation between hunt success and the percentage of juveniles in the bag, which has ranged from 22 to 76. The correlation between the state's breeding dove index and hunt success (D. Brown and Smith 1976) suggests that productivity is relatively constant from year to year and that changes in fall population levels are more dependent on variations in overwinter survival, long-term production trends, and timing of the onset of migration than on any fluctuations in the success of the hatch.

Mourning Doves are short-lived; fewer than 5 percent live to be four years of age (Kufeld 1963). Annual mortality varies by year and location, but mean mortality rates of banded adults range from 45 percent statewide to 68 percent locally, and mortality rates for immatures average about 60 percent in all areas (Stair 1960b; Kufeld 1963; D. Brown 1978b). Little of this mortality is directly attributable to hunting, however, as annual harvest levels in even the most heavily hunted areas average less than 10 percent of the population, and less than 2 percent of desert-dwelling doves are taken by hunters (Kufeld 1963; D. Brown 1977c, 1978b).

Harvest levels vary by sex and age class. Banding studies in Arizona have shown that adults are more likely to be shot than juveniles, and males more

than females (Kufeld 1963; D. Brown 1978b). These differences in vulnerability are believed to be because of the earlier migration of juveniles and the
males' tendency to feed earlier in the morning. Second-year birds, however,
are recovered at a greater rate than older adults (D. Brown 1978b).

Harvest and mortality rates reported for Arizona are well within the
species's ability to replace itself. Populations have been known to increase
when subject to harvest rates of up to 8 percent (D. Brown 1978b). Given
even the low productivity rate of 0.77 young Mourning Doves successfully
fledged per nesting attempt found by Swank (1955b), and the average 4.4
nestings per pair per year reported by Webb (1967b), 3.4 young doves
would be produced each year, enough to survive to nest the following year
even with the high annual mortality rate of 68 percent for adults and 60
percent for juveniles in the highest hunted areas.

This worst-case scenario does not consider the greater mortality rate of
adult males than females, the possibility of surplus males in the population,
and the potential for excess birds from adjacent populations to move into
vacant nesting habitat. The possibility that a small number of early hatched
juveniles will nest late in the summer is also ignored (Irby and Blankenship
1966; R. Brown 1967). Population declines are therefore dependent on factors other than hunting. In Arizona the most obvious reasons are habitat
changes, disease, and pesticide poisoning.

Parasites, Diseases, and Chemical Losses

Doves are prone to a number of parasites and diseases, including louse
flies, mites, intestinal roundworms, and bird malaria (Hanson et al. 1957;
Couch et al. 1962; Couch 1963). The only causes of significant mortality
recorded in Arizona, however, are fowlpox and trichomoniasis.

Fowlpox is an infectious pox-virus (*Borreliota avium*) spread by mos-
quitos and by contact. In chronic cases pox nodules and lesions appear on
the head (often about the eyes), beak, and sometimes the feet. Wounded or
distressed birds are more prone to infection than healthy ones. In the more
serious cases the birds become debilitated and listless, and eventually die
from asphyxiation or starvation (Locke 1961). Blankenship et al. (1966) reported pox in a number of Mourning Doves and Gambel's Quail near
Tucson during the summer and fall of 1963, with most cases noted in October. Of several hundred trapped doves examined, 2.1 percent were infected and 40 percent of these died. This disease is a relatively minor cause
of concern in Arizona in comparison to trichomoniasis, however.

Trichomoniasis, or "canker," is caused by a flagellate protozoan (*Trichomonas gallinae*) and has resulted in severe die-offs of doves in Arizona and throughout the United States. The early symptoms are oral lesions, which may develop and spread throughout the anterior portions of the digestive tract. In chronic infections these lesions form firm curdlike lumps that can obstruct the food and air passages. In severe infestations the birds die of starvation and/or suffocation.

Typical trichomoniasis outbreaks are in residential areas where doves are concentrated at artificial sources of food and water and involve dead Mourning Doves and an occasional Inca Dove. Rock Doves, or domestic pigeons, and White-winged Doves have high incidences of infection without displaying any debilitating symptoms and are probably carriers of the disease (Straus 1966; Toepfer et al. 1966). The number of incidences usually increases in spring, with sporadic occurrences reported throughout the summer. Few cases are received from September through January. Examination of the dead doves reveals cheeselike lumps in the esophagus and pharynx, and the mouth has a fetid odor.

Investigations by Straus (1966) showed incidence levels throughout Arizona populations ranging from 4 to 41 percent and averaging about 20 percent. Males had a higher rate of incidence than females, and juveniles were more prone to infection than adults. Sileo (1970) later found 15 to 58 percent of the populations he studied to be infected and noted that the less severe outbreaks in terms of mortality were associated with high incidence levels. An epizootic in the Scottsdale area in mid-March resulted in a 27 percent mortality rate in which adult males suffered the highest morbidity. Sileo concluded that the doves had various immunological responses to different strains of the disease and that at least one strain was more virulent than others. There is no acquired immunity to virulent strains, and infected populations cannot be effectively treated. Epizootics soon disappear, however, with the cessation of artificial feeding and the dispersing of mixed flocks of pigeons and doves.

The improper use of pesticides has occasionally been a cause of significant dove mortality in Arizona. Although doves normally do not succumb to routine field applications of toxophene and other farm toxicants, the species is susceptible to aldrein, dieldrin, and other chlorinated hydrocarbons (Young et al. 1952). Lead poisoning from ingested shot is another possible cause of death. Preliminary studies show significant residues of spent shot in heavily hunted fields and up to 6 percent of doves to have ingested lead shot (Arizona Game and Fish Department files).

A GENTLEMAN'S HUNT

My first impression was that we were too late. No birds were flying, and the few hunters in attendance were just standing around visiting. The morning sun was in our eyes as we turned off the canal bank and onto a two-track road that led into the desert. My partner and guide was not the least dismayed by our lateness and pointed to a small wash supporting ironwoods and mesquite at decent intervals. Kelly Neal had been here before.

"Pull over about there," he said. "We can leave the truck here and station ourselves in the cover of the wash."

Still, no doves were flying. I fished around in the camper for my lawn chair and checked out a plastic bottle of frozen water from the ice chest. Two boxes of Double AAs in my hunting vest, and I was almost ready. I was debating whether to use the Winchester Model 12 or the superimposed Citori when I heard Kelly shoot from the cover of the wash. Maybe the flight was not over yet. I hurried to the shade of a big mesquite that I had appropriated. No sooner had I gotten there than three doves whistled by, thirty yards overhead. Too late to shoot, I settled in for the next flight.

I did not have long to wait. Within minutes there were doves on the horizon. No matter that I missed the first four shots straight off—more of the dodging and weaving speedsters were on the way. The small flocks of twos and threes were numerous and low to the ground, and I could pick my targets and choose easy or difficult shots. Within a half hour I was busy cleaning my limit of twelve birds. By the looks of the piles of feathers scattered about, ours was not the first limit of the season. There were too many shell casings and empty shell boxes lying about. In a ritual homage, we policed a two-hundred-yard perimeter around the site of our shoot. It was our way of showing respect for the hunt we had just enjoyed.

Examination of the doves' crops showed them to have been feeding on the seeds of an annual forb growing on the creosote plains of the desert. Having gorged on these hard and angular bits, the doves were coming in to drink. The flight was at its height between eight-thirty and nine o'clock—time enough to sleep in and early enough to avoid the stifling heat of the September sun . . . a gentleman's hunt.

Dove hunting *is* a gentleman's sport, requiring no great outlay of time and energy. Such shoots are also great recreation and an ideal way to initiate novice shooters into the world of real game. Even the most accomplished big-game hunter probably tasted his first success on a dove. And even though dove hunting is more properly termed a shoot than a hunt, this is so only because the hunting is done *before* the season.

Finding Mourning Doves is usually no problem, not in the Southwest anyway. Preseason scouting trips to almost any farming community will locate several concentrations of these common game birds. Doves habitually follow flight corridors when going about their daily activities and have favorite crossings that they regularly pass over. Many of these so-called flyways are used throughout the summer and into September so that dove hunting can actually begin in June.

Particularly good places to scout are along canals and streams where doves come to roost and water. Even when no birds are flying, doves perched on fence lines and telephone wires can provide a clue to the whereabouts of these aerial highways. But to really know the doves' movements, it is best to follow the morning flights to a feeding field. Follow the birds out of the roost at dawn. Field glasses can be used to advantage. Unless food is especially scarce, doves do not fly more than ten miles from their nighttime cover to feed. Usually they will be feeding in more than one field. Pick one that is bordered with trees or that at least has some cover.

The key to a successful shoot is to avoid Arizona's opening-day crowds by finding a secondary field. A small flight, one that will not attract hordes of other hunters is ideal. After all, the bag limit is only a dozen birds, and you will want to string them out. A good strategy is to locate several flights; pick one with fewer birds but with pleasant surroundings.

Doves roost at night in mesquite and saltcedar thickets, in citrus groves, cemeteries, windrows, and other tree-supporting locales. Wooded floodplains and brushy riverbottoms next to agricultural tracts are especially productive sites. Some better-known roosting areas in south-central Arizona are the "Green Belt" along the Gila River between Buckeye and Gillespie Dam, Picacho Lake, and the mesquite bosque on the Santa Cruz River near Redrock. Good secondary places are remnant patches of brush, irrigation sumps, and other "leave" areas.

Should you have gotten too late a start for this tactic, simply drive farm laterals until you note passing doves or locate a plot of recently harvested barley, maize, or safflower. Mourning Doves prefer waste grain to standing crops and recently cut fields are always likely locales—even those that have been plowed under once. If the summer rains were generous, a waste field of careless-weed or sunflowers might attract these small seed eaters. This is especially so in northern Arizona, where weed patches provide most of the dove hunting.

Now comes the critical part. Is the field posted? If so, you need to ask the rancher for permission or seek another spot. As important as whether doves are coming in or not is the selection of a shooting stand. From which

direction are the birds coming? Will the sun be in your eyes? Is there any
hiding cover? Is there an open area away from cotton and other standing
crops so that you will not waste time looking for downed birds in an area
that you should not be in anyway? When hunting with a dog, you will
want to know if there is a canal or other water available. These factors
should all be noted and an actual hunt simulated. Unless the field is plowed
under or posted at the last minute, you should now be in business.

There are variations to this technique. Doves can be intercepted en route
to feedlots and other crowded or posted areas. Or you can ambush them
on their way to desert feeding sites or water. Watering sites may be located
the same way as feeding areas—by following doves about their business
prior to the opening of the season. If you plan to spend the midmorning
hours shooting at water holes, make sure that a cottonwood or other shade
is present.

Midday finds the doves perched at the edges of fields and in other temporary roosts. Shooting doves as they flush out of trees is hot work and
indicates poor planning. The idea is to let the doves come to you. If you
have missed the morning flight, wait for the pace to pick up in the evening.
Feeding birds usually begin trickling in at about three o'clock and continue
to arrive until about five or so. Awaiting these post-siesta feeders makes for
a warm vigil, and waylaying them on their evening return to the roost can
be risky. These late flights are short and the doves often fly so high that
they may be out of range. Shooting doves at water in the evening can also
be frustrating. More often than not the birds come in just before dark, and
the entire flight may be concentrated in the closing minutes of the legal
shooting hour. This does not mean that you cannot have some enjoyable
and challenging shoots late in the day. I have had some of my best shoots
then—and some of my sparsest bags.

Pick your shots, but not just the easy ones. Doves usually fly in ones,
twos, and threes. Once shot at, the birds dip down and rocket off at speeds
up to forty miles an hour. A tail wind can make for some difficult shooting
and the Mourning Dove's tendency to dodge and weave can embarrass
even an experienced shooter. Few hunters can bag two "tail-wind charlies"
or "artful dodgers" in a row. Try for doubles and take some of the high
flyers.

Because of their variable speed, doves require a wide range of lead. Fast
flyers need a fast-swinging muzzle and two to three lengths. Shot size is
not all that important. I am partial to high-base #7½s but #8s are fine,
too. Doves are not heavily feathered and come to earth relatively easily, if
you are "on" and have not misjudged the distance. I am always surprised at

how many forty-yard shots turn out to be fifty yards—a point brought home when I mark off the distance to one knocked down at that range. You need a good load to hold up under those distances, and I prefer a modified choke to an open one.

Two hours of shooting will get you any angle of shot imaginable: cross-cuts, straightaways, three-quarter shots, and incoming birds. Try them all and then concentrate on your weakest shot. Doves are the best practice there is, and a little investment now can pay big dividends during duck season when game is a lot harder and shells are more expensive.

Between 80 and 85 percent of the dove harvest is during the early season, which is unfortunate given the pleasant surroundings and numbers of doves often available in late November and December. Because of the September heat, it is good practice to retrieve and clean each bird immediately. I usually place the doves in two piles in the shade—one of adults and the other of juveniles (identified by the white edges on their wing coverts). I pick and dress them while I wait for incoming arrivals. Keep the adults in one bag, the youngsters in another. Being so engaged may cost an opportunity or two, but promptly cleaned birds not only keep better, they taste better.

Should time be a factor, the birds can be "breasted." Simply cut off the wings with a tin shears or wire-cutter, insert a thumb in the bird's vent, and pull the entire sternum of breast muscle forward. The skin and crop are then peeled away. Rinse the breasts off in water and the operation is complete. This procedure eliminates the need to pluck and dress your birds and allows a limit of doves to be cleaned in less than ten minutes. Although "breasting" may be more desirable than facing your cleaning task later at home, such shortcuts are not for the dove gourmet. Plucked doves with their skin intact retain their juices better while cooking. The more meticulous hunter will receive his just rewards at the dinner table.

By cooking up doves of the same age class together, all the birds will be done at the same time. Simmered either in a thick wine sauce with mushrooms or in chicken-rice soup, doves rank as one of the most delectable of game dishes. As the first game of the season and fine cuisine, they deserve nothing but the most attentive preparation.

Should time be a factor, the birds can be "breasted." Simply cut off the wings with a tin shears or wire-cutter, insert a thumb in the bird's vent, and pull the entire sternum of breast muscle forward. The skin and crop are then peeled away. Rinse the breasts off in water and the operation is complete. This procedure eliminates the need to pluck and dress your birds and allows a limit of doves to be cleaned in less than ten minutes. Although "breasting" may be more desirable than facing your cleaning task later at home, such shortcuts are not for the dove gourmet. Plucked doves with their skin intact retain their juices better while cooking. The more meticulous hunter will receive his just rewards at the dinner table.

By cooking up doves of the same age class together, all the birds will be done at the same time. Simmered either in a thick wine sauce with mushrooms or in chicken-rice soup, doves rank as one of the most delectable of game dishes. As the first game of the season and fine cuisine, they deserve nothing but the most attentive preparation.

Bibliography

Alcorn, S. M., S. E. McGregor, and G. Olin. 1961. Pollination of saguaro cactus by doves, nectar-feeding bats, and honey bees. *Science* 133:1594–95.

Aldrich, J. W. 1979. Status of the Canadian Sandhill Crane. *Proc. 1978 Int. Crane Workshop* 139–48.

Aldrich, J. W., and A. J. Duvall. 1955. Distribution of American gallinaceous game birds. *USDI Fish and Wildl. Serv. Circ.* 34:1–30.

———. 1958. Distribution and migration of races of the Mourning Dove. *Condor* 60:108–28.

Allen, J. A. 1886a. The Masked Bobwhite (*Colinus ridgwayi*) in Arizona. *Auk* 3:275–76.

———. 1886b. The Masked Bobwhite (*Colinus ridgwayi*) of Arizona and its allies. *Bull. Amer. Mus. Nat. Hist.* 7:273–91.

———. 1886c. The type specimen of *Colinus ridgwayi*. *Auk* 3:483.

———. 1887. A further note on *Colinus ridgwayi*. *Auk* 4:74–75. American Ornithologists' Union. 1983. *The A.O.U. check-list of North American birds*, 6th ed. Lawrence, Kansas: Allen Press.

Amundson, T. E. 1985. Health management in Wild Turkey restoration programs. *Proc. National Wild Turkey Symp.* 5:285–94.

Anderson, W. L. 1974. Scaled Quail: Social organization and movements. M.S. thesis, Univ. of Arizona, Tucson.

Anonymous. 1923. Mourning Dove a migratory game bird, court decides. *Calif. Fish and Game* 9:34.

Anthony, R. 1970. Ecology and reproduction of California Quail in southeastern Washington. *Condor* 72:276–87.

Arney, J. 1959a. Turkey survey. F.A. Proj. W-53-R. Ariz. Game and Fish Dept.
———. 1959b. Turkey hunt information. F.A. Proj. W-53-R. Ariz. Game and Fish
    Dept.
Arnold, J. F. 1942. Forage consumption and preferences of experimentally fed
    Arizona and antelope jack rabbits. *Ariz. Agr. Exp. Sta. Tech. Bull.* 98:51–86.
Arnold, L. 1941. Mesquite forest and the whitewing. *Ariz. Wildl. Sportsman*
    3:5–6.
———. 1943. A study of the factors influencing the management of and a
    suggested management plan for the Western White-winged Dove in Arizona.
    P.R. Proj. 9-R. Ariz. Game and Fish Comm.
Arrington, O. N. 1942a. Pheasant restocking. F.A. Proj. 11-D. Ariz. Game and Fish
    Comm.
———. 1942b. A report on a land inspection survey of proposed Gambel Quail
    release areas in the vicinity of Prescott, Arizona. F.A. Proj. 11-D. Ariz. Game
    and Fish Comm.
———. 1942c. A survey of possible refuge areas for Masked Bobwhite in the
    Arivaca and Altar Valleys. F.A. Spec. Rept. Proj. 11-D. Ariz. Game and Fish
    Comm.
———. 1942d. A survey of the Mt. Graham Merriam Turkey release. F.A. Proj.
    11-D, Spec. Rept. Ariz. Game and Fish Comm.
———. 1943. Status of restoration areas stocked with game species under Federal
    Aid in Wildlife Restoration in Arizona. F.A. Proj. 11-D, Compl. Rept. Ariz.
    Game and Fish Comm.
———. 1946. The status of restoration areas stocked with game species under
    Federal Aid in Wildlife Restoration in Arizona. F.A. Proj. 11-D, Spec. Rept.
    Ariz. Game and Fish Comm.
Audubon, J. W. 1906. *Audubon's western journal: 1849–1850*, ed. F. H. Hodder.
    Cleveland: Arthur H. Clark.
Bahre, C. J. 1977. Land use history of the Research Ranch, Elgin, Arizona. *J.
    Ariz. Acad. Sci.* 12(suppl. 2): 1–32.
Bailey, F. M. 1928. *Birds of New Mexico.* Santa Fe: New Mexico Dept. of Game
    and Fish.
———. 1939. *Among the birds in the Grand Canyon country.* Washington, D.C.:
    U.S. Government Printing Office.
Baird, S. F. 1859. Birds of the boundary. In Emory, W. H., *United States and
    Mexican Boundary Survey*, vol. 2. 34th Cong., 1st sess. H. Doc. 135.
Banks, R. C. 1975. Plumage variation in the Masked Bobwhite. *Condor* 77:486–87.
Barnes, W. 1936. Our Thanksgiving turkey: An American bird and an American
    festal day. *Cattleman* 23:19, 22.
Bartholomew, G. A., and R. E. MacMillen. 1960. The water requirements of
    Mourning Doves and their use of sea water and NaCl solutions. *Physiol. Zool.*
    33:171–78.
Bastin, E. W. 1952. Flight speed of the Mourning Dove. *Wilson Bull.* 64:47.
Battye, C. 1909. Reminiscences of a southern trip. *The Needle's Eye* 21(21–25).
Beale, E. F. 1858. The report of the superintendent of the wagon road from Fort
    Defiance to the Colorado River. 35th Cong., 1st sess. H. Doc. 124.

Bendell, J. F., and P. W. Elliot. 1967. Behavior and regulation of numbers in Blue Grouse. *Can. Wildl. Serv. Ser. Rept.* 4:1–76.

Bendire, C. 1892. Life histories of North American birds with special reference to their breeding habits and eggs, with twelve lithographic plates. *Special Bull. U.S. National Mus.* 1:1–446.

Bennitt, R. 1951. Some aspects of Missouri quail and quail hunting, 1938–1948. *Missouri Conserv. Comm., Tech. Bull.* 2:1–51.

Bent, A. C. 1932. Life histories of North American gallinaceous birds; Orders Galliformes and Columbiformes. *U.S. National Mus. Bull.* 162:1–420.

Bishop, R. A. 1964. The Mearns' Quail (*Cyrtonyx montezumae mearnsi*) in southern Arizona. M.S. thesis, Univ. of Arizona, Tucson.

Bishop, R. A., and C. R. Hungerford. 1965. Seasonal food selection of Arizona Mearns' Quail. *J. Wildl. Manage.* 29:813–19.

Blaisdell, J. P. 1958. Seasonal development and yield of native plants on the upper Snake River plains and their relation to certain climatic factors. *USDA Tech. Bull.* 1190:1–68.

Blankenship, L. H., R. E. Reed, and H. D. Irby. 1966. Pox in Mourning Doves and Gambel's Quail in southern Arizona. *J. Wildl. Manage.* 30:253–57.

Blankenship, L. H., and H. M. Reeves. 1970. Mourning Dove recoveries from Mexico. *USDI Fish and Wildl. Serv., Spec. Sci. Rept.—Wildl.* 135:1–25.

Blankenship, L. H., and R. E. Tomlinson. 1967. Arizona dove wing survey. *USDI Fish and Wildl. Serv., Spec. Sci. Rept.—Wildl.* 116:1–34.

Boag, D. A. 1965. Indicators of sex, age, and breeding phenology in Blue Grouse. *J. Wildl. Manage.* 29:103–08.

Boeker, E. L., and V. E. Scott. 1969. Roost tree characteristics for Merriam's Turkey. *J. Wildl. Manage.* 33:121–24.

Brandt, H. 1951. *Arizona and its birdlife*. Cleveland: Bird Research Foundation.

Braun, C. E. 1973. Studies of Band-tailed Pigeons in wintering areas of Mexico, December 1972 to April 1973. Mimeo Rep., Contract No. 14-16-0008-626. Colo. Div. Wildl.

Braun, C. E., D. E. Brown, J. C. Pedersen, and T. P. Zapatka. 1975. Results of the Four Corners cooperative Band-tailed Pigeon investigation. *USDI Fish and Wildl. Serv. Resour. Publ.* 125:1–20.

Brewster, W. 1885. Additional notes on some birds collected in Arizona and the adjoining province of Sonora, Mexico. *Auk* 2:196–200.

———. 1887. Further notes on the Masked Bobwhite (*Colinus ridgwayi*). *Auk* 4:159–60.

Britt, T. L. 1978. Blue Grouse introduction. F.A. Proj. W-53, R-28. Ariz. Game and Fish Dept.

———. 1979. Blue Grouse introduction. F.A. Proj. W-53, R-29. Ariz. Game and Fish Dept.

Britt, T. L., and D. E. Brown. 1977. Blue Grouse introduction. F.A. Proj. W-53, R-27. Ariz. Game and Fish Dept.

Brooks, S. C. 1943. Speed of flight of Mourning Doves. *Condor* 45:119.

Brown, D. E. 1968a. Tortolita-Owlhead quail management information. F.A. Proj. W-53-R. Ariz. Game and Fish Dept.

———. 1968b. Avra Valley dove information. F. A. Proj. W-53-R, Ariz. Game and
Fish Dept.

———. 1969. Band-tail Pigeon management information. F.A. Proj. W-53, R-19.
Ariz. Game and Fish Dept.

———. 1970a. Gambel Quail management information. F.A. Proj. W-53-R. Ariz.
Game and Fish Dept.

———. 1970b. Scaled Quail habitat evaluation. F.A. Proj. W-53, R-20. Ariz. Game
and Fish Dept.

———. 1970c. Endangered species investigations: Masked Bobwhite. F.A. Spec.
Rept. W-53, R-21, Ariz. Game and Fish Dept. 5 pp.

———. 1970d. Bandtail management information. F.A. Proj. W-53, R-20. Ariz.
Game and Fish Dept.

———. 1970e. Summary of White-wing Dove banding and hunt information in
Arizona. F.A. Proj. W-53, R-20, Spec. Rept. Ariz. Game and Fish Dept.

———. 1971a. Endangered species investigations: Masked Bobwhite. F.A. Special
Rept. W-53-R. Ariz. Game and Fish Dept.

———. 1971b. Bandtail Pigeon management information. F.A. Proj. W-53, R-21.
Ariz. Game and Fish Dept.

———. 1972a. Proposal for the introduction of Blue Grouse into spruce-fir
communities of the San Francisco Peaks. F.A. Proj. W-53, R-22, Spec. Rept.
Ariz. Game and Fish Dept.

———. 1972b. Afghan Whitewing Pheasant management information. F.A. Proj.
W-53, R-22. Ariz. Game and Fish Dept.

———. 1972c. Quail management information. F.A. Proj. W-53, R-22. Ariz. Game
and Fish Dept.

———. 1972d. Bandtail Pigeon management information. F.A. Proj. W-53, R-22.
Ariz. Game and Fish Dept. 15 pp.

———. 1972e. Dove management information. F.A. Proj. W-53, R-22. Ariz. Game
and Fish Dept.

———. 1973a. Afghan Whitewing Pheasant management information. F.A. Proj.
W-53, R-23. Final Rept. Ariz. Game and Fish Dept.

———. 1973b. Western range extensions of Scaled Quail, Montezuma Quail and
Coppery-tailed Trogon in Arizona. *West. Birds* 4:59–60.

———. 1973c. Bandtail Pigeon management information. F.A. Proj. W-53, R-23.
Ariz. Game and Fish Dept.

———. 1974a. Blue Grouse introduction. F.A. Proj. W-53, R-24. Ariz. Game and
Fish Dept.

———. 1974b. Quail management information. F.A. Proj. W-53, R-24. Ariz. Game
and Fish Dept.

———. 1974c. Bandtail Pigeon management information. F.A. Proj. W-53, R-24.
Ariz. Game and Fish Dept.

———. 1975. Migratory upland game bird banding investigations. F.A. Proj. W-53,
R-25. Ariz. Game and Fish Dept.

———. 1976a. Blue Grouse introduction. F.A. Proj. W-53, R-26. Ariz. Game and
Fish Dept.

——. 1976b. Migratory upland game bird banding investigations. F.A. Proj. W-53, R-26. Ariz. Game and Fish Dept.

——. 1977a. Scaled Quail investigations. F.A. Proj. W-53, R-27, Ariz. Game and Fish Dept.

——. 1977b. Tree squirrel investigations. F.A. Proj. W-53, R-27, Ariz. Game and Fish Dept.

——. 1977c. Migratory upland game bird banding investigations. F.A. Proj. W-53, R-27. Ariz. Game and Fish Dept.

——. 1978a. Grazing, grassland cover and game birds. *Trans. N. Amer. Wildl. Nat. Resour. Conf.* 43:477–85.

——. 1978b. Migratory upland game bird banding investigations. F.A. Proj. W-53, R-28, Final Rept. Ariz. Game and Fish Dept.

——. 1978c. Where are all the whitewings? *Arizona Wildl. Views* 21:1–12.

——. 1979. Factors influencing reproductive success and population densities in Montezuma Quail. *J. Wildl. Manage.* 43:522–26.

——. 1980. Migratory game bird banding analysis. F.A. Proj. W-53, R-30. Ariz. Game and Fish Dept.

——. 1981. Migratory game bird banding analysis. F.A. Proj. W-53, R-31. Ariz. Game and Fish Dept.

——. (ed.) 1982a. Biotic communities of the American Southwest—United States and Mexico. *Desert Plants* 4:1–342.

——. 1982b. Special report on the status of the Arizona White-winged Dove in Mexico. F.A. Proj. W-53, R-31, Spec. Rept. Ariz. Game and Fish Dept.

——. 1984. Arizona's tree squirrels. Ariz. Game and Fish Dept.

——. 1985a. *Arizona wetlands and waterfowl*. Tucson: Univ. of Arizona Press.

——. 1985b. *The grizzly in the Southwest*. Norman: Univ. of Oklahoma Press.

Brown, D. E., D. R. Blankenship, P. K. Evans, W. H. Kiel, Jr., G. L. Waggerman, and C. K. Winkler. 1977. White-winged Dove (*Zenaida asiatica*). In *Management of migratory shore and upland game birds in North America*. ed. G. C. Sanderson, pp. 246–72. Washington, D.C.: International Association of Fish and Wildlife Agencies.

Brown, D. E. (chair.), D. Bunnell, G. Herron, C.D. Littlefield, D.L. Perkins, R. W. Schlorff, and R. Vanderberge. 1983. Pacific Flyway management plan: Colorado River Valley population of Greater Sandhill Cranes. U.S. Fish and Wildlife Service, Portland, Oregon.

Brown, D. E., C. L. Cochran, and T. E. Waddell. 1978. Using call-counts to predict hunting success for Scaled Quail. *J. Wildl. Manage.* 42:281–87.

Brown, D. E., and D. H. Ellis. 1977. Masked Bobwhite recovery plan. U.S. Fish and Wildlife Service Office of Endangered Species, Region 2, Albuquerque. Revised by S. W. Hoffman, 1984.

——. 1984. Masked Bobwhite recovery plan. Revised by S. W. Hoffman. U.S. Fish and Wildlife Service Office of Endangered Species, Region 2, Albuquerque.

Brown, D. E., and R. J. Gutiérrez. 1980. Sex ratios, sexual selection, and sexual dimorphism in quails. *J. Wildl. Manage.* 44:198–202.

Brown, D. E., C. H. Lowe, and C. P. Pase. 1979. A digitized classification system for the biotic communities of North America with community (series) and association examples for the Southwest. *J. Ariz.-Nev. Acad. Sci.* 14 (Suppl. 1): 1–16.

Brown, D. E., and J. O'Neil. 1975. Blue Grouse. F.A. Proj. W-53, R-26. Ariz. Game and Fish Dept.

Brown, D. E., and Project Personnel. 1971. Afghan Whitewing Pheasant information. F.A. Proj. W-53, R-21. Ariz. Game and Fish Dept.

Brown, D. E., and R. H. Smith. 1976. Predicting hunting success from call counts of Mourning and White-winged doves. *J. Wildl. Manage.* 40:743–49.

———. 1980. Winter-spring precipitation and population levels of Blue Grouse in Arizona. *Wildl. Soc. Bull.* 8:136–41.

Brown, D. E., and R. W. White. 1971. Blue Grouse management information. F.A. Proj. W-53, R-21. Ariz. Game and Fish Dept.

Brown, H. 1884. *Ortyx virginianus* in Arizona. *Forest and Stream* 22(6):104.

———. 1885. Arizona quail notes. *Forest and Stream* 25(23): 445.

———. 1887. Arizona bird notes. *Forest and Stream* 27:462.

———. 1900. Conditions governing bird life in Arizona. *Auk* 17:31–34.

———. 1904. Masked Bobwhite (*Colinus ridgwayi*). *Auk* 21:209–13.

Brown, R. L. 1967. The extent of breeding by immature Mourning Doves (*Zenaidura macroura marginella*) in southern Arizona. M.S. thesis, Univ. of Arizona, Tucson.

———. 1975. Mearns' Quail capture method. F.A. Proj. W-78, R-15, Final Rept. Ariz. Game and Fish Dept.

———. 1976. Mearns' Quail census technique. F.A. Proj. W-78, R-15, Final Rept. Ariz. Game and Fish Dept.

———. 1978. An ecological study of Mearns' Quail. F.A. Proj. W-78, R-22, Final Rept. Ariz. Game and Fish Dept.

———. 1982. Effects of livestock grazing on Mearns' Quail in southeastern Arizona. *J. Range Manage.* 35:727–32.

Browning, B. M. 1962. Food habits of the Mourning Dove in California. *Calif. Fish and Game Bull.* 48:91–115.

Buller, R. J. 1976. Recent studies of age ratios of Sandhill Cranes in the Central Flyway. *Proc. 1976 Int. Crane Workshop* 1:78–85.

Bunnell, S. D., and D. W. Olson. 1978. Utah upland game annual report. F.A. Proj. W-65, R-E-25, Publ. 78–8.

Bunnell, S. D., J. A. Rensel, J. F. Kimball, Jr., and M. L. Wolfe. 1977. Determination of age and sex of Dusky Blue Grouse. *J. Wildl. Manage.* 41:662–66.

Butler, W. I. 1977. A White-winged Dove nesting study in three riparian communities on the Lower Colorado River. M.S. thesis, Arizona State Univ., Tempe.

Cable, D. R. 1975. Influence of precipitation on perennial grass production in the semidesert Southwest. *Ecology* 56:981–86.

Campbell, H. 1960. An evaluation of gallinaceous guzzlers for quail in New Mexico. *J. Wildl. Manage.* 24:21–26.

———. 1968. Seasonal precipitation and Scaled Quail in eastern New Mexico. *J. Wildl. Manage.* 32:641–44.

———. 1972. A population study of Lesser Prairie Chickens in New Mexico. *J. Wildl. Manage.* 26:689–99.

Campbell, H., and B. K. Harris. 1965. Mass population dispersal and long distance movements in Scaled Quail. *J. Wildl. Manage.* 29:801–05.

Campbell, H., and L. Lee. 1956. Notes on the sex ratio of Gambel's and Scaled quail in New Mexico. *J. Wildl. Manage.* 20:93–94.

Campbell, H., D. K. Martin, P. E. Ferkovich, and B. K. Harris. 1973. Effects of hunting and some other environmental factors on Scaled Quail in New Mexico. *Wildl. Monogr.* 34:1–49.

Carr, J. 1960. Mourning Dove and White-winged Dove nest surveys during the summer of 1960. F.A. Proj. W-53-R. Supplemental Report. Ariz. Game and Fish Dept.

Christensen, G. C. 1970. The Chukar Partridge. *Nevada Dept. of Wildl. Bull.*, No. 4:1–82.

Cosper, P. M. 1949a. A trend census technique for Merriam's Turkey in the Coconino National Forest of Arizona. F.A. Proj. Spec. Rept. Ariz. Game and Fish Comm.

———. 1949b. Merriam's Turkey population trend survey technique. F.A. Proj. 25-R. Ariz. Game and Fish Comm.

———. 1952. Statewide trapping and transplanting project. F.A. Proj. 11-D. Ariz. Game and Fish Comm.

Cottam, C. P., and P. Knappen. 1939. Food of some uncommon North American birds. *Auk* 56:138–69.

Cottam, C. P., and J. B. Trefethen, eds. 1968. *Whitewings: The life history, status and management of the White-winged Dove*. Princeton: D. Van Nostrand.

Couch, A. B., Jr. 1963. Notes on the biology of *Microlynchia pusilla* Speiser, a lousefly of Mourning Doves. *J. Parasitol.* 49:140–46.

Couch, A. B., Jr., B. Grabstald, and K. J. Kimbrough. 1962. Nasal mites of the Mourning Dove. *J. Grad. Research Center* 30:42–43.

Coues, E. 1866. List of the birds of Fort Whipple, Arizona, with which are incorporated all other species ascertained to inhabit the Territory; with brief critical and field notes, descriptions of new species, etc. *Proc. Acad. Nat. Sci. Phila.* 18:39–100.

———. 1874. *Birds of the Northwest*. U.S. Geo. Surv. Misc. Publ. No. 3.

———. 1903. *Key to the North American birds . . .*, 5th ed., vol. 2. Boston: Dana Estes and Co.

Cutts, J. J. 1965. *The conquest of California and New Mexico*. Albuquerque: Univ. of New Mexico Press.

Darwin, C. 1871. *The descent of man, and selection in relation to sex*. 2 vols. New York: Appleton.

Davis, C. A., and M. W. Anderson. 1973. Seasonal food use by Mourning Doves in the Mesilla Valley, south-central New Mexico. *Agri. Exp. Sta. Bull.* 612:1–21.

Davis, C. A., R. C. Barkley, and W. C. Haussamen. 1975. Scaled Quail foods in southeastern New Mexico. *J. Wildl. Manage.* 39:496–502.

Davis, D. E., and R. L. Winstead. 1980. Estimating the numbers of wildlife populations. In *Wildlife management techniques manual*, ed. S. D. Schemnitz, pp. 221–45. Washington, D.C.: The Wildlife Society.

Davis, G. P., Jr. 1982. Man and wildlife: The American exploration period, 1824–1865, ed. N. B. Carmony and D. E. Brown. Ariz. Game and Fish Dept.

Day, G. I., S. D. Schemnitz, and R. D. Taber. 1980. Capturing and marking wild animals. In *Wildlife management techniques manual*, ed. S. D. Schemnitz, pp. 61–88. Washington, D.C.: The Wildlife Society.

Delacour, J. T. 1951. *The pheasants of the world*. London: Country Life Ltd.; New York: Charles Scribner's Sons.

Denniston, C. 1978. Small population size and genetic diversity. In *Endangered birds: Management techniques for preserving threatened species*, ed. S. A. Temple, pp. 281–89. Madison: Univ. of Wisconsin Press.

Dice, L. R. 1943. *The biotic provinces of North America*. Ann Arbor: Univ. of Michigan Press.

Dickens, G. 1979. Pheasant distribution and numbers along the Virgin River in Management Unit 13B. F.A. Proj. W-53, R-29. Spec. Rept. Ariz. Game and Fish Dept.

Dobrott, S. J. 1985. Masked Bobwhite Quail release program. Memorandum to Regional Director.

Drewien, R. C. 1973. Ecology of Rocky Mountain Greater Sandhill Cranes. Ph.D. diss., Univ. of Idaho, Moscow.

Drewien, R. C., and E. G. Bizeau. 1974. Status and distribution of Greater Sandhill Cranes in the Rocky Mountains. *J. Wildl. Manage.* 38:720–42.

Drewien, R. C., R. J. Oakleaf, and W. H. Mullins. 1976. The Sandhill Crane in Nevada. *Proc. 1976 Int. Crane Workshop* 1:130–38.

Dunning, J. B., Jr. 1984. Body weights of 686 species of North American birds. *West. Bird Band. Assoc. Monogr.* 1:1–38.

Durivage, J. E. 1937. *Southern trails to California in 1849*, ed., R. P. Bieber. Glendale: Arthur H. Clark. *Southwest Historical Series* 5:1–386.

Earl, J. C. 1952. Statewide trapping and transplanting project. F.A. Proj. W-11, D-12. Ariz. Game and Fish Comm.

Eicher, G. J., Jr. 1943a. Annual mid-summer statewide Gambel Quail survey, 1943. F.A. Proj. 9-R: Quail. Ariz. Game and Fish Comm.

———. 1943b. Correlation of the fall hunting season with the midsummer quail survey, 1943. F.A. Proj. 9-R. Special Report: Quail. Ariz. Game and Fish Comm.

———. 1943c. Ecological study of Cochise County quail headquarters. F.A. Proj. 9-R. Special Report: Quail. Ariz. Game and Fish Comm.

———. 1944a. Survey of conditions in Cochise County quail areas. F.A. Proj. 9-R. Special Report: Quail. Ariz. Game and Fish Comm.

———. 1944b. Ecological study of Cochise County quail headquarters areas. F.A. Proj. 9-R. Special Report: Quail. Ariz. Game and Fish Comm.

———. 1944c. White-winged Dove survey. F.A. Proj. 9-R. Ariz. Game and Fish Comm.

———. 1944d. Report on the 1943 White-winged Dove investigations. F.A. Proj. 9-R. Ariz. Game and Fish Comm.

———. 1945. Midsummer quail survey, July 5 to 31, 1944. F.A. Proj. 9-R: Special Quail. Ariz. Game and Fish Comm.

Ellis, D. H., and J. W. Carpenter. 1981. A technique for vasectomizing birds. *J. Field Ornith.* 52:69–71.

Ellis, D. H., S. J. Dobrott, and J. G. Goodwin, Jr. 1978. Reintroduction techniques for Masked Bobwhites. In *Endangered birds: Management techniques for preserving threatened species*, ed. S. A. Temple, pp. 345–54. Madison: Univ. of Wisconsin Press.

Ellis, D. H., and J. A. Serafin. 1977. A research program for the endangered Masked Bobwhite. *J. World Pheasant Assoc.* 2:16–33.

Emlen, J. T., Jr. 1940. Sex and age ratios in survival of the California Quail. *J. Wildl. Manage.* 4:92–99.

Emlen, S. T., and L. W. Oring. 1977. Ecology, sexual selection, and the evolution of mating systems. *Science* 197:215–23.

Emory, W. H. 1848. *Notes of a military reconnaissance from Fort Leavenworth, in Missouri, to San Diego, in California, including parts of the Arkansas, Del Norte, and Gila rivers.* 30th Congr., 1st sess. Exec. Doc. 41. Washington, D.C.: Wendell and Van Benthuysen.

Evans, J. 1972. Bandtail Pigeon trapping techniques in Arizona. F.A. Proj. W-53, R-22. Ariz. Game and Fish Dept.

Falvey, E. B. 1936. His majesty the Mearns' Quail. *Game Breeder and Sportsman* 40:226–27, 241.

Ffolliot, P. F., R. E. Thill, W. P. Clary, and F. R. Larson. 1977. Animal use of ponderosa pine forest openings. *J. Wildl. Manage.* 41:782–84.

Fisher, R. A. 1958. *The genetical theory of natural selection*, 2nd ed. New York: Dover.

Fitzhugh, E. L. 1970. Literature review and bibliography of the Band-tailed Pigeons of Arizona, Colorado, New Mexico and Utah. Spec. Rept., Ariz. Game and Fish Dept.

———. 1974. Chronology of calling, egg laying, crop gland activity, and breeding among wild Band-tailed Pigeons in Arizona. Ph.D. diss., Univ. of Arizona, Tucson.

Francis, W. J. 1970. The influence of weather on population fluctuations in California Quail. *J. Wildl. Manage.* 34:249–66.

Fredrickson, L. H., J. M. Anderson, F. M. Kozlik, and R. A. Ryder. 1977. American coot (*Fulica americana*). In *Management of migratory shore and upland game birds in North America*, ed. G. C. Sanderson, pp. 122–47. Washington, D.C.: International Association of Fish and Wildlife Agencies.

Freeman, L. R. 1923. *The Colorado River: Yesterday, today and tomorrow.* New York: Dodd, Mead.

French, W. 1965. *Some recollections of a western ranchman: New Mexico, 1883–1899.* 2 vols. New York: Argosy-Antiquarian Ltd.

Gallizioli, S. 1951a. Annual midsummer quail survey. F.A. Proj. 53-R-2. Ariz. Game and Fish Comm.

———. 1951b. Sectional quail hunts. F.A. Proj. 53, R-2. Spec. Rept. Ariz. Game and Fish Comm.

———. 1951c. Graham Mountains special turkey-squirrel hunt. F.A. Proj. W-53-R. Ariz. Game and Fish Comm.

———. 1952a. Pre-season and post-season survey of the Oracle Junction area quail range. F.A. Proj. 53, R-2. Compl. Rept. Ariz. Game and Fish Comm.

———. 1952b. White-winged and Mourning dove banding. F.A. Proj. 53-R-1. Compl. Rept. Ariz. Game and Fish Dept.

———. 1953a. Annual quail survey and investigations. F.A. Proj. W-53, R-3. Compl. Rept. Ariz. Game and Fish Comm.

———. 1953b. Dove investigations. F.A. Proj. W-53, R-3. Ariz. Game and Fish Dept. Compl. Rept.

———. 1954a. Quail hunt information. F.A. Proj. W-53-R. Ariz. Game and Fish Comm.

———. 1954b. Hunting season information on the Mourning and Whitewing doves of Arizona. Spec. Rept. Ariz. Game and Fish Dept.

———. 1955a. Quail hunt information. F.A. Proj. W-53-R. Ariz. Game and Fish Dept.

———. 1955b. Hunting season information on the Mourning and White-winged doves of Arizona. *Proc. West. Assoc. State Game and Fish Comm.* 35:226–35.

———. 1955c. Dove hunt information. F.A. Proj. W-53, R-5. Compl. Rept. Ariz. Game and Fish Dept.

———. 1957a. Gambel's Quail population trend technique. F.A. Proj. W-78-R. Ariz. Game and Fish Dept.

———. 1957b. The influence of hunting upon quail populations. F.A. Proj. W-78-R. Ariz. Game and Fish Dept.

———. 1957c. The influence of hunting upon quail populations. F.A. Proj. W-78-R. Ariz. Game and Fish Dept.

———. 1961a. Water and Gambel Quail. Ariz. Game and Fish Dept. Bull.

———. 1961b. Gambel Quail population trend techniques. F.A. Proj. W-78-R. Ariz. Game and Fish Dept.

———. 1961c. The current status and management of the Mourning Dove in the western management unit. *Trans. N. Amer. Wildl. Nat. Resour. Conf.* 26:395–406.

———. 1965. Quail research in Arizona. Ariz. Game and Fish Dept. F.A. Proj. W-78-R, Special Bull.

———. 1967. Sex and age differential vulnerability to trapping and shooting in Gambel's Quail. *Proc. West. Assoc. State Game and Fish Comm.* 47:262–71.

Gallizioli, S., and G. Day. 1954. Quail survey and investigations. F.A. Proj. W-53, R-4. Ariz. Game and Fish Dept.

Gallizioli, S., S. Levy, and J. Levy. 1967. Can the Masked Bobwhite be saved from extinction? *Audubon Field Notes* 2:571–75.

Gallizioli, S., and R. Smith. 1960. Gambel Quail and cottontail rabbit population trend techniques. F.A. Proj. W-78-R. Ariz. Game and Fish Dept.

———. 1962. Quail survey and hunt information. F.A. Proj. W-53-R. Ariz. Game and Fish Dept.

Gallizioli, S., and E. L. Webb. 1958. The influence of hunting upon quail populations. F.A. Proj. W-78. Ariz. Game and Fish Dept.

———. 1959. The influence of hunting upon quail populations. F.A. Proj. W-78-R. Ariz. Game and Fish Dept.

———. 1960. The influence of hunting upon quail populations. F.A. Proj. W-78-R. Ariz. Game and Fish Dept.

———. 1961. The influence of hunting upon quail populations. F.A. Proj. W-78-R. Ariz. Game and Fish Dept.

Gambrell, R. 1940a. Catalina, Chiricahua and Pinaleño mountain turkey restocking project. F.A. Proj. 2-D. Ariz. Game and Fish Comm.

———. 1940b. Catalina, Chiricahua, Pinaleño, and Bradshaw mountain turkey restocking project. F.A. Proj. 8-D. Ariz. Game and Fish Comm.

———. 1941. Trapping and transplanting. F.A. Proj. 11-D. Ariz. Game and Fish Comm.

———. 1942. Trapping and transplanting. F.A. Proj. 11-D. Ariz. Game and Fish Comm.

Gilman, M. F. 1911. Doves on the Pima Reservation. *Condor* 13:51–56.

Glading, B. 1943. A self-filling quail watering device. *Calif. Fish and Game* 29:151–64.

Goforth, W. R. 1971. The three-bird chase in Mourning Doves. *Wilson Bull.* 83:419–24.

Goldman, E. A., and R. T. Moore. 1945. The biotic provinces of Mexico. *J. Mammal.* 26:347–60.

Goodwin, J. G., Jr. 1982. Habitat needs of Masked Bobwhites in Arizona. Univ. of Ariz. contract report to U.S. Fish and Wildlife Service.

———. 1983. Potential release sites for Masked Bobwhites in Arizona. Arizona Nat. Herit. Progr. Contract report to U.S. Fish and Wildlife Service.

Goodwin, J. G., Jr., and C. R. Hungerford. 1977. Habitat use by native Gambel's and Scaled quail and released Masked Bobwhite Quail in southern Arizona. USDA For. Serv. Res. Paper RM-197.

———. 1981. 1981 releases and surveys of Masked Bobwhite. Univ. of Ariz. contract report to U.S. Fish and Wildlife Service.

Gorsuch, D. M. 1934. Life history of the Gambel Quail in Arizona. *Univ. of Arizona Bull.* 2:1–89.

Grater, R. K. 1937. Check list of birds of Grand Canyon National Park. *Grand Canyon Nat. Hist. Assoc. Nat. Hist. Bull.* 8:1–55.

Greenwalt, L. A. 1955. Mobility of Gambel's Quail (*Lophortyx gambeli gambeli*) in a desert-grassland–oak woodland area in southeastern Arizona. M.S. thesis, Univ. of Arizona, Tucson.

Griffing, J. P. 1972. Population characteristics and behavior of Scaled Quail in southeastern New Mexico. M.S. thesis, New Mexico State Univ., Las Cruces.

Griner, L. A. 1940a. Proposed quail management plan for Cochise County, Arizona. F.A. Proj. 9-R. Ariz. Game and Fish Comm.

———. 1940b. Report of field trip to Cochise and Santa Cruz counties, May 15–25, 1940. F.A. Report 4-D: Quail. Ariz. Game and Fish Comm.

———. 1940c. Proposed quail refuge area in Pinal County, June 12–17, 1940. F.A. Proj. 4-D: Quail. Ariz. Game and Fish Comm.

———. 1940d. Quail investigations of Wickenburg–Congress Junction area. F.A. Proj. 4-D: Quail. Ariz. Game and Fish Comm.

———. 1940e. Investigations of quail problems in Yuma Valley, May 8–11, 1940. F.A. Proj. 4-D. Ariz. Game and Fish Comm.

———. 1940f. Lake Imperial quail range survey, May 10, 1940. F.A. Proj. 4-D. Ariz. Game and Fish Comm.

———. 1941. Quail survey of the Verde Valley. F.A. Proj. 9-R. Ariz. Game and Fish Comm.

Griner, L. A., T. L. Kimball, and A. A. Nichol. 1941. Gambel Quail in Arizona: A preliminary report. F.A. Proj. 9-R. Ariz. Game and Fish Comm.

Griner, L. A., and A. A. Nichol. 1940b. Preliminary report on a quail survey of certain parts of Mohave County. F.A. Proj. 9-R: Quail. Ariz. Game and Fish Comm.

Grinnell, G. B. 1884. A quail new to the United States fauna. *Forest and Stream*: 243.

Grinnell, J. 1914. An account of the mammals and birds of the Lower Colorado Valley with special reference to the distributional problems presented. *Univ. Calif. Pub. Zool.* 12:51–294.

———. 1927. A critical factor in the existence of southwestern game birds. *Science* 64:528–29.

Grinnell, J., H. C. Bryant, and T. I. Storer. 1918. *The game birds of California.* Berkeley: Univ. of California Press.

Gullion, G. W. 1954. Management of Nevada's Gambel Quail resource. *Proc. Annual Conf. West. Assoc. State Game and Fish Commissioners* 32:234–39.

———. 1956a. Evidence of double-brooding in Gambel Quail. *Condor* 58:232–34.

———. 1956b. Let's go desert quail hunting. *Nevada Fish and Game Comm. Biol. Bull.* 2:1–76.

———. 1957. Gambel Quail disease and parasite investigation in Nevada. *Amer. Midl. Nat.* 57:414–20.

———. 1958. The proximity effect of water distribution on desert small game populations. *Proc. West. Assoc. State Game and Fish Comm.* 38:187–89.

———. 1960a. The ecology of Gambel's Quail in Nevada and the arid Southwest. *Ecology* 41:518–36.

———. 1960b. Gambel's Quail: Their social behaviors at waterholes. *Naturalist* 10–13.

———. 1962. Organization and movements of coveys of a Gambel Quail population. *Condor* 64:402–15.

Gullion, G. W., and G. C. Christensen. 1957. A review of the distribution of gallinaceous game birds in Nevada. *Condor* 59:128–38.

Gullion, G. W., and A. M. Gullion. 1964. Water economy of Gambel Quail. *Condor* 66:32–40.

Gullion, G. W., W. M. Pulich, and F. G. Evenden. 1959. Notes on the occurrence of birds in southern Nevada. *Condor* 61:278–97.

Gutiérrez, R. J. 1973. Reproductive biology of the Band-tailed Pigeon (*Columba fasciata*). M.S. thesis, Univ. of New Mexico, Albuquerque.

———. 1977a. A preliminary evaluation of potential habitat for Mountain Quail in Arizona. F.A. Proj. W-53, R-27, Spec. Rept. Ariz. Game and Fish Dept.

————. 1977b. Comparative ecology of the Mountain and California quail in the Carmel Valley, California. Ph.D. diss., Univ. of California, Berkeley.

Hall, J. M. 1948. Turkey sex, age ratio and population trend survey. F.A. Proj. 25-R. Ariz. Game and Fish Comm.

————. 1950a. An evaluation of the Sitgreaves turkey habitat restoration plots. F.A. Proj. 25-R. Ariz. Game and Fish Comm.

————. 1950b. Turkey sex, age ratio and population trend survey. F.A. Proj. 25-R. Ariz. Game and Fish Comm.

————. 1952. Turkey hunt information. F.A. Proj. 53-R. Ariz. Game and Fish Comm.

Hand, G. O. 1862. George O. Hand's diary. Arizona Historical Society, Tucson.

Hanson, H. C., and C. W. Kossack. 1963. The Mourning Dove in Illinois. *Ill. Dept. Conserv. Tech. Bull.* 2:1–133.

Hanson, H. C., N. D. Levine, C. W. Kossack, S. Kantor and L. J. Stannard. 1957. Parasites of the Mourning Dove (*Zenaidura macroura carolinensis*) in Illinois. *J. Parasitol.* 43:186–93.

Hardy, J. W., and C. A. McConnell. 1967. Bobwhite Quail: Propagation, conditioning and habitat management. Tenn. Game and Fish Comm.

Hargrave, L. L. 1939. Reconnaissance report of turkey food on a portion of the winter range of the Wild Turkey in Arizona. F.A. Proj. 3-R. Ariz. Game and Fish Comm.

————. 1940. Data on grouse and quail. F.A. Proj. R-3. Ariz. Game and Fish Comm.

Harrison, B. 1893. Arizona gun clubs and game. *Arizona Magazine* 2:55–58.

Harrison, C. 1978. *A field guide to the nests, eggs and nestlings of North American birds.* Glasgow: William Collins' Sons.

Hart, D. 1933. Stocking with day-old quail. *Game Breeder and Sportsman* 37.

Hastings, J. R., and R. R. Humphrey. 1969. Climatological data and statistics for Sonora and northern Sinaloa. *Univ. Ariz. Inst. Atmos. Physics., Tech. Reports Meteor. Climat. Arid Regions* 19:1–96.

Hastings, J. R., and R. M. Turner. 1965. *The changing mile: An ecological study of vegetation change with time in the lower mile of an arid and semi-arid region.* Tucson: Univ. of Arizona Press.

Hayes, B. 1850. Diary of Judge Benjamin Hayes. Bancroft Library, Univ. of California, Berkeley, and Arizona Historical Society, Tucson.

Heller, E. 1901. Notes on some little known birds of southern California. *Condor* 3:100.

Henderson, C. W. 1971. Comparative temperature and moisture responses in Gambel and Scaled quail. *Condor* 73:430–36.

Henshaw, H. W. 1875. Report upon the ornithological collections made in portions of Nevada, Utah, California, Colorado, New Mexico, and Arizona, during the years 1871, 1872, 1873, and 1874. In G. M. Wheeler, *Annual Report Geol. Surv. West of 100th Meridian* 5:120, 131–507, 977–89.

Hewitt, O. H., ed. 1967. *The Wild Turkey and its management.* Washington D.C.: Wildlife Society.

Hickey, J. J. 1952. Survival studies of banded birds. *U.S. Fish and Wildl. Serv., Spec. Sci. Rept.* 15:1–177.

Hoffman, D. M. 1965. The Scaled Quail in Colorado: Range, population, status, harvest. *Colo. Game, Fish and Parks Dept. Tech. Publ.* 18:1–47.

———. 1968. Roosting sites and habits of Merriam's Turkeys in Colorado. *J. Wildl. Manage.* 32:859–66.

———. 1978. Population dynamics and habitat relationships of Blue Grouse. Colo. F.A. Proj. W-37, R-31.

Hollon, W. E. 1966. *The Great American Desert: Then and now.* New York: Oxford Univ. Press.

Howard, O. W. 1900. Nesting of the Mexican Wild Turkey in the Huachuca Mtns., Ariz. *Condor* 2:55–57.

Howe, H. F. 1977. Sex ratio adjustment in the Common Grackle. *Science* 198:744–45.

Humphrey, R. R. 1958. The desert grassland: A history of vegetational change and an analysis of causes. *Botan. Rev.* 24:193–252.

Hungerford, C. R. 1955. A preliminary evaluation of quail malaria in southern Arizona in relation to habitat and quail mortality. *Trans. N. Amer. Wildl. Nat. Resour. Conf.* 20:209–19.

———. 1960a. The factors affecting the breeding of Gambel's Quail *Lophortyx gambelii gambelii* in Arizona. Ph.d. diss., Univ. of Arizona, Tucson.

———. 1960b. Water requirements of Gambel's Quail. *Trans. N. Amer. Wildl. Nat. Resour. Conf.* 25:231–40.

———. 1962. Adaptions shown in selection of food by Gambel's Quail. *Condor* 64:213–19.

———. 1964. Vitamin A and productivity in Gambel's Quail. *J. Wildl. Manage.* 28:141–47.

Irby, H. D. 1964. The relationship of calling behavior to Mourning Dove populations and production in southern Arizona. Ph.D. diss., Univ. of Arizona, Tucson.

Irby, H. D., and L. H. Blankenship. 1966. Breeding behavior of immature Mourning Doves. *J. Wildl. Manage.* 30:598–604.

Jantzen, R. A. 1954. Turkey hunt information. F.A. Proj. W-53-R. Ariz. Game and Fish Comm.

———. 1955a. Turkey hunt information. F.A. Proj. W-53-R. Ariz. Game and Fish Comm.

———. 1955b. Turkey survey. F.A. Proj. W-53-R. Ariz. Game and Fish Comm.

———. 1956a. Turkey survey. F.A. Proj. W-53-R. Ariz. Game and Fish Comm.

———. 1956b. Turkey hunt information. F.A. Proj. W-53-R. Ariz. Game and Fish Comm.

———. 1957a. Turkey survey. F.A. Proj. W-53-R. Ariz. Game and Fish Dept.

———. 1957b. Turkey hunt information. F.A. Proj. W-53-R. Ariz. Game and Fish Dept.

———. 1958a. Turkey survey. F.A. Proj. W-53-R. Ariz. Game and Fish Dept.

———. 1958b. Turkey hunt information. F.A. Proj. W-53-R. Ariz. Game and Fish Dept.

Jeffrey, R. G., C. E. Braun, D. E. Brown, D. R. Halliday, P. M. Howard, C. E. Kebbe, D. H. Nish, W. A. Smith, and T. P. Zapatka. 1977. Band-tailed Pigeon (*Columba fasciata*). In *Management of migratory shore and upland game birds in*

North America, ed. G. C. Sanderson, pp. 208–45. Washington, D.C.: International Association of Fish and Wildlife Agencies.

Johnsgard, P. A. 1973. *Grouse and quails of North America*. Lincoln: Univ. of Nebraska Press.

———. 1975. *North American game birds of upland and shoreline*. Lincoln: Univ. of Nebraska Press.

———. 1983. *Cranes of the world*. Bloomington: Indiana Univ. Press.

Jones, K. H. 1981. Effects of grazing and timber management on Merriam's Turkey habitat in mixed conifer vegetation of south central New Mexico. M.S. thesis, New Mexico State Univ., Las Cruces.

Kabat, C., and D. R. Thompson. 1963. Wisconsin quail, 1834–1962: Population dynamics and habitat management. *Wisc. Conserv. Dept. Tech. Bull.* 30:1–135.

Kearny, T. H., and R. H. Peebles. 1960. *Arizona flora*. Berkeley: Univ. of California Press.

Keeler, J. E., C. C. Allin, J. M. Anderson, S. Gallizioli, K. E. Gamble, D. W. Hayne, W. H. Kiel, Jr., F. W. Martin, J. L. Ruos, K. C. Sadler, L. D. Soileau, and C. E. Braun. 1977. Mourning Dove (*Zenaida macroura*). In *Management of migratory shore and upland game birds in North America*, ed. G. C. Sanderson, pp. 274–98. Washington, D.C.: International Association of Fish and Wildlife Agencies.

Kendeigh, S. C. 1961. *Animal ecology*. Englewood Cliffs, N.J.: Prentice-Hall.

Kennerly, C. B. R. 1856. Report on the zoology of the [Whipple] expedition. In *Reports of explorations and surveys . . .* 33rd Congr., 2nd sess. H. Doc. 91. Washington, D.C.: A. O. P. Nicholson.

Kimball, T. L. 1940a. Quail survey of the Queen Creek–Superstition Mountain area. F.A. Rept. 9-R. Ariz. Game and Fish Comm.

———. 1940b. Quail survey of the Gila River Valley. F.A. Proj. 9-R. Ariz. Game and Fish Comm.

———. 1940c. Quail survey of the Congress Junction–Date Creek area, June 22–30, 1940. F.A. Proj. 9-R: Quail. Ariz. Game and Fish Comm.

———. 1941a. Restoration reconnaissance in Cochise County. Part I. F.A. Proj. 9-R: Quail. Ariz. Game and Fish Comm.

———. 1941b. Maricopa County quail program. Part 1: Paradise Valley Area. F.A. Proj. Arizona 9-R: Quail. Ariz. Game and Fish Comm.

———. 1941c. Supplementary survey of the Congress Junction–Date Creek area—July 6, 1941. F.A. Proj. 9-R: Quail. Ariz. Game and Fish Comm.

———. 1941d. Investigation of crop damage by quail on the J. Fred Hoover Ranch. F.A. Proj. 9-R: Special Rept. Ariz. Game and Fish Comm.

———. 1942a. 1942 midsummer survey to determine the current production of quail. F.A. Proj. 9-R. Special Report: Quail. Ariz. Game and Fish Comm.

———. 1942b. Quail survey of Maricopa County. F.A. Proj. 9-R. Ariz. Game and Fish Comm.

———. 1942c. Ecological study of quail headquarter areas in Cochise County. F.A. Proj. 9-R. Special Report: Quail. Ariz. Game and Fish Comm.

———. 1943. A standardized method of conducting the annual midsummer quail survey. F.A. Proj. 9-R. Special Report: Quail. Ariz. Game and Fish Comm.

―――. 1945. Survey of conditions in Cochise County quail areas. F.A. Proj. 9-R. Ariz. Game and Fish Comm.

―――. 1946a. Experimental quail watering devices, February–March, 1946. F.A. Proj. 9-R. Special Report: Quail. Ariz. Game and Fish Comm.

―――. 1946b. 1946 midsummer survey to determine the current production of quail. F.A. Proj. 9-R. Special Report: Quail. Ariz. Game and Fish Comm.

―――. 1946c. Superstition Mountain experimental quail water development. F.A. Proj. 9-R. Special Report: Quail. Ariz. Game and Fish Comm.

―――. 1947. Turkey age ratio classification survey on the Apache National Forest. F.A. Proj. 25-R. Ariz. Game and Fish Comm.

Kimball, T. L., and L. K. Griner. 1942. Cochise County quail management. *Ariz. Wildl.* 4:12, 16.

Knopp, T. B. 1956. Factors affecting the abundance and distribution of Merriam's Turkey (*Meleagris gallopavo merriami*) in southeastern Arizona. M.S. thesis, Univ. of Arizona, Tucson.

Kufeld, R. C. 1962a. Quail survey and hunt information. F.A. Proj. W-53-R. Ariz. Game and Fish Dept.

―――. 1962b. Turkey management information. F.A. Proj. W-53-R. Ariz. Game and Fish Dept.

―――. 1963. Summary and analysis of data for Mourning and White-winged doves banded in Arizona. F.A. Proj. W-53, R-13, Spec. Rept. Ariz. Game and Fish Dept.

―――. 1964. Quail survey and hunt information. F.A. Proj. W-53-R. Ariz. Game and Fish Dept.

―――. 1965. Quail management information. F.A. Proj. W-53-R. Ariz. Game and Fish Dept.

―――. 1966. Dove management information. F.A. Proj. W-53-R. Ariz. Game and Fish Dept.

Lawson, L. L. 1940a. Investigation of pheasant release area in the South Mountain–Phoenix region of the Salt River. F.A. Special Rept. Ariz. Game and Fish Comm.

―――. 1940b. Statewide pheasant restocking. F.A. Proj. 10-D: Ariz. Game and Fish Comm.

―――. 1940c. Quail survey of the Desert Wells Refuge. F.A. Proj. 4-D: Quail. Ariz. Game and Fish Comm.

―――. 1940d. Quail survey of the Camelback Refuge. F.A. Proj. 4-D: Quail. Ariz. Game and Fish Comm.

―――. 1940e. Reports on quail damage in Lower Gila River Valley, Yuma County. F.A. Proj. 4-D: Quail. Ariz. Game and Fish Comm.

―――. 1941. Turkey trapping activities. F.A. Proj. 11-D. Ariz. Game and Fish Comm.

―――. 1949a. Chukar Partridge investigations. F.A. Proj. W-40, R-1. Ariz. Game and Fish Comm.

―――. 1949b. Annual midsummer quail survey. F.A. Proj. 40-R. Ariz. Game and Fish Comm.

―――. 1949c. Whitewing Dove study. F.A. Proj. 40-R. Ariz. Game and Fish Dept.

———. 1950. Quail research and investigations in southern Arizona. F.A. Proj. 40-R-2. Ariz. Game and Fish Comm.

———. 1951a. Special investigations on the status of Pheasant and Chukar Partridge in Arizona. F.A. Proj. W-40, R-2. Ariz. Game and Fish Comm.

———. 1951b. Masked Bobwhite and Benson Quail trapping in Sonora, Mexico. F.A. Proj. W-40, R-2. Ariz. Game and Fish Comm.

LeCount, A. L. 1966. Blue Grouse—Unit 1. F.A. Special Rept. Ariz. Game and Fish Dept.

———. 1969. Blue Grouse management information. F.A. Proj. W-53, R-19. Ariz. Game and Fish Dept.

———. 1970a. Blue Grouse management information. F.A. Proj. W-53, R-20. Ariz. Game and Fish Dept.

———. 1970b. Fall food preferences of the Blue Grouse in the White Mountains of Arizona. M.S. thesis, Univ. of Arizona, Tucson.

Lehmann, V. M. 1953. Bobwhite fluctuations and vitamin A. *Trans. N. Amer. Wildl. Nat. Resour. Conf.* 18:199–246.

Leopold, A. 1933. *Game management*. New York: Charles Scribner's Sons.

———. 1939. Age determination in quail. *J. Wildl. Manage.* 3:261.

———. 1945. Sex and age ratios among Bobwhite Quail in southern Missouri. *J. Wildl. Manage.* 9:30–34.

———. 1949. *A Sand County almanac and sketches here and there.* New York: Oxford Univ. Press.

Leopold, A. S. 1959. *Wildlife of Mexico.* Berkeley: Univ. of California Press.

———. 1977. *The California Quail.* Berkeley: Univ. of California Press.

———. 1979. Field identification of juvenile Sandhill Cranes. *J. Wildl. Manage.* 43:211–14.

Leopold, A. S., and R. A. McCabe. 1957. Natural history of the Montezuma Quail in Mexico. *Condor* 59:3–26.

Levy, S. H., and J. J. Levy. 1984. Report of a brief reconnaissance of the Buenos Aires Ranch during August 1982 and 1983 in search of the Masked Bobwhite. Report to the U.S. Fish and Wildlife Service.

Lewis, J. C. 1967. Physical characteristics and physiology. In *The Wild Turkey and its management*, ed. O. H. Hewitt, pp. 45–72. Washington, D.C.: Wildlife Society.

———. 1976. Roost habitat and roosting behavior of Sandhill Cranes. *Proc. 1976 Int. Crane Workshop* 1:93–104.

———. 1979a. Field identification of juvenile Sandhill Cranes. *J. Wildl. Manage.* 43:211–14.

———. 1979b. Taxonomy, food and feeding habitat of Sandhill Cranes, Platte Valley, Nebraska. *Proc. 1978 Int. Crane Workshop* 2:21–28.

Lewis, J. C., G. W. Archibald, R. C. Drewien, C. R. Frith, E. A. Gluesing, R. D. Klataske, C. D. Littlefield, J. Sands, W. J. D. Stephen, and L. E. Williams, Jr. 1977. Sandhill Crane (*Grus canadensis*). In *Management of migratory shore and upland game birds in North America*, ed. G. C. Sanderson, pp. 4–43. Washington, D.C.: International Association of Fish and Wildlife Agencies.

Ligon, J. S. 1927. *Wildlife of New Mexico: Its conservation and management.* Santa Fe: New Mexico State Game Commission.

———. 1942. Masked Bobwhite Quail in southern Arizona and notes on efforts at restoration. Memorandum, July 3.

———. 1946. *History and Management of Merriam's Wild Turkey.* Albuquerque: New Mexico Game and Fish Comm.

———. 1952. The vanishing Masked Bobwhite. *Condor* 54:48–50.

———. 1961. *New Mexico birds and where to find them.* Albuquerque: Univ. of New Mexico Press.

Littlefield, C. D. 1973. Report on Sandhill Cranes for Baja California, California, Oregon, Washington, and Alaska. Sandhill Crane Committee Report.

Locke, L. N. 1961. Pox in Mourning Doves in the United States. *J. Wildl. Manage.* 25:211–12.

Lockwood, D. R., and D. H. Sutcliffe. 1984. Distribution, mortality, and reproduction of Merriam's Turkey in New Mexico. *Proc. National Wild Turkey Symp.* 5:309–16.

Lowe, C. H., Jr. 1955. Gambel Quail and water supply in Tiburón Island, Sonora, Mexico. *Condor* 57:244.

Lumholtz, C. 1912. *New trails in Mexico.* Reprint. Glorieta, N.M.: Rio Grande Press, 1971.

McCarthy, J. 1899. Biennial report of the Fish and Game Commissioners to the governor of the Territory of Arizona for the years 1897–1898. Phoenix.

McCormick, D. P. 1975. Effect of mesquite control on small game populations. M.S. thesis, Univ. of Arizona, Tucson.

MacGregor, W. G. 1953. An evaluation of California Quail management. *Proc. West. Assoc. State Game and Fish Comm.* 33:157–60.

MacGregor, W. G., and M. Inlay. 1951. Observations on failure of Gambel Quail to breed. *Calif. Fish and Game* 37:218–19.

Mackey, J. P. 1965. Cooing frequency and permanence of pairing of Mourning Doves. *J. Wildl. Manage.* 29:824–29.

McLean, D. D. 1930. The quail of California. *Calif. Div. of Fish and Game Bull.* 2:1–47.

———. 1959. O'er deserts and mountains band returns trace doves. *Outdoor Calif.* 20:3, 7.

MacMillen, R. E. 1961. The minimum water requirements of Mourning Doves. *Condor* 64:165–66.

Marshall, J. T. 1957. The birds of pine-oak woodland in southern Arizona and adjacent Mexico. *Cooper Ornith. Club, Pac. Coast Avifauna* 32:1–123.

Martin, E. M. 1979. Hunting and harvest trends for migratory game birds other than waterfowl, 1964–76. *USDI Fish and Wildl. Serv., Spec. Sci. Rept.* 218:1–37.

Mearns, E. A. 1884–86. Unpublished field notes. U.S. National Museum, Washington, D.C.

———. 1890. Observations on the avifauna of portions of Arizona. *Auk* 7:45–55, 251–64.

———. 1914. Diagnosis of a new subspecies of Gambel's Quail from Colorado. *Proc. Biol. Soc. Washington* 27:133.

Merriam, C. H. 1890. Results of a biological survey of the San Francisco Mountain region and desert of the Little Colorado, Arizona. *USDA N. Amer. Fauna* 3:1–112.

Miles, A. K. 1976. Fall migration of Mourning Doves in the Western Management Unit. M.S. thesis, Oregon State University, Corvallis.

Miller, L. 1943. Notes on the Mearns' Quail. *Condor* 45:104–09.

Mills, S. G., and F. W. Reichenbacher. 1982. Status of the Masked Bobwhite (*Colinus virginianus ridgwayi*) in Sonora, Mexico. Ariz. Nat. Heritage Progr. contract report to U.S. Fish and Wildlife Service.

Mollhausen, H. B. 1858. *Diary of a journey from the Mississippi to the Pacific with a United States government expedition.* 2 vols. London: Longman, Brown, Green, Longman, and Roberts.

Monson, G., and A. R. Phillips. 1981. *Annotated checklist of the birds of Arizona,* 2nd ed. Tucson: Univ. of Arizona Press.

Moore, T. C. 1965. Origin and disjunction of the alpine tundra flora on San Francisco Mountains, Arizona. *Ecology* 46:860–64.

Moran, G. H. 1878. Sonora Pigeon and Arizona Quail. *Forest and Stream* 11:310.

Mosby, H. S., and C. O. Handley. 1943. *The Wild Turkey in Virginia: Its status, life history, and management.* Richmond: Va. Comm. Game and Inland Fish.

Mullins, W. H., and E. G. Bizeau. 1978. Summer foods of Sandhill Cranes in Idaho. *Auk* 95:175–78.

Murie, A. 1946. The Merriam Turkey on the San Carlos Indian Reservation. *J. Wildl. Manage.* 10:329–33.

Mussehl, T. W. 1963. Blue Grouse brood cover selection and land-use implications. *J. Wildl. Manage.* 27:547–55.

Neff, J. A. 1940a. Notes on nesting and other habits of the White-winged Dove in Arizona. *J. Wildl. Manage.* 4:279–90.

———. 1940b. Range, population and game status of the Western White-winged Dove in Arizona. *J. Wildl. Manage.* 4:117–27.

———. 1941. Arboreal nests of the Gambel Quail in Arizona. *Condor* 43:117–18.

———. 1942. The White-winged Dove in Sonora, Mexico—summer of 1942. Ariz. Game and Fish Dept. Mimeographed.

———. 1947. Habits, food and economic status of the Band-tailed Pigeon. *U.S. Fish and Wildl. Serv., N. Amer. Fauna* 58:1–76.

Nelson, A. L., and A. C. Martin. 1953. Gamebird weights. *J. Wildl. Manage.* 17:36–42.

Nelson, E. W. 1885. Annual report of the Board of Regents of the Smithsonian Institution for the year 1884. In S. F. Baird, *Report of the Secretary,* p. 22. Washington, D.C.: U.S. Government Printing Office.

———. 1927. Vanishing migratory birds. *Saturday Evening Post* 199:12–13, 92, 94, 97.

Nickerson, M. F., G. E. Brink, and C. Fedennia. 1976. Principal range plants of the central and southern Rocky Mountains. USDA Forest Service Gen. Tech. Rep. RM-20:1–121.

Norton, H. W., T. G. Scott, W. R. Hanson, and W. D. Klimstra. 1961. Whistling-cock indices and Bobwhite populations in autumn. *J. Wildl. Manage.* 25:398–403.

O'Connor, J. 1939. *Game in the desert.* New York: Derrydale Press.

Ough, W. D., and J. C. deVos, Jr. 1984. Masked Bobwhite investigations on the Buenos Aires Ranch in August 1982. Report to the U. S. Fish and Wildlife Service.

Palmer, W. C. 1965. Meteorological drought. *U.S. Weather Bureau Res. Paper* 45:1–58.

Perkins, D. L., and D. E. Brown. 1981. The Sandhill Crane in Arizona. *Ariz. Game and Fish Dept. Spec. Publ.* 11:1–47.

Phelps, J. E. 1955. The adaptability of the Turkish Chukar Partridge (*Alectoris graeca* Meisner) in central Utah. M.S. thesis, Utah State Agricultural College.

Phillips, A. R. 1959. Las subspecies de la codorniz de Gambel y el problema de los cambros climáticos en Sonora. *Sobretiro de los Anales de Instituto de Biologia* 29:361–74.

Phillips, A. R., J. T. Marshall, and G. Monson. 1964. *The birds of Arizona.* Tucson: Univ. of Arizona Press.

Phillips, F. E. 1980. A basic guide to roost site management for Merriam's Turkeys. *Ariz. Game and Fish Dept. Wildl. Digest* 12:1–6.

———. 1982. Wild Turkey investigations and management recommendations for the Bill Williams Mountain area. *Ariz. Game and Fish Dept. Spec. Rept.* 13:1–50.

Phillips, P. 1937. Dusky Grouse in the Chuskai Mountains of northeastern Arizona and northwestern New Mexico. *Auk* 54:203–04.

Pitelka, F. A. 1948. Notes on the distribution and taxonomy of Mexican game birds. *Condor* 50:121–22.

Potter, T. D., S. D. Schemnitz, and W. D. Zeedyk. 1984. Status and ecology of Gould's Turkey in the Peloncillo Mountains of New Mexico. *Proc. National Wild Turkey Symp.* 5:1–24.

Price, W. W. 1899. Some winter birds of the Lower Colorado Valley. *Bull. Cooper Ornith. Club* 1:89–93.

Project Personnel. 1954. Turkey survey. F.A. Proj. W-53-R. Ariz. Game and Fish Comm.

———. 1961. Turkey management information. F.A. Proj. W-53-R. Ariz. Game and Fish Dept.

———. 1963. Turkey management information. F.A. Proj. W-53-R. Ariz. Game and Fish Dept.

———. 1964. Turkey management information. F.A. Proj. W-53-R. Ariz. Game and Fish Dept.

———. 1968a. Afghan Whitewing Pheasant management information. F.A. Proj. W-53, R-18. Ariz. Game and Fish Dept.

———. 1968b. Scaled Quail habitat evaluation. F.A. Proj. W-53-R. Ariz. Game and Fish Dept.

———. 1969. Afghan Whitewing Pheasant management information. F.A. Proj. W-53, R-19. Ariz. Game and Fish Dept.

———. 1970. Afghan Whitewing Pheasant management information. F.A. Proj. W-53, R-20. Ariz. Game and Fish Dept.

Pulich, W. M. 1948. White-winged Dove survey. F.A. Proj. 24-R-2. Ariz. Game and Fish Dept.

Raitt, R. J., and R. E. Genelly. 1964. Dynamics of a population of California Quail. *J. Wildl. Manage.* 28:127–40.

Raitt, R. J., and R. D. Ohmart. 1966. Annual cycle of reproduction and molt in Gambel Quail of the Rio Grande Valley, southern New Mexico. *Condor* 68:6:541–61.

————. 1968. Sex and age ratios in Gambel Quail of the Rio Grande Valley, southern New Mexico. *Southwest. Nat.* 13:27–34.

Rasmussen, D. I. 1941. Biotic communities of Kaibab Plateau. *Ecol. Monogr.* 11:229–75.

Rea, A. M. 1973. The Scaled Quail (*Callipepla squamata*) of the Southwest: Systematic and historical consideration. *Condor* 75:322–29.

————. 1977. Historic changes in the avifauna of the Gila River Indian Reservation. Ph.D. diss., Univ. of Arizona, Tucson.

————. 1980. Late Pleistocene and Holocene turkeys in the Southwest. *Contrib. Sci. Nat. Hist. Mus. Los Angeles County* 330:209–24.

Reeves, H. M. (comp.) 1975. A contribution to an annotated bibliography of North American cranes, rails, woodcock, snipe, doves, and pigeons. Washington, D.C.: Office of Migrat. Bird Manage. PB-240999.

Reeves, R. H. 1951. Turkey management practices directed toward increased turkey populations. F.A. Proj. 49-R. Ariz. Game and Fish Comm.

————. 1953a. Man as an influencing factor on Merriam's Turkey. F.A. Proj. W-49-R. Ariz. Game and Fish Comm.

————. 1953b. Turkey hunt information. F.A. Proj. W-53-R. Ariz. Game and Fish Comm.

————. 1953c. Range and distribution of Merriam's Wild Turkey on the Coconino, Sitgreaves, Tonto, and Apache national forests. F.A. Proj. W-49. Ariz. Game and Fish Comm.

————. 1953d. Habitat and climatic factors as an influence on Merriam's Turkey. F.A. Proj. W-49-R. Ariz. Game and Fish Comm.

————. 1953e. Merriam's Turkey–predator relationship. F.A. Proj. W-49-R. Ariz. Game and Fish Comm.

————. 1953f. Merriam's Turkey management recommendations. F.A. Proj. W-49-R. Ariz. Game and Fish Comm.

————. 1953g. Merriam's Turkey survey techniques. F.A. Proj. W-49-R. Ariz. Game and Fish Comm.

————. 1954. Turkey trapping and banding. F.A. Proj. W-53, R-4. Ariz. Game and Fish Comm.

Reeves, R. H., and W. G. Swank. 1955. Food habits of Merriam's Turkey. F.A. Proj. W-49-R. Ariz. Game and Fish Comm.

Reinecke, K. J., and G. L. Krapu. 1979. Spring food habits of Sandhill Cranes in Nebraska. *Proc. 1978 Int. Crane Workshop* 2:13–20.

Ridgway, R. R. 1884. *Ortyx virginianus* not in Arizona. *Forest and Stream* 22:124.

————. 1886. Arizona quail. *Forest and Stream* 25:484.

————. 1887. *A manual of North American birds*. Philadelphia: J. P. Lippincott.

Robbins, C. S., B. Brunn, and H. S. Zim. 1966. *A guide to field identification: Birds of North America*. New York: Golden Press.

Rosene, W., Jr. 1957. A summer whistling cock count of Bobwhite Quail as an index to wintering populations. *J. Wildl. Manage.* 21:153–58.

————. 1969. *The Bobwhite Quail: Its life and management*. New Brunswick, N.J.: Rutgers Univ. Press.

Russell, P. 1932. The Scaled Quail in New Mexico. M.S. thesis, Univ. of New Mexico, Albuquerque.

Russo, J. P. 1957. Kaibab turkey transplant. Special Report. Ariz. Game and Fish Dept.

Saunders, G. B. 1968. Seven new subspecies of White-winged Doves from Mexico, Central America and southwestern United States. *USDI Bureau of Sport Fisheries and Wildl., N. Amer. Fauna* 65:1–30.

Schemnitz, S. D. 1961. Ecology of the Scaled Quail in the Oklahoma panhandle. *Wildl. Monogr.* 8:1–47.

———. (ed.) 1980. *Wildlife management techniques manual*, 4th rev. ed. Washington, D. C.: Wildlife Society.

Schemnitz, S. D., D. L. Goerndt, and K. H. Jones. 1984. Habitat needs and management of Merriam's Turkey in south-central New Mexico. *Proc. National Wild Turkey Symp.* 5:199–231.

Schwartz, C. C. 1974. Analysis of survey data collected on Bobwhite in Iowa. *J. Wildl. Manage.* 38:674–78.

Scott, V. E., and E. L. Boeker. 1975. Ecology of Merriam's Wild Turkey on the Fort Apache Indian Reservation. In *Proc. Third National Wild Turkey Symp.*, ed. L. K. Hall, pp. 141–58. Austin: Texas Chapter of the Wildlife Society.

Scott, W. E. D. 1886. On the avi-fauna of Pinal County, Arizona, with remarks on some birds of Pima and Gila counties, Arizona. *Auk* 3:1–421.

Seber, G. A. F. 1973. *The estimation of animal abundance and related parameters.* New York: Hafner Press.

Secrist, F. P. 1896. Hunting big game in Arizona. *Amer. Field* 46:1–2.

Senteney, P. F. 1957. Factors affecting the nesting of Gambel Quail in southern Arizona. M.S. thesis, Univ. of Arizona, Tucson.

Severson, K. E. 1986. Spring and early summer habitats and foods of Blue Grouse, Arizona. *J. Ariz.-Nev. Acad. Sci.* 21:13–18.

Shaw, H. 1961a. Influence of salt cedar on White-winged Doves in the Gila Valley. F.A. Proj. W-53-R, Special Rept. Ariz. Game and Fish Dept.

———. 1961b. Dove management information. F.A. Proj. W-53-R. Ariz. Game and Fish Dept.

———. 1966a. Investigation of factors influencing Merriam's Turkey populations. F.A. Proj. W-78-R. Ariz. Game and Fish Dept.

———. 1966b. Effects of timber management practices on turkey habitat. F.A. Proj. W-78-R. Ariz. Game and Fish Dept.

———. 1967a. Investigation of factors influencing turkey populations. F.A. Proj. W-78-R. Ariz. Game and Fish Dept.

———. 1967b. Effects of timber management practices on turkey habitat. F.A. Proj. W-78-R. Ariz. Game and Fish Dept.

———. 1968a. Investigations of factors influencing turkey populations. F.A. Proj. W-78-R. Ariz. Game and Fish Dept.

———. 1968b. Effects of timber management practices on turkey habitat. F.A. Proj. W-78-R. Ariz. Game and Fish Dept.

———. 1969. Effects of hunting on turkeys. F.A. Proj. W-78-R. Ariz. Game and Fish Dept.

———. 1970. Activity patterns of turkeys in ponderosa pine vegetation type. F.A. Proj. W-78-R. Ariz. Game and Fish Dept.

———. 1971. Activity patterns of turkeys in ponderosa pine vegetation type. F.A. Proj. W-78-R. Ariz. Game and Fish Dept.

———. 1977. Habitat use patterns of Merriam's Turkey in Arizona. F.A. Proj. W-78-R. Ariz. Game and Fish Dept. Final Report.

Shaw, H., and J. Jett. 1960. Mourning Dove and White-winged Dove nesting in the Gila River bottom between Gillespie Dam and the junction of the Salt and Gila rivers, Maricopa County, Arizona. F.A. Proj. W-53-R. Special Rept. Ariz. Game and Fish Dept.

Sheldon, C. 1979. *The wilderness of desert bighorns and Seri Indians.* Phoenix: Ariz. Desert Bighorn Sheep Society.

Shreve, F. 1942. The desert vegetation of North America. *Botan. Rev.* 8:195–246.

———. 1951. Vegetation and flora of the Sonoran Desert. Vol. 1. Vegetation. *Carnegie Inst. Wash. Publ.* 591:1–192.

Shreve, F., and I. L. Wiggins. 1964. *Vegetation and flora of the Sonoran Desert.* 2 vols. Stanford: Stanford Univ. Press.

Sibley, C. G. 1957. The evolutionary and taxonomic significance of sexual dimorphism and hybridization in birds. *Condor* 59:166–91.

Sileo, L., Jr. 1970. The incidence and virulence of *Trichomonas gallinae* (Rivolta) in Mourning Dove (*Zenaidura macroura*, Linnaeus) populations in southern Arizona. Ph.D. diss., Univ. of Arizona, Tucson.

Sileo, L., Jr., and F. L. Fitzhugh. 1969. Incidence of trichomoniasis in the Band-tailed Pigeons of southern Arizona. *Bull. Wildl. Disease Assoc.* 5:146.

Silovsky, G. D. 1969. Distribution and mortality of Pacific Coast Band-tailed Pigeons. M.S. thesis, Oregon State Univ., Corvallis.

Silovsky, G. D., H. M. Wright, L. H. Sisson, T. L. Fox, and S. W. Harris. 1968. Methods for determining age in Band-tailed Pigeons. *J. Wildl. Manage.* 32:421–24.

Sinn, J. 1978. Surveys and management of Bobwhite Quail. F.A. Proj. W-15-R Rep. Nebr. Game and Parks Comm.

Skutch, A. G. 1940. Some aspects of Central American bird-life. II. Plumage, reproduction and sound. *Sci. Month.* 41:500–511.

Slonaker, J. L. 1912. Two new Arizona records. *Condor* 14:154.

Smith, P. M. 1984. Report on three years of experimental Sandhill Crane hunting in southeastern Arizona. F.A. Proj. W-53, R-34. Ariz. Game and Fish Dept.

Smith, R. H. 1961a. Age classification of the Chukar Partridge. *J. Wildl. Manage.* 25:84–86.

———. 1961b. Turkey population trend techniques. F.A. Proj. W-78-R. Ariz. Game and Fish Dept.

———. 1962. Turkey population trend techniques. F.A. Proj. W-78-R. Ariz. Game and Fish Dept.

Smith, R. H., and S. Gallizioli. 1957. Gambel's Quail population trend technique. F.A. Proj. W-78-R. Ariz. Game and Fish Dept.

———. 1958. Gambel Quail population trend techniques. F.A. Proj. W-78-R. Ariz. Game and Fish Dept.

———. 1963. Gambel Quail population trend techniques. F.A. Proj. W-78-R. Ariz. Game and Fish Dept.

———. 1965. Predicting hunter success by means of a spring call count of Gambel Quail. *J. Wildl. Manage.* 29:806–13.

Snyder, W. D. 1967. Experimental habitat improvements for Scaled Quail. *Colo. Game, Fish and Parks Dept. Publ.* 19:1–65.

Sowls, L. K. 1960. Results of a banding study of Gambel's Quail in southern Arizona. *J. Wildl. Manage.* 24:185–90.

Spicer, R. L. 1959. Wild turkey in New Mexico: An evaluation of habitat development. *New Mexico Dept. of Game and Fish Bull.* 10:1–64.

Stabler, R. M. 1951. A survey of Colorado Band-tailed Pigeons, Mourning Doves, and wild common pigeons for *Trichomonas gallinae*. *J. Parasitol.* 37:470–72.

Stabler, R. M., and C. P. Matteson. 1950. Incidence of *Trichomonas gallinae* in Colorado Mourning Doves and Band-tailed Pigeons. *J. Parasitol.* 36:25–26.

Stair, J. 1956a. Quail hunt information. F.A. Proj. W-53-R. Ariz. Game and Fish Dept.

———. 1956b. Dove investigations. F.A. Proj. W-53, R-6, W.P. 3, Job 9. Ariz. Game and Fish Dept.

———. 1957a. Quail survey and investigations. F.A. Proj. W-53-R. Ariz. Game and Fish Dept.

———. 1957b. Quail hunt information. F.A. Proj. W-53-R. Ariz. Game and Fish Dept.

———. 1957c. Dove investigations. F.A. Proj. W-53, R-7, W.P. 3, Job 9. Compl. Rept. Ariz. Game and Fish Dept.

———. 1957d. Dove hunt information. F.A. Rept. W-53, R-7. Ariz. Game and Fish Dept.

———. 1958a. Quail hunt and survey information. F.A. Proj. W-53-R. Ariz. Game and Fish Dept.

———. 1958b. Dove hunt information and dove investigations. F.A. Rept. W-53, R-8. Ariz. Game and Fish Dept.

———. 1959b. White-winged Dove die-off at Maricopa. F.A. Special Rept. W-53, R-9, W.P. 3. Ariz. Game and Fish Dept.

———. 1960a. Quail hunt and survey information. F.A. Proj. W-53-R. Ariz. Game and Fish Dept.

———. 1960b. Dove management information. F.A. Proj. W-53-R, Completion Rept. Ariz. Game and Fish Dept.

———. 1961a. Quail management information. F.A. Proj. W-53-R. Ariz. Game and Fish Dept.

———. 1961b. Dove management information. F.A. Proj. W-53-R. Ariz. Game and Fish Dept.

———. 1970. Chronology of the nesting season of White-winged Doves *Zenaida asiatica mearnsi* (Ridgway) in Arizona. M.S. thesis, Univ. of Arizona, Tucson.

Stanford, J. A. 1952. An evaluation of the adoption method of Bobwhite Quail propagation. *Trans. N. Amer. Wildl. Nat. Resour. Conf.* 17:330–37.

State Game Warden Reports, 1917–21. Mimeo. Ariz. Game and Fish Dept. files.

Stephen, W. J. D., R. S. Miller, and J. P. Hatfield. 1966. Demographic factors affecting management of Sandhill Cranes. *J. Wildl. Manage.* 30:581–89.

Stephens, F. P. 1885. Notes of an ornithological trip in Arizona and Sonora. *Auk* 2:225–31.

————. 1903. Bird notes from southern California and western Arizona. *Condor*
5:75–78, 100.

Stirling, I., and J. F. Bendell. 1970. The reproductive behavior of Blue Grouse.
Syesis 3:161–71.

Stoddard, H. L. 1931, 1946. *The Bobwhite Quail: Its habits, preservation and increase.*
New York: Charles Scribner's Sons.

Stokes, A. W. 1961. Voice and social behavior of the Chukar Partridge. *Condor*
63:111–27.

Stone, W. 1905. On a collection of birds and mammals from the Colorado delta,
Lower California. *Proc. Acad. Nat. Sci. Phila.* 57:676–90.

Straus, M. A. 1966. Incidence of *Trichomonas gallinae* in Mourning Dove,
Zenaidura macroura, populations of Arizona. M.S. thesis, Univ. of Arizona,
Tucson.

Sumner, E. L. 1935. A life history study of the California Quail, with
recommendations for conservation and management. *Calif. Fish and Game*
21:185–342.

Swank, W. G. 1955a. Feather molt as an ageing technique for Mourning Doves.
J. Wildl. Manage. 19:412–13.

————. 1955b. Nesting and production of the Mourning Dove in Texas. *Ecology*
36:495–505.

Swank, W. G., and S. Gallizioli. 1953. The influence of hunting and of rainfall upon
Gambel's Quail. Ariz. Game and Fish Dept. Spec. Rept.

————. 1954. The influence of hunting and of rainfall upon Gambel's Quail
populations. *Trans. N. Amer. Wildl. Nat. Resour. Conf.* 19:283–96.

Swarth, H. S. 1904. Birds of the Huachuca Mountains, Arizona. *Pac. Coast
Avifauna* 4:1–70.

————. 1905. Summer birds of the Papago Indian Reservation and of the Santa
Rita Mountains, Arizona. *Condor* 7:22–28.

————. 1909. Distribution and molt of the Mearns Quail. *Condor* 1:39–43.

————. 1914. A distributional list of the birds of Arizona. *Cooper Ornith. Club,
Pac. Coast Avifauna* 10:1–133.

————. 1920. *Birds of the Papago, Saguaro National Monument and the neighboring
region, Arizona.* Washington, D.C.: National Park Service.

Tacha, T. C. 1981. Behavior and taxonomy of Sandhill Cranes from mid-continental
North America. Ph.D. diss., Oklahoma State Univ., Stillwater.

Tacha, T. C., D. C. Martin, and C. G. Endicott. 1979. Mortality of Sandhill Cranes
associated with utility highlines in Texas. *Proc. 1978 Int. Crane Workshop*
2:175–76.

Tharp, J. E. 1971. A study of Scaled and Bobwhite quail with special emphasis on
habitat requirements and brush control. M.S. thesis, Texas Technical Univ.,
Austin.

Tinkham, E. R. 1941. An ecological study of the Western White-winged Dove
Melopelia asiatica mearnsi in the saguaro-palo verde, mesquite and oak zones of
Pima County in south central Arizona. Spec. Repts. F.A. Division. Ariz. Game
and Fish Comm.

————. 1942. White-winged Dove investigations in Pima County, Arizona. F.A.
Proj. 9-R. Ariz. Game and Fish Comm.

Todd, R. L. 1986. A salt water marsh hen in Arizona. F.A. Proj. W-95-R, Compl.
    Rept. Ariz. Game and Fish Dept.
Toepfer, E. W., L. N. Locke, and L. H. Blankenship. 1966. The occurrence of
    Trichomonas gallinae in White-winged Doves in Arizona. *Bull. Wildl. Disease
    Assoc.* 2:13.
Tomlinson, R. E. 1963. A method for drive-trapping Dusky Grouse. *J. Wildl.
    Manage.* 24:563–66.
———. 1972a. Review of literature on the endangered Masked Bobwhite. *U.S. Fish
    and Wildl. Serv. Resour. Publ.* 108:1–28.
———. 1972b. Current status of the endangered Masked Bobwhite Quail. *Trans.
    N. Amer. Wildl. Nat. Resour. Conf.* 37:294–311.
———. 1975. Weights and wing lengths of wild Sonoran Masked Bobwhite
    during fall and winter. *Wilson Bull.* 87:180–86.
Trivers, R. L. 1972. Parental investment and sexual selection. In *Sexual selection
    and the descent of man, 1871–1971*, ed. B. G. Campbell, pp. 137–79. Chicago:
    Aldine.
Truett, J. C. 1966. Movements of immature Mourning Doves, *Zenaidura macroura
    marginella*, in southern Arizona. M.S. thesis, Univ. of Arizona, Tucson.
Turner, G. I., and H. A. Paulsen, Jr. 1976. Management of mountain grasslands in
    the central Rockies: The status of our knowledge. USDA For. Serv., Rocky
    Mtn. For. and Range Exp. Sta. Res. Pap. RM-161.
Van Rossem, A. J. 1911. Winter birds of the Salton Sea Region. *Condor* 13:129–37.
———. 1925. Flight feathers as age indicators in *Dendrogapus. Ibis* 12:417–22.
———. 1945. A distributional survey of the birds of Sonora, Mexico. *Occ. Papers
    Mus. Zool.* 21:1–379.
Viers, C. E., Jr. 1970. The relationship of calling behavior of White-winged Doves
    to population and production in southern Arizona. Ph.D. diss., Univ. of
    Arizona, Tucson.
Vorhies, C. T. 1928. Do southwestern quail require water? *Amer. Nat.* 62:446–52.
Vorhies, C. T., and W. P. Taylor. 1933. The life histories and ecology of *Lepus alleni*
    and *Lepus californicus* ssp., in relation to grazing in Arizona. *Ariz. Agr. Exp. Sta.
    Tech. Bull.* 49:471–587.
Walker, L. W. 1964. Return of the Masked Bobwhite. *Zoonooz Fed.*:10–15.
Walkinshaw, L. H. 1949. *The Sandhill Cranes.* Cranbrook Inst. Sci. Bull. No. 29.
———. 1956. Sandhill Cranes killed by flying into power lines. *Wilson Bull.*
    68:325–26.
———. 1965a. Attentiveness of cranes at their nest. *Auk* 82:465–76.
———. 1965a. A new Sandhill Crane from central Canada. *Can. Field Nat.*
    79:181–84.
———. 1965b. Territories of cranes. *Mich. Acad. of Science, Arts and Letters*, 75–88.
———. 1973. *Cranes of the world.* New York: Winchester Press.
Wallmo, O. C. 1954. Nesting of Mearns' Quail in southeastern Arizona. *Condor*
    56:125–28.
———. 1956a. Determination of sex and age of Scaled Quail. *J. Wildl. Manage.*
    20:154–58.
———. 1956b. *Ecology of Scaled Quail in west Texas.* Austin: Texas Game and Fish
    Comm.

Wauer, R. H. 1973. *Birds of Big Bend National Park and vicinity.* Austin: Univ. of
    Texas Press.
Weaver, H., and W. L. Haskell. 1968. Age and sex determination of the Chukar
    Partridge. *J. Wildl. Manage.* 32:46–50.
Webb, L. G. 1949. The life history and status of the Mourning Dove, *Zenaidura
    macroura carolinensis* (L.) in Ohio. Ph.D. diss., Ohio State Univ.
Webb, P. M. 1953a. Introduction and study of exotic bird species. F.A. Proj. W-58,
    R-1. Ariz. Game and Fish Comm.
———. 1953b. Statewide wildlife restocking. F.A. Proj. W-11-D. Ariz. Game and
    Fish Comm.
———. 1953c. Trapping, tagging, and releasing quail on the Three Bar area. F.A.
    Proj. W-11-D. Ariz. Game and Fish Comm.
———. 1954a. A study of the introduction, release and survival of Chukar
    Partridge, Sand Grouse, and other game species. F.A. Proj. W-58, R-2. Ariz.
    Game and Fish Dept.
———. 1954b. Quail restocking. F.A. Proj. W-11-D. Ariz. Game and Fish Comm.
———. 1955. Statewide wildlife restocking project. F.A. Proj. W-11, D-15. Ariz.
    Game and Fish Comm.
———. 1956a. A study of the introduction, release and survival of Chukar
    Partridge, Sand Grouse, and other game species. F.A. Proj. W-58, R-4. Ariz.
    Game and Fish Comm.
———. 1956b. Statewide wildlife restocking project. F.A. Proj. W-11, D-16. Ariz.
    Game and Fish Dept.
———. 1957a. A study of the introduction, release and survival of Chukar
    Partridge, Sand Grouse, and other game species. F.A. Proj. W-85, R-5. Ariz.
    Game and Fish Dept.
———. 1957b. Arizona wildlife restocking project. F.A. Proj. W-11-D. Ariz. Game
    and Fish Dept.
———. 1958a. A study of the introduction, release and survival of Chukar
    Partridge, Sand Grouse, and other game species. F.A. Compl. Rept. W-58,
    R-6. Ariz. Game and Fish Dept.
———. 1958b. The effect of water development on the distribution and abundance
    of quail. F.A. Proj. W-78-R. Ariz. Game and Fish Dept.
———. 1959a. Distribution, survival and reproduction of introduced species. F.A.
    Compl. Rept. W-78, R-3. Ariz. Game and Fish Dept.
———. 1959b. Statewide wildlife restocking project. F.A. Proj. W-11, D-18. Ariz.
    Game and Fish Dept.
———. 1960. Statewide wildlife restocking project. F.A. Proj. W-11, D-19. Ariz.
    Game and Fish Dept.
———. 1961a. The effect of water development on the distribution and abundance
    of quail and deer. F.A. Proj. W-78-R. Ariz. Game and Fish Dept.
———. 1961b. Statewide wildlife restocking project. F.A. Proj. W-11-D. Ariz.
    Game and Fish Dept.
———. 1962. Statewide wildlife restocking project. F.A. Proj. W-11-D. Ariz. Game
    and Fish Dept.
———. 1967a. Bandtailed Pigeon management information. F.A. Proj. W-53, R-17.
    Ariz. Game and Fish Dept.

———. 1967b. Dove management information. F.A. Proj. W-53-R. Compl. Rept. Ariz. Game and Fish Dept.

———. 1968a. Chukar Partridge management information. F.A. Proj. W-53, R-18. Ariz. Game and Fish Dept.

———. 1968b. Bandtail Pigeon management information. F.A. Proj. W-53, R-18. Ariz. Game and Fish Dept.

Webb, P. M., and R. Robeck. 1962. Statewide wildlife restocking project. F.A. Compl. Rept. Proj. W-11-D. Ariz. Game and Fish Dept.

———. 1963. Statewide wildlife restocking project. F.A. Proj. W-11-D. Ariz. Game and Fish Dept.

Wetmore, A. 1920. Observations on the habits of White-winged Doves. *Condor* 22:140–46.

White, J. A. 1973. Molt of Colorado Band-tailed Pigeons. M.S. thesis, Colorado State Univ., Fort Collins.

White, R. W. 1965. Blue Grouse—Unit 1. F.A. Spec. Rept. Ariz. Game and Fish Dept.

Wigal, D. D. 1973. A survey of the nesting habitats of the White-winged Dove in Arizona. *Ariz. Game and Fish Dept. Spec. Rept.* 2:1–37.

Wight, H. M., R. U. Mace, and W. M. Batterson. 1967. Mortality estimates of an adult Band-tailed Pigeon population in Oregon. *J. Wildl. Manage.* 31:519–25.

Wiley, L. 1916. Bird notes from Palo Verde, Imperial County, California. *Condor* 18:230–31.

Wiley, R. H. 1974. Evolution of social organization and life-history patterns among grouse. *Quart. Rev. Biol.* 49:201–27.

Willard, F. C. 1912. A week a-field in south Arizona. *Condor* 14:53.

———. 1914. Report of the State Game Warden of Arizona. Ariz. Board of Control. Phoenix.

Williams, G. R. 1957. Changes in sex ratio occurring with age in young California Quail in central Otago, New Zealand. *Bird-Banding* 28:145–50.

Williams, L. E., Jr. 1961. Notes on wing molt in the yearling Wild Turkey. *J. Wildl. Manage.* 25:439–40.

Wilson, E. O. 1975. *Sociobiology: The new synthesis*. Cambridge: Harvard Univ. Press.

Wilson, R. 1976. Cattle died by thousands. *Arizona Republic*, October 17, "Arizona Days."

Wrakestraw, G. (chair.), L. Serdiuk, E. Bizeau, C. E. Braun, D. E. Brown, D. Bunnell, R. Croft, R. Drewien, P. Johnson, C. Peck, D. Perkins, L. Smith, and T. Zapatka. 1983. Pacific Flyway management plan: Rocky Mountain population of Greater Sandhill Cranes. U.S. Fish and Wildlife Service, Portland, Oreg.

Wright, J. T. 1951. Evaluation of the quail restoration plots in Cochise County. F.A. Proj. 40-R-2. Spec. Rept. Ariz. Game and Fish Comm.

———. 1953. Quail rainwater catchments and their evaluation. *Proc. West. Assoc. State Game and Fish Comm.* 33:220–23.

———. 1959. Desert wildlife, a research study. *Ariz. Game and Fish Dept. Wildl. Bull.* 6:78.

Yeager, W. M. 1966. Mearns' Quail management information. F.A. Spec. Rept. W-53, R-16. Ariz. Game and Fish Dept.

————. 1967. Mearns' Quail management information. F.A. Spec. Rep. W-53, R-17. Ariz. Game and Fish Dept.

Young, H. A. Hulsey, and R. Moe. 1952. Effects of certain insecticides on the Mourning Dove. *Proc. Ark. Acad. Sci.* 43–45.

Zeigler, D. L. 1971. Crop-milk cycles in Band-tailed Pigeons and losses of squabs due to hunting pigeons in September. M.S. thesis, Oregon State Univ., Corvallis.

Zwickel, F. C. 1958. Fall studies of forest grouse in northcentral Washington. M.S. thesis, Washington State Univ., Pullman.

————. 1973. Dispersion of female Blue Grouse during the brood season. *Condor* 75:114–20.

————. 1975. Nesting parameters of Blue Grouse and their relevance to populations. *Condor* 77:423–30.

Zwickel, F. C., J. H. Brigham, and I. O. Buss. 1975. Autumn structure of Blue Grouse populations in north-central Washington. *J. Wildl. Manage.* 39:461–67.

Zwickel, F. C., I. O. Buss, and J. H. Brigham. 1968. Autumn movements of Blue Grouse and their relevance to population and management. *J. Wildl. Manage.* 32:456–68.

Index

About the Author

David E. Brown was Small Game Management Supervisor for the Arizona Game and Fish Department from 1968 through 1979, and he spent twenty-six years in the department studying and managing wildlife. He taught Advanced Wildlife Management at Arizona State University in 1981 and was the Outdoor Editor for *City Magazine* in Tucson in 1988. He has written several books on wildlife, including *Arizona Wetlands and Waterfowl* (University of Arizona Press, 1985), and has published numerous articles on small game and small-game hunting in *Sports Illustrated*, *Gray's Sporting Journal*, *Shooting Sportsman*, and other periodicals.

About the Illustrator

Paul Bosman was born in South Africa in 1929 and studied at art schools in Johannesburg and London. After an advertising career in England, Canada, and South Africa, he settled in Rhodesia (now Zimbabwe) in 1969, where he and his family built and operated a safari lodge. He became a professional wildlife artist in 1973, with his work being shown in South Africa, West Germany, Canada, and the United States. Bosman has designed numerous wildlife postage stamps and is the recipient of an international stamp award. He and his family now make their home in Scottsdale, Arizona, where he paints wildlife of the Southwest.